THE DOMINION OF CHRIST

BEING THE SECOND PART OF A TREATISE ON

THE FORM OF THE SERVANT

BY THE SAME AUTHOR

THE COMMON LIFE
IN THE BODY OF CHRIST

A Study of some of the Biblical Materials
for a Doctrine of the Church

Fourth edition

*

REVELATION AND
THE MODERN WORLD

Being the first part of a treatise on
The Form of the Servant

*

DACRE PRESS: A. AND C. BLACK

THE DOMINION OF CHRIST

being the second part
of a treatise on

THE FORM OF THE SERVANT

by

L. S. THORNTON, C.R.

D.D. CAMBRIDGE, HON. D.D. DURHAM

dacre press
westminster

FIRST PUBLISHED 1952

DACRE PRESS: A. AND C. BLACK LTD.
4, 5 AND 6 SOHO SQUARE, LONDON, W.1

PRINTED IN GREAT BRITAIN BY ROBERT MACLEHOSE AND CO. LTD.
THE UNIVERSITY PRESS, GLASGOW

To fellow-members

in

The Fellowship of St. Alban and St Sergius

who have listened patiently

to the exposition of themes

contained in this book

PREFACE

In the preface to the first part of this treatise a hope was expressed that it would be completed in a second volume containing the substance of some Scott Holland Memorial lectures. In the present work this hope is only partially fulfilled. For since the original lectures were given the subject-matter has grown in bulk to such an extent that it seemed best to divide it up. This 'second part' covers some of the earlier lecture-material together with an even larger proportion of new matter. The general theme is indicated in the title; but that theme has very varied aspects. In the present volume 'the dominion of Christ' is surveyed primarily in its exercise as a sovereign process of divine activity restoring the original plan of creation. During the present century considerable advance has been made in our apprehension of what might be called 'theological unities'. An example of this would be our present-day appreciation of the truth that Christology, soteriology and ecclesiology are all bound together in an indissoluble whole, so that no one of these three mysteries can be rightly appreciated apart from the other two.

The more synoptic standpoint thus indicated is rooted in scripture itself where all mysteries are interwoven. In that respect biblical studies are likely to have a continuously beneficial effect upon the more systematic departments of theology. For there is always a danger that 'system' will become too 'departmental' to represent adequately either the unity of revelation or its inexhaustible mystery. Whenever that happens it becomes only too likely that the unchanging character of the historical revelation will be obscured, because its sovereign authority has been usurped by some all-too-human factor in the ever-changing complex of Christian life and thought. By such means the genuinely human factors which convey and embody the revelation may be unwittingly discounted and displaced, or simply ignored. Such a procedure, however unintentional, is essentially unscientific. For it is precisely the human element in historical revelation which is being progressively disclosed to us by the biblical sciences to-day.

In the present work considerations of space have severely limited the range of treatment. Other aspects of Christ's dominion will, it is hoped, be considered in a further volume. For the rest this instalment constitutes an exercise in biblical exegesis which attempts to apply in detail some principles of interpretation laid down in the preceding volume. The book was nearly completed before I had an opportunity of reading *A Study in St Mark* by Dr A. M. Farrer. I was particularly glad, however, to have read that very interesting volume before attempting to write my own concluding chapter on 'The Divine Victory'. My other obligations will be sufficiently obvious. To all who have had a share in producing this book I express my thanks. But a special word of gratitude is due to Miss Margaret Webb for the skill and accuracy with which she typed the whole of these first two volumes concerning *The Form of the Servant*.

L. S. T.

January, 1952.

CONTENTS

BOOK I

CHRIST AND CREATION

BOOK II

CONFLICT AND VICTORY

NOTE

Abbreviations are for the most part the same as in my previous works, *The Common Life in the Body of Christ* and *Revelation and the Modern World*. Those two books are, in the present volume, referred to, respectively, as *The Common Life* and *Revelation*.

Other references to the previous volume of this series (*Revelation*) refer to 'Vol. I' or simply 'I'; so that, for example, a reference to I. IX. v would indicate 'the fifth section of Chapter IX in that volume, and so on.

Readers are reminded that 'LC' refers to Lake and Cadbury, editors of Vol. iv of *The Beginnings of Christianity Part I*, and that 'Tr. LC.' refers to the translation of the Acts of the Apostles given in that volume.

AJV = American Jewish Version.

EGT = Expositor's Greek Testament.

Hebrew words or roots (referred to in Latin script) have, in a few instances, been indicated by their consonants only.

H. or Heb. refers to the Hebrew text. MT = Masoretic Text.

In references to LXX texts from the four books of 'Kingdoms' (1 and 2 Sam., 1 and 2 Kings) the abbreviated symbol: *Reg.* is employed.

ERRATA

Page *line*

8 18. *For* in *read* In.

30, 2nd line from bottom. *For* σκιρτὴσατε *read* σκιρτήσατε.

33 15. *For* 5^6 *read* 5^b.

34 28. *For* dignifies *read* signifies.

38, note 1. *For* εἴς *read* εἰς.

66 14, 17. *For* ἀναπαύσις *read* ἀνάπαυσις.

74, 2nd line from bottom. *For* $8^{17, 8}$ *read* $8^{17, 18}$.

80 11. *For* had *read* has.

100, note 3. *For* καλά *read* καλοί.

113 29. *For* preliminary *read* a preliminary.

BOOK I

CHRIST AND CREATION

CHAPTER I

CREATION AND RESTORATION

A. The Two Creations

i

The scriptural way of thinking in contrast to ours. The plan of creation centred in Christ (Eph. 1^{3-10}). Two ways of life (two orders of being) in history and in ourselves.

In this series we are concerned with the Gospel of Christ in its relation to human life. For genuine Christian faith it is, of course, a basic assumption that in Jesus of Nazareth lies the clue to the solution of all human problems, theoretical and practical. To those who do not share our faith this claim may, and perhaps must, seem fantastic. For the believer, however, the question at issue is not the vastness of Christ's claim, but rather the baffling complexity of its application. The Gospel has a divine simplicity which does not change, whereas human life is a panorama of complex problems, changing issues and intricate motives. How is the one to be related to the other? Clearly our starting-point must be in Christ. For in man we see an unsolved enigma, whereas in Christ faith can discern the mystery which illuminates the puzzle and dispels obscurity. Something was said upon this subject in the preceding volume;[1] and its more metaphysical aspects have recently been discussed in a series of Gifford Lectures.[2] But a brief resumé may not be amiss at this point.

In popular speech a 'mystery' is something which mystifies, itself a puzzle which we cannot solve until we find the clue.

[1] I. II. i, pp. 30 ff.

[2] *The Mystery of Being* by Gabriel Marcel. See also his earlier volume: *Être et avoir*

Our statement, however, reverses this way of speaking. In its theological meaning a mystery is something which throws light upon other things, a revealed truth which illuminates other truths, like a bright lamp showing clearly the relation between the various objects which surround it. Our eyes, indeed, cannot bear to look directly at the light; yet its rays are the medium in which we see all things clearly. Baffled by the human enigma, we can with St Paul bend our minds towards 'the mystery of God, even Christ, in whom are hidden all the treasures of wisdom and knowledge' (Col. $2^{2,3}$). There is a paradox here; for the Christian mystery which dispels obscurity must ever remain mysterious. For faith mystery and rationality are not contradictory but complementary. Reason feeds upon mysteries which yet transcend our understanding. This is a universal truth of human life. So too the God of the Bible dwells 'in the thick darkness;' yet 'he reveals his secrets unto his servants the prophets'[1] until at length the whole mystery of his hidden purpose is laid open in the Christ.

In the earlier volume a recovered sense of mystery in our approach to revelation was connected with a corresponding recovery in our attitude to the unity of scripture. The Bible is now seen to be a single universe of discourse in which, while the speech is human, it is yet divinely authenticated. God speaks to us in language of his own choosing, yet upon terms of profound intimacy with our nature. Not only the revelation, but also the form in which it is given, is of divine appointment. This, however, involves no inhibition upon our thought or reasoning powers. On the contrary, by resting securely upon the appointed form our minds are set free from their own fettering restrictions,[2] so that they may be opened to receive the rich nourishment of the divine Word. We cannot fully *com*prehend that Word; for God is inscrutable. But, to adapt a phrase of St Paul's, we may learn to *ap*prehend that by which we are already apprehended; and that is surely the better way. The Bible constitutes that world of thought and action, that order of light and life to which as Christians we properly belong.

Here we may recall an apostolic warning. Although of necessity we have to live in this present age, yet we are not to be

[1] i Kings 8^{12}; Amos 3^{7}.

[2] Some examples were given in Vol. I, Chs. II and III.

conformed to it (Rom. 12[2]). Its fashions of thought are all too human and transitory. They cannot therefore provide for our minds a permanent background. To us the Word of God has come (John 10[35]), taking us into its own ordered cosmos, where the disorder of our poor thoughts falls under judgement, to be tested, reformed and transformed. Such considerations suggest an urgent necessity that we should bring biblical theology to bear upon our social thinking. For in this sphere nothing of human systems can be taken for granted. Behind them all, transcending and judging them all, is the mystery of God in Christ. When we turn to the Scriptures, we find, for example, that they are not concerned with human society as such, but rather with man in his relation to God his Creator. Once more, interest may seem to centre at times upon this or that individual or social group. But the controlling interest is always occupied with God's plan for the world and with the part assigned in that plan to the People of his choice.

The New Testament has nothing to say about the preservation, development or reform of 'the social order' as such. It has on the other hand much to say about a 'new creation' which has taken place in Christ and about a particular community with which this new creation is mysteriously identified. We may well pause to consider the significance of this difference in language; for behind it lies a radical difference of outlook. *We* are all too consciously, and perhaps somewhat nervously, engrossed to-day in 'problems' of human society. *Our* attention is fixed upon the immediate mundane fortunes of man, upon his self-development, upon his mutual relations with his fellows, and upon the protection of both from menacing dangers. For these we anxiously make plans; and the successful issue of such planning seems, in turn, to depend mainly upon *our* manipulation of nature's resources. The bible, however, speaks in terms of a single plan, and that not ours but God's. Again, it speaks of creation as a single whole within which man is included. It emphasizes his frailty as a creature amongst other creatures. Yet in the same context it will exalt him by placing him at the heart of God's plan for creation.

Once more, the biblical story is not chiefly occupied with 'every man', but rather, in the first instance with the chosen People. In Israel the divine plan is concentrated after its initial frustration by man's disobedience and self-will. To Israel, in a sense, the plan is actually entrusted. But finally the plan is brought to its fulfilment in the Christ, not by any process of intrinsic development, but by an unparalleled entry of God himself into the world of his creation. In Christ the chosen people is re-created, because in him there is a re-making of the whole world. In a biblical interpretation of our subject, therefore, the primary question confronting us is not: 'What has Christianity to say about human society or about international order?' but rather: 'What is the relation of the new creation in Christ to the original plan of creation?' Can 'the mystery of the Christ' throw light upon that plan which God framed 'in the beginning'? The apostolic writers have no doubt that it can do so. Indeed, it would scarcely be possible to over-emphasize the strength of their conviction upon this matter.

In their statements we can distinguish three strands of thought. First of all, the purpose of God in creation, although frustrated and thwarted by the powers of evil, has none the less been brought to fruition in Christ through his great act of restoration. Secondly, in the new creation thus brought into being there is disclosed the outline of the original plan. That which was obscured and distorted in the broken mirror of a fallen world can now be seen in Christ in its true proportions and in its original integrity. Consequently, in the third place, what stands revealed in the New Testament is not two plans but one. The mystery of the Christ is not an after-thought, supplementary to the original purpose of God. It was present 'in the beginning'. The whole design of creation was Christ-centred from the first. It is in its very essence Christological. Jesus is the goal towards which creation moves, because he is also the source of its movement. So too he is the matrix within which creation received its form, because the Father saw in him the actual design from which he would fashion it. Only in Jesus, therefore, can man become that significant whole for which he was originally created.

In the New Testament, however, these vast perspectives belong to the wider setting of the picture. At its centre, inseparably united with Jesus, stands the community of the redeemed. The connexion between this human foreground and that cosmic background appears in a typical statement of the

Epistle to the Ephesians,[1] where it is declared that God 'chose us in Christ before the foundation of the world', having already, in his love, 'predestined us unto the adoption of sons through Jesus Christ'. The form in which creation is to attain its destiny is thus the form of sonship; and this is, perhaps, the most important truth implied in our previous statement that the design of creation is in essence Christological. For Christ is the beloved Son; and the plan which proceeds from the Father's love must find its consummation in him who is the object of that love, that is the Son. In this passage, as constantly in other contexts, our filial relation to God is regarded from within the standpoint of the redeemed community. We know God's fatherhood in Christ, in whom we have forgiveness of sins and spiritual illumination through participation in his life of sonship.

We see then that in the apostolic view the destiny of the universe is interpreted through insight into God's plan for the redeemed; and this insight is generated within the new life in Christ. Similarly from the same source comes knowledge concerning the starting-point of the Creator's purpose. We know God's love for us in the beloved Son. The Father's love for the Son is the source of his love for us, just as the loving response of the Son to the Father is the sphere in which the response of our love is born. From that mysterious background the divine love for us proceeds; upon that eternal background God chose us to be his children before the worlds were made. With this decisive choice he predestined us 'in love'; and therefore our adoption is 'through Jesus Christ'. In the Son, the unchanging object of his love, the Father saw mirrored all the possibilities of creation, He saw, as in a single pattern, the participation of all his creatures, each according to its due measure, in the many glories of that 'very varied wisdom' which delights him in the beloved Son.[2]

Our life in Christ is the sphere in which the secrets of creation become manifest. Through our undeserved release from sin we know our predestination and our destiny. For those 'whom God foreknew he also foreordained to be conformed to the image of his Son' (Rom. 8^{29}). Our election to sonship in

[1] Eph. 1^{3-10}.
[2] cp. Eph. 3^{10}; see also Prov. $8^{22, 30, 31}$.

Christ is, therefore, not a consequence of God's plan for creation, but rather the fundamental presupposition of the plan. Creation is the means through which God's fatherly intention towards his predestined children is brought to fulfilment. From this, also, it follows that all men are in some sense sons of God by creation. Moreover, universal implications are clearly integral both to the plan itself and to the meaning of the redeemed community in which the secret of the plan becomes manifest. From this line of thought there follows a further corallary of great importance. It is this: the title of Father is more fundamental than the title of Creator. The former is the presupposition of the latter.[1]

Fatherhood is the first word of God's creative design, as sonship is its last word; and the meaning of both words is disclosed in Christ. For he is 'the first and the last', in whose relation to the Father all creation has its being, in whose incarnate response to the Father all things are to be summed up. What then is the relationship of the new sonship which we enjoy in Christ to that wider sonship which is at least a possibility of all mankind? Once again, the answer must come from the foreground of the picture, from the place where the secret of the Christ is disclosed. If the key to the passage which we have been considering lies in the mystery of *Christus consummator* at its conclusion, the heart of that mystery in turn lies in the central phrase about the remission of sins (Eph. 1⁷). The filial relation to God is something which *we* know only as a restoration of lost privileges. The Church is the home to which lost sons return from their sojourn in a far country. Membership in God's family is not something upon which we can presume. It is ours only through undeserved grace. This is the point at which the light shines most clearly for those who are in Christ. It is only in the bright beams of God's forgiving love that we can discern clearly those distant horizons of sonship which indicate the true source of our being.[2]

[1] For fuller details on this point see I. VIII. Addit. Note B (1).

[2] Here we may find the explanation of much that is puzzling in the language of scripture. St Paul taught that sonship by adoption is a privilege granted to sinners who have been reconciled to the Father through the death of Christ and who are also made partakers in the Saviour's resurrection (Details in *The Common Life*, Chs. iv–vi). Yet in his speech at Athens

We see then a certain contrast in scripture. There is, on the one hand, the contraction of the divine purpose narrowing down in concentration upon Christ and the church; and again, on the other hand, there is a corresponding expansion of that same purpose to include in its scope the utmost bounds of creation. These two themes might be regarded as the systole and diastole of the divine action in sacred history were it not for the fact that, although sometimes alternating at least from the standpoint of human interest, they must, none the less, on a deeper view be conceived to be actually and permanently compresent. The tension involved in this contrast constitutes one of the great problems of religious history, one which overshadows the centuries and which to-day still envelopes us. In one form, for example, it confronts us in a popular demand that the Church should expend her energies upon the humane tasks of peace, justice, fellowship and social order rather than upon the promotion of specifically religious beliefs and practices. Such an attitude would imply that the duty of loving God can be resolved, wholly and without remainder, into the duty of loving our neighbour.

The Church, however, stands for the truth that the two duties are one in the sense that these two forms of activity, although always distinct, should be inseparably one in their

the apostle is represented as endorsing the sentiment that all men are God's offspring (the universal application is clear in Acts 17^{24-30}). It has been too easily assumed that two such opinions are mutually inconsistent. Yet the context of this statement in Acts shows that in the speaker's mind, at any rate, there was no consciousness of any incompatibility. Moreover the speech actually gives a notable indication of the way in which the two modes of speech may be brought together, so that their congruity becomes manifest. The acknowledgement of a universal sonship through creation is certainly here made to be the ground of a universal sentence against sin and the basis also of a summons to repentance. This was an appropriate method of appealing to that particular audience. On the other hand, the summons to repentance derived its urgency and its authority, not from the truth of universal sonship but from the facts of the gospel. For the summons was supported by a proclamation that a day of judgement was impending for which the appointed judge had already been installed. It will be remembered that this speech originated in the curiosity aroused by the apostle's preaching of 'Jesus and the resurrection'. That gospel was once more reiterated at the close of the speech, when the fact of Christ's resurrection was adduced as the concrete evidence for believing in the imminence of approaching judgement (Acts $17^{18-20, 29-32}$).

exercise, each always implying the other. The creed of Christendom is the guarantee of that universal fellowship for which we hope. For just so far as our ideals lose vital connexion with the gospel of Jesus they tend to lose their universality. They begin to undergo a distortion and a restriction, so that the humanism which they represent becomes less truly human. They become principles of human action divorced from the mysteries of divine revelation. Presently they pass into ideologies which exhibit their weakness precisely in that which gives them their appeal, namely their undue simplification of human facts and needs. For us Christ is the touchstone of earthly ideas and ideals; and to his teaching we must turn. The question at issue, however, shall first be restated in a rather different form.

There is in the bible and in Christian history a contrast, sometimes sharpened to an antithesis, between the church and human society, between their respective aims and interests and between the two forms of life and activity which they represent. in his treatise on *The City of God* St Augustine showed that this antithesis is not simply political or ecclesiastical, as between two social institutions. The African father's theme corresponds much more closely to the biblical conception of the two creations as represented by the contrasted figures of Adam and Christ, the former being understood to stand for a spiritual order crippled and disintegrated by the Fall, whereas Christ fulfils and comprehends the vocation of the true Israel of God in all ages. The contrast, therefore, is not primarily between two alternative forms of society, but rather between two modes of created being. In us who are the heirs of Christian history both modes of being are present, whether we recognize that fact or not. For us, also, both modes have validity, whether we acknowledge it or not.

Moreover, the relationship between these two orders is profoundly complex. The one is like leaven at work in the other. The Gospel of Christ has become interwoven with our history and our civilization, but also with our very nature as individuals. We can never wholly evade it, although we all seek to do so in this or that degree. We are, it seems, altogether unable to do without the gospel, yet our nature is ever in conflict with it. The dialectic of the two creations, therefore, goes on in each one of us as a great silent, internal dialogue; and the same process works itself out on a vaster scale in the world around us. We may, indeed, dissociate ourselves from the Church; but it is much harder to dissociate ourselves from the Christ. To do so entirely we should have to root out much which has entered deeply into our innermost being. On biblical presuppositions all of this is seen to be inevitable. Since Christ is the source and matrix of both the creations, they must clearly be complementary to one another. Just so far as they are forced apart both will suffer damage. Our nature is incomplete apart from Christ; but also, in taking that nature for his own he who is Very God made himself dependent upon us for his creaturely completion.

ii

The family of Jesus as wide as creation, yet realized only in him through an identification of sinners with their Redeemer.

It is recorded of Jesus that once, when a crowd of people sat round him listening to his words, he was summoned by a message from his mother and his brethren. He replied with the question: 'Who are my mother and my brethren?' and then looking round upon those seated about him, he said: 'Behold my mother and my brethren; whosoever shall do the will of God, the same is my brother and sister and mother' (Mark 3^{31-35}). Jesus here recognizes a family relationship between himself and all who do God's will. His hearers are so acknowledged because they are learning God's will from him. In them he sees what he desires to see in all men. For he interprets the genuine vocation of every man and woman in terms of his own unswerving obedience to the Father. In this incident Jesus sets aside the natural claims of near kinship to a privileged position with respect to himself, giving the priority to a yet higher kind of relationship. Perfect Man as he is, his unique status as the only-begotten Son detaches him from all merely particularist claims upon his manhood. Yet that same unique relation as Son to the Father also brings him into kinship with all who follow him in doing God's will. He saw in all those whose flesh and blood he shared the possibility of union with himself in one family, subject to the one indispensable condition that they were learning from him to participate in his filial obedience to his Father.

This saying of our Lord's, therefore, points in two directions. It suggests, on the one hand, that Jesus regarded all men as in some sense children of God. On the other hand, the fulfilment of this universal possibility is wholly conditioned by relationship to himself, and mediated through that relationship. If we ask what is the precise connexion between these two aspects of the saying we may find the beginnings of an answer by noting the variations between two of the three gospels which record the incident. St Mark says that 'Jesus looked round upon those who were seated about him in a circle', referring apparently to the whole company. St Matthew, however, says that 'he stretched forth his hands towards *his disciples* and said, Behold my mother and my brethren'. In St Mark all the company present are learning God's will by listening to Jesus; the saying, therefore, may become true of any one of them. None the less St Matthew's interpretation is not excluded; and it actually receives emphatic support elsewhere in St Mark's Gospel.[1] If Jesus saw possibilities of kinship with himself in all men, he saw these possibilities being realized in those who permanently acknowledged his leadership. For *they* had found in him the true life of sonship to the heavenly Father. By conforming their lives to his they became sharers in his unique relation to God's fatherhood. Thus they entered a new family group of which Jesus himself is both the head and the nucleus.

Attention must now be drawn to two dominical sayings, both recorded in St Matthew's Gospel, which, when taken together, illustrate further this particular facet of divine revelation. The first of these occurs in the great sermon, and strikes the universal note. There the disciples are told to love men as God loves them, without partiality, 'that ye may become sons of your Father which is in heaven'. This family relationship is one into which men enter through participating, in some sense, in the divine perfection; and it is precisely this high goal to which Jesus calls them: 'Ye therefore shall be perfect as your heavenly Father is perfect' (Matt. 5^{43-48}). Secondly, in the parable of the sheep and the goats (Matt. 25^{31ff}) those who have fulfilled the

[1] St Luke (8^{21}) has: 'these who hear and do', which mediates between the other two.

precept of impartial love to all men enter into the bliss of eternal life. Yet, once again, there is a Christological connexion. Jesus calls them 'the blessed of my Father' because, in their universal charity to those in need, they have ministered to the beloved Son himself. Here we are in the presence of the same mystery, yet developed more fully. In the sermon Jesus points men to the true life of sonship in God's human family, a life inseparable from brotherly love. In the parable the objects of such love (in principle all mankind) are identified (as his brethren) with Jesus himself, so that the fraternal conduct of children in God's family is directed towards the beloved Son in whose filial life they share.

Our Lord, then, teaches that an exalted destiny awaits all mankind. Yet he holds out no hope of men attaining this destiny except upon the conditions which he lays down. The universal promise of sonship which he sees in men can be fulfilled only through entry into that unique sonship which he possesses. Moreover, this implies a certain identification of mankind with Jesus, and that again at two levels. There is an original connexion of every man with the divine Son by virtue of our creation in the image. In all true human relationships therefore he identifies himself with both sides of the relationship, that is, with those who give and with those who receive. The divine image, however, in all its flawless perfection, is now incarnate. The beloved Son has become the Son of man who resumes the lost sceptre of humanity (Matt. $25^{31, 32}$).[1] The plan of creation comes to fulfilment in the very body of the Christ. That particular implication of the parable (25^{40}) actually becomes more explicit in the incident which follows almost immediately (26^{6-13}), where the mortal flesh of Jesus is honourably anointed at the supper in Bethany. In view of the first evangelist's careful grouping of his material, this arrangement may well be deliberate.

Next, we must take note of the fact that in the story of our Lord's baptism, the mystery of his sonship is connected, by the Voice from heaven, with the whole sacrificial destiny of Israel as Servant of the Lord.[2] *This* is the central theme of scripture;

[1] For this and what follows cp.: I, pp. 160–163 and I, p. 180 f., note 2. In Daniel 7 the Man resumes his rule over the Beasts (Ps. 8, Gen. 1, 2).

[2] cp. Mark 1^{11} with Isa. 42^{1}.

and its two stages of development are united in the person of Jesus. Fulfilling all lines of biblical anticipation he recreated Israel in himself, while he summoned all men to receive from him, and by union with him, that sonship of lowly service to which Israel had originally been called. Here, once more, as in the saying about kinship with Jesus through the doing of God's will, we hear two notes struck, a note of universality and again a note of complete particularity. Moreover, the two notes together make a concord, notwithstanding their diversity. This, then, is typical of our Lord's whole message. He issued an invitation to all on the basis of that common humanity which he had made his own. Yet with equal emphasis he declared that 'narrow is the gate, and straightened the way that leadeth unto life, and few be they that find it' (Matt. 7^{14}). We conclude, then, that the appeal to human nature as such, in whatever form it occurs in the New Testament, receives its authentication solely from Christ and in him.

There are many passages in scripture which illustrate the doctrine of the divine image in man. Amongst these one may include especially those which are concerned with the moral accountability of the Gentile world.[1] Yet all these elements of biblical teaching concerning the first creation derive their final significance for faith solely from the revelation in Christ, in whom all things are summed up. Jesus shares our common humanity because by his own act he identified himself with it. By that same act he shows us the true significance of that which he then took into union with himself. He shows its greatness and its littleness, its high promise and its constant need. One of the cardinal facts about human nature as we know it is the contrast between its grandiose aims and its pitiful failure to achieve those aims. Hope springs eternal in us, but is perpetually falsified by events. This is in part due to the fact that we are infected by ambitions which the New Testament condemns as foolish and idolatrous. So much of our activities resembles the building of a tower of Babel. We try to reach up to heaven; and the result is confusion and disintegration. The march of per-

[1] e.g. Amos 1; Rom. 1^{14-32}, 2^{12-16}. In these NT passages the authentication in Christ occurs at $1^{16,17}$ and 2^{16}, which correspond to Acts 17^{31}. See above, p. 6, n. 2.

petual progress issues in the chaos of a cracking and rending civilization.

The gospel was not intended to provide palliatives for such a situation. Our Lord did not become incarnate in order to prop up a falling Babylon. He did not clothe himself in our nature in order to supply patches for an old and worn out garment. His purpose was altogether different. We may venture to diagnose it as manifested in a series of stages. First he came to expose the desperate evil of our present state, to lay bare the roots of evil, and to show us precisely how and where we have strayed away from that divine plan, traces of which he still finds present in us. Secondly he came to restore the design of created sonship in all men; and this, again, involves a radical transformation of our nature until it bears his own likeness for which it was originally created. Finally, his redemptive action in both of these respects is effected through his complete identification of himself with us and through a corresponding identification of us with him. In this attempt to describe the stages of our Lord's redeeming work there are two key-words about which a good deal will have to be said. 'Restoration' and 'identification' need to be further clarified.

Thus far we have traced out in the New Testament some fuller justification for a thesis prominent in the first part of this treatise as a characteristic contribution of St Irenaeus, namely his tendency to affirm an identity between the new creation in Christ and the original plan of creation. Besides this, however, we have observed in one section of our Lord's teaching an affirmation of nothing less than physical identification between himself and his 'brethren' (Matt. 25^{40}). This saying may fairly be regarded as a dominical equivalent of the Pauline doctrine concerning the Body of Christ, indicating clearly the sense in which that doctrine has its roots in our Lord's own teaching. Moreover, according to St Luke this total identification between Christ and his people was the first truth brought home to Saul of Tarsus in the hour of his conversion. He learnt it, indeed, from the lips of the risen Lord himself, when he heard the words: 'I am Jesus whom thou persecutest' (Acts $9^{4,5}$). That sentence, then, would seem to be the historic starting-point of a train of thought which reached its ripest conclusion in the Epistle to the Ephesians, providing there, in turn, a foundation for what one might call the 'Irenaean' development.

What we have now to do is to trace the revelation of identity between the two creations through its various scriptural forms; and in particular to follow out the theme of restoration which provides a link between the two covenants, as also between the old order and the new. For the mysterious identity between Christ and his members which is signified in the apostolic doctrine of the one organism is something which is both new and not new. Indeed, we can only affirm with safety its exceeding newness, if we have securely traced the connexion between this newness and that which was 'from the beginning' and 'in the beginning'. Any other course would lead us back into the arms of Marcion and his kind. Fallen humanity is now in process of 'being renewed after the image of him that created' it (Col. 3^{9}). The renewal, therefore, takes the form of a work of restoration, already accomplished, yet still in process of completion. In the new creation every step forwards towards the End is also and equally a movement back to the Beginning. For Christ is both the one and the other. He embodies the restoration which he is now effecting in us; and when he has accomplished that work we shall find that we have returned to what he ever is and to what he always intended us to be.

B. Restoration to Wholeness

iii

Two meanings of 'restore' in scripture. The symbolism of healing (Mark 3^{5} and parallels). The background in OT. Types of restoration: the hand of Moses and the heart of Jeremiah. The enlightenment of the Twelve (Mark 8^{25}).

In a volume devoted to 'The dominion of Christ' we shall find it worth while to take note of the question addressed to the risen Christ by 'the apostles': 'Lord, dost thou at this time *restore* the Kingdom to Israel?' (Acts 1^{6}; cp. 1^{2}). The word here rendered 'restore' is employed in the Septuagint in reference to a future restoration of Israel from captivity to the Holy Land. The word is so used in a number of prophetic passages, and is especially noticeable in the writings attributed to Jeremiah and Ezekiel, both of whom witnessed the Babylonian exile. In Acts 1^{6} the disciples ask if these prophetic oracles are now to be fulfilled by an immediate inauguration of the messianic kingdom. The dominion of Christ is clearly conceived on the background of the Davidic monarchy and its earthly theocracy. In his reply our Lord deprecates the form of the question with its reflexion of popular implications and expectations. He diverts the minds of his hearers instead to an alternative form of the prophetic hope, namely the promised gift of the Spirit issuing in the conversion of the Gentile world (cp. Luke 24^{45-49}). That is his last recorded utterance before the ascension (Acts 1^{7-9}).

Next, it should be noticed that this same word[1] has also another connotation in the Septuagint which has an important bearing upon its use in the New Testament. This second meaning is connected with the idea of restoration to health. For example, it is applied to the restoration of healthy flesh in the case of a leper who is pronounced to be clean (Lev. 13^{16}). This second use of the word is repeated in the record of a particular gospel healing. The incident in question is recorded in all three synoptic gospels; and attention must be drawn to the fact that all the three evangelists employ the same word in their descriptions of the healing (Mark 3^{5}, Matthew 12^{13}, Luke 6^{10}). There are reasons for thinking that this unanimity is deliberate and theologically significant. Indeed there is good ground for believing that what might be called a theological pattern of 'restoration' runs through the bible, and that the pattern can be traced out by careful observation of language. A familiar example of this exploitation of a key-word must by now be beyond dispute. I refer to the double use of *paradidômi* in the Greek version of Isaiah 53^{12} ('he was delivered up'—Cp. Rom. 4^{25}). In English its recurrence in the New Testament is concealed under a variety of synonyms.[2]

At first sight a connexion between restoration of the Holy Land to its former glories (Acts 1^{6}) and restoration of a sick person to health might seem to be purely verbal. But there is more than this beneath the surface. For example, the book of

[1] ἀποκαθιστάνω(= ἀποκαθίστημι)

[2] For details in my earlier works see the following: *The Common Life*, (edd. 2 and 3), index, under *paradidomi* and *paradosis; The Apostolic Ministry*, pp. 61 and 95 with n. 2; *Revelation*, p. 285 with n. 1.

Isaiah opens with a picture of Israel as a sick person;[1] and the picture symbolizes the moral corruption of the Judaean State and its consequent humiliation. Then the scene changes and we see 'the daughter of Zion' under a series of images signifying dereliction (Isaiah 1^{2-10}). The personification of a people under an individual figure is as familiar in the bible as the corresponding idiom by which a representative individual stands for the whole community.[2] Moreover the prophecies of restoration to the Holy Land are, as we shall see, deeply conditioned by a 'return' of the people to their God. Such moral 'restoration', again, is not infrequently described under the metaphor of healing. A good example of this combination is to be found in Hosea 6^{1-3}. Here we have a characteristic blending of images. The 'returning' Israelites hope that after timely repentance they will experience a healing of their sick condition, so that their national life will shortly revive under the ministrations of the divine Healer.[3] Then, as in Isaiah 1^7, the picture changes; Israel is to become a land watered by the dew of heaven. As often in Hebrew thought, spiritual and material transformations are conceived to be inseparable.

These subtle interchanges are facilitated by the variety of possible meanings attaching to a single Hebrew verb.[4] The complex idea represented by this word (and by its two Greek equivalents) is implicit in its various meanings, just as in the literary forms which the biblical revelation assumes the whole is implicit in its various parts.[5] Yet, in its own way, each one of the parts represents the whole;[6] and this involves us in a diffi-

[1] This rendering of 1^5 suits the analogy between 1^6 and 1^7. But the plural in 1^5, if accepted, would simply indicate 'oscillation' from many to one in 1^6. Cp. the *Soncino* (Jewish) comm. *ad. loc.*, and I. p. 337 (index), under 'oscillation'.

[2] For 'the daughter of Zion' see an article by Fr Hebert, S.S.M. in *Theology*, Vol. LIII, No. 365. For the idioms generally see I. p. 338 (index) under 'representation'.

[3] The insincerity of their repentance, as judged by the prophet, does not affect the validity of the illustration.

[4] On this point see I. VI, p. 157 (§ 1, par. 1, last sentence). The Hebrew verb in question (*shûbh*) means (i) 'to return' (literally or metaphorically). (ii) (in the *hiphil* mood) 'to cause to return', 'to bring back', 'to restore'. In LXX the usual equivalent for (i) is ἐπιστρέφω and for (ii) ἀποκαθίστημι But ἐπιστρέφω can have both meanings; e.g. Zech. $10^{9,10}$.

[5] For this see I. V. pp. 153 ff.

[6] cp. I. VIII. § ii.

culty of procedure. For in following out a biblical pattern of thought through its verbal associations, as we are now trying to do, it is never possible to say of any given picture or of any one strand in the pattern: 'here is all of the whole.' Yet how can we handle them all together? A way out of the dilemma was suggested in Volume I, where it was pointed out (p. 153) that the Whole given in Christ provided its own 'central ideas'. The New Testament writers reassemble Old Testament images according to a new pattern given in Christ. The shape of revelation is now Christological; so we have only to discern its outlines as traced by the evangelical writers. In this we have one important clue. The prominence of the 'repetition *motif*', already explained extensively in Volume I, should enable us to trace the continuity of the pattern by virtue of its recurrence throughout scripture in successive forms.

This, then, will be our immediate line of advance; and we shall begin by assuming that for the evangelists the healing miracles are 'saving' events of a peculiar kind. They are typical acts of divine power which embody and manifest the truth that messianic salvation consists in 'restoration to wholeness'. Readers of Volume I will remember that the story of the blind man restored to sight in John 9 illustrates this characteristic gospel theme.[1] There the 'new creation' healing was connected with the idea that the original work of creation was both completed and manifested in Christ. It is, however, a characteristically biblical notion that in redemptive history there is a renewal of God's creative activity. In the historic acts of saving power 'chaos' is once more replaced by 'cosmos'. So in the Exodus all creation seems to co-operate with its Creator in Israel's deliverance; and in prophetic oracles of 'restoration' a 'repetition' of this cosmic co-operation is confidently expected. In our Lord's inaugural sermon in the synagogue at Nazareth a 'new creation' prophecy of this type is cited as now about to be fulfilled. In the prophecy and in the sermon based upon it allusions to physical healing are prominent; and in prophecy, here and elsewhere, such healings are incidental to a wider restoration of Israel's polity to messianic glories.

With these considerations in mind we will proceed to corre-

[1] I. VI. iv (2), pp. 177 ff. For what follows the reader is also referred to *The Common Life*, pp. 358 f., with reference to Isa. 35.

late 'restoration' incidents of the New Testament with typical situations in the Old Testament to which they seem to correspond. We begin, then, with the story of that sabbath-healing in the synagogue which the three synoptic evangelists connect with the 'restoration' idea (Mark 3^{1-6}, Matthew 12^{9-14}, Luke 6^{6-11}). This event has a critical significance for the whole plan of our Lord's ministry as told in these three gospels. It is not the first healing, nor the first occasion of conflict with the authorities. But, coming as it does as the last of a series of such incidents,[1] it is represented as finally determining the Pharisees to combine forces with the Herodians with a view to the Saviour's destruction. The 'restoration' effected involves a declaration of war on the old order. As, therefore, the healing is symbolic of a new creation and a restored Israel, so also its circumstances are symbolic of the ensuing conflict which comes to its climax only at the conclusion of the gospel story, in the crucifixion and its sequel. A fuller survey of the context will, I believe, serve to confirm this interpretation.

In all three gospels this incident is preceded by another involving a corresponding break with the Pharisaic view of the sabbath. A precedent is cited which implies that David, as the Lord's anointed, stood above the Mosaic Law. That bears upon the concluding words of Jesus (Mark $2^{27,28}$). The issue is not primarily humanitarian but Christological, the lesser issue depending upon the greater, as in Mark 7^{9-13}. Usurped authority is always tyrannical. Thus the reference to David makes the lordship of the Son of man messianic (Mark 2^{28}).[2] If this conclusion is sound, it is supported by further indications that David's story forms the background. The conflict of David's Son with current Jewish authority 'repeats' the conflict of David with Saul. In both cases 'the Spirit' has been transferred to a new ruler; yet at first the new king is an outlaw in danger of death. The high Christology is woven on to that background. The Son of man who forgives sins (Mark 2^{10}) is also the messianic bridegroom, destined, however, to premature separation from

[1] In Mark and Luke. Matthew's order represents an alternative collocation of ideas to which we shall return.

[2] On this see further the timely article by Prof. T. W. Manson in the Rylands' Library Bulletin, Vol. 32, No. 2. But see also above, Ch. I, § ii, par. 4 with note.

his bride (2^{20}; cp 1 Sam. $19^{11,12}$). The explicit parallel which follows (1 Sam. 21^{1-6}; Mark 2^{23-28}) is succeeded by others more lightly traced. David was accounted mad, and so was Jesus (1 Sam. 21^{12-15}; Mark 3^{21}); outlawry brings a band of followers, some of whom will one day be princes in a new theocracy; yet it also involves family separations (1 Sam. 22^{1-5}; Mark $3^{13-18, 31-35}$).

We are, then, in a position to compare the restoration healings of the two covenants. Immediately before the Marcan sequence just now traced out, *and therefore at the beginning of his mission*, our Lord heals a leper and bids him observe the Mosaic law laid down in Leviticus. Behind this law of 'restoration' (Lev. 13^{16}), again,[1] lies a traditional incident of the Exodus narrative. After the theophany of the burning bush, *and therefore at the beginning of his mission*, Moses is encouraged with three 'signs' by means of which he is to authenticate that mission to Israel. The middle sign of the three is a 'restoration' of his hand from leprosy (Exod. 4^{7}. LXX). Moreover, it is further differentiated from the first and the third. The 'restoration' sign is not (like the other two) repeated before Pharaoh. Its sole use is to induce in Israel belief in the genuineness of Moses' commission (Exod. $4^{30, 31}$). The three signs have this effect; but the other two leave Pharaoh in unbelief. Thus there is a certain general correspondence between the inaugural signs of the two covenants in the old Exodus and in the new; and the gospel sequence introducing a new historical redemption culminates in a 'restoration' healing which is a test for dividing the true Israel from its present oppressors.

There is a further parallel with the Exodus story which deserves attention as it shows a threefold verbal echo. In the gospel incident our Lord said to the man 'stretch out thy hand'. 'And he stretched it out'; and his hand 'was restored'. In the story of the Red sea crossing the Lord says twice to Moses 'stretch out thy hand'. 'And Moses stretched out his hand.' On the second occasion the water 'was restored' to its wonted flow, overwhelming the Egyptians. The narrative concludes with two relevant comments: (1) The Lord delivered Israel 'from the hand of the Egyptians'; (2) and Israel saw 'the

[1] see above, par. 2.

great hand which the Lord made'.[1] Further, in Exodus 14^{16} the hand of Moses is linked to the rod which turned into a serpent (cp. also $4^{17, 20}$). Thus in the hour of victorious redemption we are reminded of the preliminary signs which foreshadowed victory, the hand restored to wholeness and the magic power of the rod which the restored hand would wield. Moreover, immediately after the signs Moses is provided with a 'mouth' in the person of Aaron, to whom, in turn, Moses (rod in hand) is to be 'as God'. So it might seem that Moses himself was 'the great hand which the Lord had made'. Israel without a hand would be helpless, fitly symbolized by the man in the synagogue before the Lord spoke the creative word which enabled him to stretch out his hand once more.[2]

The analogy between the two covenants in respect of 'restoration' signs has thus far been confined to a single point. In both the two incidents considered the healing of a representative person has been found to symbolize or to foreshadow a fuller manifestation of God's redemptive power which was to follow. It will be remembered, however, that the divine acts of restoration are, in Hebrew prophecy, spiritually conditioned on the human side by a 'return' to God.[3] This aspect of the restoration theme shall now be illustrated by a fresh pairing of healing incidents in the two covenants. In Mark 8^{25} the key-word occurs once more, and for the last time, in the story of a gospel-healing. The story and its whole setting are peculiar to this evangelist; but before we examine it in detail we shall find it convenient to turn to its selected Old Testament counterpart. In Jeremiah 15^{15-21} we are given an intimate glimpse into the interior life of the prophet. The wound of which he complains is

[1] Exod. 14^{16-31} LXX. The three phrases: (1) ἔκτεινον τὴν χεῖρά σου, (2) ἐξέτεινεν and (3) ἀπεκατέστη correspond verbally to those in Mark 3^{5} and Matt. 12^{13}. Luke 6^{10} is the same for (1) and (3), but has a verbal synonym for the second phrase.

[2] For what it may be worth I add the following comparison between the miracles of the Exodus: At the Red sea there is a double miracle. The ebb and flow of the water are both abnormal, the former for Israel's escape, the latter for Pharaoh's destruction. This corresponds to the two double miracles of Exod. 4 (hand and rod), in which nature is (*a*) suspended and (*b*) restored to normal. It also corresponds to the third miracle of Exod. 4 (water into blood = the first plague). For both in Exod. 4^{9} and in ch. 14 the natural functions of water are superseded to assist Israel.

[3] see above, par. 3.

spiritual rather than physical; and the divine answer to his complaint has a corresponding significance.

This is one of those passages in which Jeremiah's biography foreshadows the later 'Servant' songs. The prophet's wound is a spiritual estrangement from his companions, because he alone is treading the path of the true Servant. Yet he is tempted to doubt the faithfulness of God. His solitude is therefore partly due to a defect of faith; and for this he suffers rebuke. He must undergo a conversion if he is once more to be the mouthpiece of deity. All the key-words are used.[1] 'If thou wilt return and I cause thee to return' says the Hebrew text, using two moods of the same verb, while the Septuagint has: 'if thou are converted I will restore thee'. Moreover this 'return' to God will give him courage and strength to endure his isolation, and may possibly end it. If so, it will be through *their* 'return' to him.[2] The passage, however, ends on a note of conflict which once more points towards the 'Servant' theme. Jeremiah is here representative of Israel's true vocation. The healing which is spiritual restoration involves also a sacrificial destiny. For, as an earlier passage shows (8^{4}–9^{1}), the prophet cannot separate himself from sinful Israel whose 'hurt'[3] consists in their refusal to 'return'.

At first sight the healing of a blind man at Bethsaida bears no relation to the spiritual travail of Jeremiah. In St Mark's story, however (8^{22-26}), the restoration of the man's sight by a gradual process is clearly symbolical of the gradual enlightenment of the disciples. Indeed this healing comes once more at the climax of a gospel sequence which shows very clearly what the evangelist has in mind. This sequence (7^{31}–8^{26}) begins and ends with a healing, first of a deaf mute and then of a blind man, both in accord with prophetic expectation (Isaiah $35^{5,\,6}$); and the two together connect this section of the gospel once again with Moses and the Exodus. For after the three signs have been given Moses pleads that he is slow of speech and tongue,

[1] see above, par. 4, first note.

[2] Not through *his* conformity to their ways. The Hebrew text rings the changes on four possible meanings of *shûbh*. My rendering in verse 19^{a} follows the American Jewish version. But the RV rendering may be correct: 'If thou return, then will I bring thee again, that . . .', in agreement with LXX.

[3] Literally 'breach'.

and receives this reply: 'Who maketh a man dumb or deaf or seeing or blind? Is it not I the Lord?'[1] In Wisdom 10^{21} the Song of Moses after the passage of the Red Sea (Exodus 15) is mentioned with this comment: 'Wisdom opened the mouth of the dumb and made the tongues of babes to speak clearly'. To the 'babes' we shall return later. Meanwhile enough has been said to justify the view that in this section of his gospel St Mark sees the disciples undergoing an initiation which prepares them for the fuller revelations of Caesarea Philippi and the Transfiguration.

The incident of the blind man restored to sight in Mark 8 is a synoptic parallel to the story in John 9, and it has the same kind of theological significance.[2] Here the initiates are the Twelve who need to be made whole through spiritual enlightenment. That their renewal can only be gradual is abundantly shown in the second half of this gospel. It is significant, however, that their enlightenment is symbolically depicted in terms of a *restoration* to sight. Like Jeremiah they are representative of Israel returning to her true destiny. The healing of the hurt of 'the daughter of my people' can be effected only through a Remnant of those who lead the way back to what, in the divine plan, they were always intended to be.[3] Thus, at the point now reached there have come into fuller light two factors which were briefly indicated in the concluding paragraph of the chapter-division entitled 'the two creations' (above, § ii). Because (1) Christ embodies the restoration which he is now effecting in us, therefore (2) restoration to wholeness involves a return to the source of our being in him. These two truths will largely control

[1] Exod. 4^{11}. The κωφόν and τυφλόν of LXX here correspond to Mark 7^{32} and 8^{22}.

[2] see above, par. 5 with note. The reader is also referred to *The Common Life*, Ch. VIII, especially pp. 241 ff.

[3] For the healing of 'the daughter of my people' see further the following passages: (1) Jer. $8^{21,22}$, (2) Lam. 2^{13}, (3) Isa. 58^{8-12}. On these texts it should be observed that (i) The personification in (1) and (2) is paralleled in (3) by the individualized address to Israel as a particular person: (ii) the word rendered 'health' or 'healing' in (1) and (3) means literally 'the new flesh which grows over a wound' and which is said to 'go up' or 'spring up'. In these passages the healing process issues from moral reformation, and in Isa. 58^{12} it is also likened to 'restoration'. Lastly the idiom of 'the new flesh' is used in the 'healing' which 'went up' on the temple in 2 Chron. 24^{13} and on the city walls in Neh. 4^{1} (H; 4^{7} in EVV; see RV margin *ad loc.*). These are striking examples of the symbolic character of 'healing' in OT.

our further treatment of topics connected with *Christ and Creation.* We must now point out their relation to our second pair of healings.

The enlightenment of the Twelve took them along the road to Calvary and beyond. Continuing discipleship meant association with One who fulfilled the destiny of the Suffering Servant. In a fallen world this was the only way of restoration. They must share the outlaw status of David's Son and the solitude of 'the Prophet' (Deut. 18^{15-19}) prefigured variously both by Moses and by Jeremiah. What he is they must become. The ambiguity of our fallen nature makes it difficult for us to identify Jesus either with his foreshadowing types in the Old Testament or with his disciples under the new covenant. Yet he identifies himself with all mankind, and therefore with both of these groups.[1] Moreover, just so far as they are restored and see 'all things clearly' (Mark 8^{25}), they identify themselves both with the Servant's form and, as he ever does, with those whose form the Servant took. Our scrutiny of Jeremiah has shown the prophet in oscillation between the divided counsels of doubt and that wholeness of response to which he is being impelled by grace. This intermediate stage is repeated in us all until restoration is complete.[2]

iv

The 'restoration' theme in the Acts of the Apostles. Note on the Lucan technique of 'repetition'. Repetition of 'restoration' in Acts 3 and 4. St Peter's use of Psalm 16 (LXX 15) may provide a further link in the chain binding Acts 1–4 into a 'restoration' whole.

We return now to St Luke. In his gospel the key 'restoration' word occurs only at 6^{10} in the parallel with Mark 3^5. But in Acts 1^6, as we have seen, the word recurs in a question which corresponds to a whole cycle of Old Testament prophecy; and the preceding section (iii) will have made clear the connexion

[1] For the idioms see Vol. I, p. 336 (Index): *identification, identity;* also Vol. I. p. 222, note 2: 'typology of Mark', which bears on the 'single scriptural pattern' in note 2 below.

[2] In the final verse of Malachi the Hebrew text says that Elijah 'shall cause the heart of the fathers to return to the children' etc. (*hiphil* of *shûbh*). LXX (Mal. 4^5) renders this with ἀποκαταστήσει, and widens the scope of the restoration to a re-integration of society ('a man to his neighbour.)' In Mark

between this prophetic expectation and symbolic healings. But further, a typical healing miracle actually occurs in Acts 3; and in the incidents which follow immediately afterwards this healing is treated by St Peter as a 'sign' of promised restoration. The details will be considered presently. Here it is sufficient to suggest that in the opening chapters of Acts St Luke is deliberately introducing the 'restoration' idea. If this can be shown to be a fact, what might we suppose to be its purpose? A full answer to this question would take us far afield. For I believe that a detailed examination of Acts would show ground for thinking that its plan is largely governed by the 'repetition' *motif*. If this should be the case there would be reason for believing that as the 'restoration' theme, in its various forms, is carried over from the Old Testament to the gospels, so also it is 'repeated' from the gospels to the Acts.[1]

The hypothesis outlined in the last sentence must now be tested by scrutiny of the facts. After the Pentecostal events

9^{11-13} our Lord re-affirmed this prophecy emphatically ('restores all things'), but gave it a new significance. The Christ and his forerunner fulfil a single scriptural pattern. Restoration comes only through the sufferings and humiliation of the Servant. The linguistic problem touched on in Vol. I on p. 222 (note 3) will be considered afresh at the conclusion of the present chapter (Addit. Note A).

[1] See above, in § iii, end of par. 4. The most obvious example of 'repetition' from a gospel to Acts is in the dying words of St. Stephen. These consist of a prayer in two petitions (Acts 7^{60}). There is an exact correspondence here with two of our Lord's words from the Cross as recorded by St Luke in his first volume (Luke $23^{34, 46}$). Both the Lord and his servant pray for their enemies; and as Jesus commends his spirit to the Father, so Stephen to Jesus. Another example may be cited from Acts 12, where the repetition depends partly upon a symbolic interpretation. The key phrases are: 'Then were the days of unleavened bread' (verse 3) and 'after the passover' (verse 4). James meets his Good-Friday. But as Jesus, after the passover, rose from the prison of the tomb, so Peter rises up (verse 7) and goes forth as though restored to life (verse 15). Moreover James also 'continues' in the person of his namesake (verse 17). So too the gospel healings are repeated in the Acts, while Jesus suffers in his members (9^5); and the protracted account of St Paul's trials before various authorities takes on new meaning when it is seen to 'repeat' the similar trials of our Lord at a corresponding point in the gospel narrative. In *Beginnings I.*, Vol. IV, Lake and Cadbury drew attention to another form of repetition peculiar to Luke. In a number of instances words, phrases or sentences in St Mark's Gospel, which are absent from Luke's first volume, recur in Acts (*op. cit.* p. 8, note on 1^7; cp. pp. 69, 111, 134). To their list one may perhaps add 9^{33} (*κραβϐάτου* from Mark $2^{11, 12}$).

described in Acts 2 the first public action of the apostles is set forth in chapter 3. It takes a form familiar to us in the gospel narratives. A crippled man who cannot walk is healed by a word of Peter speaking in the name of Jesus Christ. The details connected with this healing are spread over the greater part of chapters 3 and 4; and throughout that section (3^{1}–4^{12}) one can discern a significant choice of language which develops the restoration theme introduced at 1^{6}. Here we can perceive a 'technique of repetition', described more fully in the preceding note. The principal clue lies in the language of Isaiah $35^{5,6}$ as rendered in the Septuagint. The passage in question is a typical oracle of restoration and new creation. As such it has clearly exercised a deep influence upon the Christian evangelists and their writings. Indeed, it must surely have been present to the mind of our Lord when he gave his answer to the disciples of the Baptist (Matt. 11^{5}, Luke 7^{22}).

It will be remembered that in his reply to John's question ('Art thou the Coming One?' etc.) Jesus described his own activities. In the list of his 'works' he mentioned the healing of blind, lame and deaf persons. These three types of healing are promised in the prophetic oracle referred to above; and to them is there added a fourth, namely the restoration of speech to the dumb. Three of these types of healing are placed among the works of Christ by St Mark in that symbolic gospel sequence which we examined in the last section.[1] For of the two 'signs' with which the sequence begins and ends the first is a double healing. The man healed recovers hearing *and* speech (Mark 7^{32-35}). Moreover, of the four words used in the Greek version of Isaiah $35^{5,6}$, three are used by St Mark in his descriptions of these two gospel healings. In 'the Marcan sequence', therefore, one word only is lacking from the Septuagint list of infirm persons to be healed, namely the word for 'a lame man'. This

This looks like one more way of emphasizing the fact that the story of Jesus is being repeated in the story of the apostolic church. Curiously enough Lake and Cadbury pass over the repetition of 'restoration' language in complete silence. In JTS, Vol. XLVI, No. 181–2, p. 54 I have suggested a 'reversed repetition' of the Passion of Jesus in the Field of Blood (Acts 1^{15-26}) by a similar technique of transference. The 'reversal' of Gethsemane in Akeldama (if intended by Luke) is the Satanic obverse of our mystical union with Christ.

[1] § iii, last par. but two.

word, however, is covered by the incident in Acts 3. With the first healing miracle of the apostolic church the full tale of prophetic healings is completed. The fulfilment of prophecy in Christ overflows from the earthly life of the incarnate Lord to its extension in the *ecclesia*.[1] For the lame man leaps![2]

The conclusions so far reached in this section can be further supported from what follows in the narrative of Acts. Addressing the gathering crowd St Peter first gives typically apostolic witness to prophecy fulfilled in the death and resurrection of Jesus. He then ascribes the healing of the lame man to faith in the Saviour's name, concluding this part of his address with the following words: 'the faith which was through him gave to him this soundness before you all'.[3] In some texts of the Greek bible (although not the best) the word here rendered 'soundness' occurs in Isaiah 1^{6}. The original Hebrew phrase: 'there is no soundness in it' is thus reproduced exactly. Unfortunately the entire phrase is absent from the most reliable manuscripts.[4] In any case, however, the story in Acts 3 reads like a symbolical reversal of Isaiah's grim parable. The Israel of God has now

[1] For theological parallels in St Paul cp. the overflow of 'the sufferings of the Christ' in 2 Cor. 1^{5} ff. and the personal application of this figure of speech in Col. 1^{24}. As the 'Marcan sequence' in question is not present in St Luke's Gospel it is relevant to quote from *Beginnings I*, Vol. IV (pp. 54 f.) the comment of Lake and Cadbury upon a parallel example of literary connexion (between Acts $5^{15,16}$ and Mark 6^{56}): 'It is almost certain that Luke knew this section, though he did not use it, so that this verse may be . . . based, as so often, on material . . . which he did not use at the place in his own narrative where it would naturally have come' (see above, note to § iv, par. 1).

[2] The linguistic argument sketched above in the text becomes even more impressive when we examine the details. The connexion between Acts 3 and Isa. 35 is based, not only upon *χωλός* in Acts 3^{2}, but also upon *ἁλλόμενος* repeating its compound (*ἐξαλλόμενος*) in 3^{8}. This corresponds to *ἁλεῖται* . . . *χωλός* in Isa. 35^{6}. The Marcan sequence had previously taken over from Isa. $35^{5,6}$ *κωφόν, μογιλάλον* and *τυφλόν*. Of these the second is a *hapax legomenon* in LXX and NT, although the Hebrew word which it renders in Isa. 35^{6} occurs also in Exod. 4^{11}. That text, as we have already noticed, provides a further background to the Marcan sequence (§ iii, last par. but two).

[3] Tr. LC

[4] *ὁλοκληρία*, the word rendered 'soundness' above, is the natural equivalent of Isaiah's Hebrew word. As such it occurs in Aquila's Jewish-Greek version of the OT (A.D. 2nd cent) at Isa. 1^{6}. The absence of the missing phrase from the text of LXX leaves the passage untranslatable. Two sug-

been restored to that wholeness of which the prophet in his day could discern no trace, but which was confidently expected in another prophetic oracle of Isaiah's book.[1] For St Luke the two prophecies of sickness and restoration (Isaiah 1 and 35) would be presumed to have a single author. If, then, our previous argument is sound the restoration to perfect wholeness signified in Acts 3^{16} might be intended to mark the completing of that reversion from sickness to health which we have seen unfolding by stages from prophecy to gospel and from Jesus to his church.

In the last ten verses of Acts 3 St Peter's address to the people comes to a practical conclusion with an appeal for repentance. In this appeal one phrase stands out as significant for our present argument. In order that this phrase may appear in its context we here set down the single lengthy sentence in which it occurs:

> Repent ye therefore, and turn again, that your sins may be blotted out, that so there may come seasons of refreshing from the presence of the Lord; and that he may send the Christ who hath been appointed for you, even Jesus: whom the heaven must receive until the times of *restoration of all things*, whereof God spake by the mouth of his holy prophets which have been since the world began (Acts 3^{19-21} as rendered in RV).

The word here translated 'restoration' is the noun corresponding to our key verb. It occurs nowhere else in the Greek Bible; but the phrase 'restoration of all things' must be connected with the corresponding phrase attributed to our Lord in Mark 9^{12}, where in answer to a question of the disciples Jesus replies that 'Elias comes first and *restores all things*'.[2]

gestions, therefore, may be made: (1) the phrase may have dropped out of LXX by accident, to be restored later by a Christian hand, possibly under the influence of Acts 3^{16}. (2) On the other hand recent researches show the possibility that St Luke was using another Greek version of Isaiah in which ὁλοκληρία was present (as in Aquila's version). For this see *The Cairo Geniza*, Schweich Lectures for 1941, by P. E. Kahle, Lecture III. § 2, especially pp. 165 ff.

[1] The imagery of recovery from wound or sickness recurs in Isa. 30^{26} and 33^{24} as an equivalent of national restoration, material and spiritual.

[2] The passage in Mark 9 has already been briefly examined, together with its OT background, in the final footnote to Section iii above. In Acts 3^{21} *πάντων* echoes Mark's *πάντα* in accordance with the Lucan technique already noticed.

We can see, then, a probable chain of connexion between Malachi 4^6 (LXX, 4^5), Mark 9^{12} and Acts 3^{21}, Malachi's prediction being first universalized in the dominical phrase 'all things' and later repeated in its new gospel form at the climax of St Peter's address.[1] Next we must notice that if St Luke's copy of the Hebrew prophets in the Greek language showed the same order as that of the Septuagint[2] he had only to glance up the column from Isaiah 1^6, and his eye would light upon the 'restoration' saying in Malachi 4. This fact may well be thought to increase the probability that when he wrote Acts 3^{16-21} he had both these prophetic oracles in mind. Moreover, when we examine more closely the correspondences between the latter part of St Peter's speech and the concluding section of Malachi in the Greek version coincidences begin to multiply. For, first, the speech passes from 'restoration' by Elijah *redivivus* to the 'Prophet' whom Moses said would come 'like unto me'. According to St Luke the apostolic preacher seems to be saying that the 'return' of Elijah in the Baptist has ushered in a 'return' of Moses in 'the Prophet' like unto himself; and this corresponds to the order in which Elijah and Moses appear in the Greek version of Malachi's concluding paragraph.[3]

The order in question reverses the Hebrew text. Moreover in the synoptic gospels this reversal is peculiar to St Mark (9^4);[4] so that once more we find a chain of connexion between Malachi 4, Mark 9 and Acts 3, characterized by its own special features; and this, too, again follows the pattern of repetition whereby St Luke makes St Mark's Gospel the connecting link between Hebrew prophecy and the apostolic church. If now we examine once more the respective patterns of Malachi and Acts we find a second range of coincidences. In Acts 3 St Peter recommends 'conversion' (using one of our three key words)[5] as the way to 'times of refreshment' which will precede the return of Jesus and the restoration of all things. The advice corresponds to that which the prophet Jeremiah

[1] See (*a*) the final note of § iii and (*b*) the note appended to the par. of the present § which immediately precedes this one.

[2] For which see the ref. to Kahle's book in the note on *ὁλοκληρία* above.

[3] Acts 3^{21-23} = Mal. 4^{4-6} (LXX). For the 'new Elijah' preceding the 'new Moses' see the final par. of § iii above with its footnotes.

[4] Contrast Matt. 17^3, Luke 9^{30}.

[5] *ἐπιστέφειν*. See above the first note attached to par. 4 of § iii.

received in a passage already considered (Jer. $15^{18,19}$). Spiritual healing involves moral conversion. In our previous analysis this process was seen to bring enlightenment as indicated by St Mark in his 'sequence' (7^{31}–8^{32}); and the same process is outlined exactly in Malachi 3^{18}–4^{5}, as set forth in the Septuagint.[1]

In the Greek version of Malachi 3^{18} we read: 'Ye shall be converted[2] and shall discern between the righteous and the wicked'. Enlightenment follows conversion; and this is also implied in Acts 3, where St Peter tells his hearers that in unwitting ignorance they had fulfilled the prophecy of the suffering Servant by crucifying Jesus (verses 13–15, 17), but that if they 'return' to him, he will return to them (verses 19, 20). If they do so, their sins will be wiped out, and yet another item in the corresponding prophecy will come to fulfilment. For in Malachi 4^{2} we read: 'And to you who fear my name shall the Sun of Righteousness arise with healing in his wings'. The spiritual healing of St Peter's hearers would then give to them that 'perfect soundness' which was effectually symbolized in the healed cripple who stood before them whole.[3] The wholeness of salvation is now fitly symbolized by a fusion of all the types and all the prophecies into a single picture. In particular Malachi 4^{2ff} is understood in the light of Isaiah 53 to mean three things: First of all, Jesus, who as the predestined Servant takes all his precursors into himself, heals us by making our sickness his own.[4] Like Moses he must become the leper in order that he may lead the Exodus. Secondly, he restores the Israel of God to its promised destiny by rising victorious over death; and this he does, thirdly, as the Righteous One by turning away his people from their sins.[5]

[1] In the EVV this corresponds to 3^{18}–4^{6},—leaving out 4^{4}.

[2] ἐπιστρέφειν here acquires a moral significance through a literalized rendering of the Hebrew idiom which means simply: 'ye shall again discern' (as once before). Cp. AJV. Similarly EVV, ignoring the idiom, have: 'Then shall ye return and discern'.

[3] For the original meaning of Mal. 4^{2} (H. 3^{20}) see ICC *ad loc.*; and for the mythological background of the 'wings' cp. *The Septuagint and Jewish Worship* by H. S. J. Thackeray, pp. 51–54.

[4] cp. Vol. I, p. 223, note 2, and above, final par. of § iii with its notes.

[5] With ἀποστρέφειν in Acts 3^{26} cp. in LXX 3 Reg. $8^{34,35}$ where this alternative compound of στρέφειν does duty for two meanings of *shûbh*: 'Thou wilt restore them to the land . . . and they will turn away from their sins'.

The theme of Acts 3^{13-26} connects healing, and the wholeness which belongs to salvation, with the death and resurrection of Jesus. So too, the same theme is more briefly resumed in the next scene where St Peter addresses the Sanhedrin. The sole difference between these two speeches lies in a shifting of the typology from the Servant prophecy to the rejected Stone (Psalm 118^{22}).[1] We must notice that this apostolic witness to the messianic death and resurrection begins in chapter 2 with the Pentecostal sermon of St Peter which also constitutes the first of a series. If then there is a connexion between the restoration of the Davidic kingdom in 1^{6} and the topic of restoration through healing in chapters 3 and 4 we might expect to find it in the intervening sections. Moreover, there is good ground for thinking that there is a close-knit unity of pattern running through these early chapters of Acts, not only in the actual course of events, but also in the continuity which is there

[1] It may prove convenient to set out here in the form of a diagram the biblical connexions of Acts 3 and 4 as set forth in the preceding argument. The refs. to Malachi follow the enumeration of LXX, where 4^{5} = EVV 4^{6}:

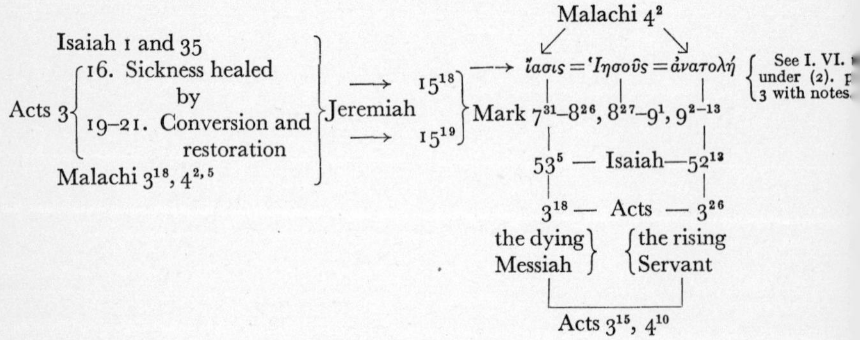

Comments:

(1) The inclusion of Mark 9^{2-13} under ἀνατολή implies that this gospel section has Mal. $4^{2,5}$ (LXX) for its prophetic background, as indicated in Vol. 1 (p. 222, note 2).

(ii) In Mal. 4^{2} ἴασις is followed by σκιρτήσετε, as of young creatures released from their bonds. Then in 4^{5} we have ἀποκαταστήσει. In Luke 6^{10ff} ἀποκατάστασις by healing has as its sequel (*a*) an inauguration of new Israel in twelve tribes and (*b*) a healing mission. Here ἰᾶτο πάντας (6^{19}) is followed by σκιρτήσατε (6^{23}) which repeats the leap (ἐσκίρτησε), in $1^{41,44}$, of the unborn John ('my messenger', Mal. 3^{1}).

manifested between the Old Testament images and their fulfilment in the story of the new Israel.[1]

In Acts 2^{22ff} St Peter announces to his Jewish hearers that the crucified Jesus of Nazareth has been raised from the dead in fulfilment of the hope expressed in the Greek version of Psalm 16^{8-11}.[2] The speaker attributes the Psalm to David; and 'the whole point of Peter's speech is that this hope was not fulfilled in the case of David but only in that of Jesus',[3] whose 'flesh' saw no 'corruption'. In the latter part of his address St Peter argues from a combination of 'Davidic' psalms (132, 16, 110) that the divine promise to David had now been fulfilled in his true heir, Jesus the ascended Messiah and bestower of the outpoured Spirit. We must not fail to note the connexion of this argument with its context in chapters 1 and 2. When the risen Christ is asked about the restoration of the kingdom originally established by David he refers his questioners to an outpouring of the Spirit such as prophecy connected with the reign of a Davidic Messiah.[4] There follow his heavenly exaltation, the filling of the vacant twelfth throne (Luke 22^{30}) and the promised illapse of the Spirit. Clearly the restoration has begun, and in the glowing description which follows the Pentecostal sermon the converts who are being 'made whole' adhere obediently to the teaching of those set over them as princes of the new Israel (2^{42}).

In view of the 'Davidic' *motif* thus recurring in Acts 1 and 2 we cannot leave out of account some earlier sentences in the Psalm which Peter quotes as David's. Here, for the third time, the Greek version is important. The following is a literal rendering:

> The Lord is the portion of my inheritance and of my cup;
> Thou art he who restores my inheritance to me.
> The lines fell to me in the best places,
> Yea my inheritance is best for me (Ps. $15^{5,6}$ LXX).[5]

[1] On some aspects of this continuity as it is exhibited especially in Acts 1 the reader is referred to my article on *The Choice of Matthias* in JTS, Vol. XLVI, No. 181–2.

[2] Ps. 15^{9} LXX (in contrast to the Hebrew), 'an indication that the speech is really based on the LXX' (LC., *ad loc.*, on Acts 2^{26}).

[3] LC., *ad loc.* At a second point the argument depends upon LXX, viz. in Ps. 15^{10}, where, instead of 'the pit' the Greek has διαφθοράν.

[4] Isa. 11, 32, Ezek. 34–37, Zech. 4^{6}, 12^{10}.

[5] For the comment of LC upon verse 5 the reader is referred to Addit. Note A below.

Viewed as a prayer of David the psalm reads like a grateful review of the past with hope for the future. In the past there was one terrible crisis when David seemed to be losing his inheritance, namely, in the rebellion of Absalom. David's own feelings at the time are described in 2 Samuel 15 ff.; and the language used is significant for its affinity with the second line quoted above. When David is in flight and is met by Zadok with the ark, the king bids him *restore* the ark to its place with these words: 'If I shall find favour in the eyes of the Lord, he will *restore* me, and show me both it and his habitation.'[1] In chapter 19 this hope is fulfilled and in verses 11–13 (EVV 10–12) the word italicized above is used three times to express the people's purpose of 'bringing back' the king. It is used once more in 19^{44} in the same sense.[2] The word in question is the key Hebrew verb for 'restoration'.

In the Hebrew idiom any state of misery can be identified with descent into the underworld of Sheol; and it is possible that escape from temporal misfortune must be read into the original thought of this psalm in verse 10 with its allusions to Hades-Sheol and 'the pit'. But for Christians after Pentecost the psalm (at least in its Greek version) had a new meaning. The return of David from exile, like the later return of Israel from captivity, foreshadowed the more mysterious return of Jesus (and that in no metaphorical sense) from the toils of death and the prison-house of the tomb. The restoration of David's inheritance was finally effected through the death and resurrection of David's Son.

Additional Note A:

Acts 3^{21}—*An Alternative Rendering*

In their commentary on Acts in Vol. iv of *Beginnings I* Lake and Cadbury render Acts 3^{21} as follows: 'Whom heaven must receive until times of establishment of all things which God spake by the mouth of his holy prophets from the beginning of the world'. They recognize that ἀποκατάστασις 'ought strictly to mean' 'restoration'; but it and its verb 'do not always have this meaning'. They then

[1] 2 Sam. 15^{25}.

[2] EVV. 19^{43}. Except for 'restore the ark' LXX uses ἐπιστρέφειν in all the above instances; and at 15^{25}, 19^{12} and 19^{43} the idiom is the same as in the Hebrew text. For the ark LXX has ἀποστρέφειν.

refer to LXX 'in passages where the Hebrew or the context' is alleged to render 'restoration' improbable. For this they cite as examples four passages: Ps. 16^5; Job 8^6; 2 Macc. 12^{39}, 15^{20} (*op. cit.*, p. 38). They next refer to contemporary linguistic support for the meaning 'establishment' so that 'in relation to prophecy' the word 'may mean the establishment of what was predicted rather than the restoration of an earlier condition'; and they cite in support of this conclusion 'the use of ἀποκαθίστημι in Mark ix. 12 = Matt. xvii. 11'. The purpose of the present note is, first to weigh the argument for 'establishment' thus briefly indicated, and then to consider its relation to the conclusions of the preceding chapter.

We will consider first the examples from LXX cited as evidence against 'restoration'.

(1) Ps. 16^5. 'The Hebrew or the context' are the two tests put forward: (*a*) The Hebrew has in 5^6 'Thou maintainest my lot' (RV, AJV). Kimchi suggested: 'Thou art the holder of my lot'; this is accepted in the *Soncino* comm: with the remark that the psalmist is content because God 'holds his destiny in His hand'. Thus the LXX rendering is not a translation nor even a paraphrase, but *a different version* of what the psalmist wrote. The fact that *gôral*, like κλῆρος, could mean 'property assigned by lot' and so 'heritage' would suggest a probable reason for the variation. But it is no adequate ground for the conclusion drawn by LC. Here we may cite from *Beginnings I*, Vol. ii, p. 16 a literary judgement ascribed to 'Henry J. Cadbury and the Editors' (see *ib.* p. 7): 'The translators of the Old Testament' 'either had a text of the Old Testament different from ours or else felt themselves at liberty to adapt, rearrange and expand or contract, to a greater degree than a modern would feel justified in doing'. Anyone who reads Kahle's recent Schweich lectures, especially his treatment of MT and LXX, will see a high probability in the first of the two alternatives just cited, wherever LXX differs from the Hebrew as greatly as in Ps 16 (15). (*b*) The context is a vaguer test for which it will be sufficient to refer the reader back to my own treatment of this psalm in Chapter I above.

(2) Job 8^6. (*a*) The *Soncino* comm. *ad loc.* quotes Buttenweiser's rendering of 8^{6b} (Hebrew): 'would make thy house prosper again in proof of thy righteousness'. This comes very near to Driver-Gray in ICC, who render 'restore' or 'properly, make whole, complete', 'the habitation which, by its prosperity, will be evidence of the righteousness of its possessor' (*op. cit.*, p. 77). This verdict connects the primary meaning of *shlm* (in *piel*) with the biblical theme of healing or salvation which 'makes whole'. Driver-Gray see that for Job the promise is one of 'restored fortune', however it be phrased.

Thus they not only endorse the LXX rendering but go on to connect ἀποκαταστήσει here with its use in Matt. 17^{11} (another of LC's cited texts!). On the other hand in Job 22^{28} the Hebrew means 'it will be established unto thee'. Curiously, however, LXX here repeats verbally its own rendering of 8^{6b}. The line in Hebrew means that Job's purpose will be brought to pass; but when we turn (*b*) to context we encounter an interesting phenomenon. Job 22^{21-30} reads like an expansion and application to Job of the advice given in Jer. $15^{18,19}$ to Jeremiah.[1] As there, so here, conversion leads to spiritual recovery and the return of good fortune which in OT is its normal concomitant. Thus the main theme of Job's friends continues: 'Take our advice, and you will be restored to prosperity'.

(3) 2 Maccabees 12^{39}, 15^{20}. In *Beginnings I*, Vol. ii, the section by W. K. L. Clarke devoted to 'the use of the Septuagint in Acts' furnishes statistical evidence for a high degree of linguistic affinity between Acts and 2 Maccabees (pp. 73–76). It is, therefore, considered highly probable that Luke may have read 2 Maccabees before writing Acts. It is all the more surprising, then, that LC have cited only two out of the four relevant passages in that book. We will take them in order. In 2 Maccabees 11^{25} (the letter of Antiochus Eupator to Lysias concerning a settlement with the Jews) the king says: 'We determine that their temple *be restored* to them, and that they live according to the customs that were in the days of their ancestors' (RV). The context shows that here no other rendering of ἀποκατασταθῆναι is possible. In 2 Macc. 12^{25} a similar verdict must be returned; for here a promise is given *to restore* hostages unharmed. In 2 Macc. 12^{39} (the first passage cited by LC) ἀποκαταστῆσαι dignifies 'to bring back' the bodies of dead soldiers to the tombs of their fathers. Here, as frequently, the English rendering of RV is a synonym for 'restore'. There remains 2 Macc. 15^{20}, the only instance in this book where the meaning of our key verb is doubtful. RV has 'the elephants brought back to a convenient post'; and this has some support from Liddell and Scott, new edition, Vol. I, pp. 200 f., where under 4. we find: 'in drill, *restore* a formation', and the imperative: 'as you were'. Possibly there is an analogy with the astronomical meaning: 'return to the original situation'.

It follows that LXX in general, and 2 Macc. in particular, afford no appreciable support to the rendering of Acts 3^{21} proposed by LC. Moreover the judgement of W. K. L. Clarke concering Acts and 2 Maccabees cited above connects the Epistle to the Hebrews with 2 Maccabees in the same way, for 'the author of Hebrews belonged to the same literary circles as Luke' (*op. cit.* pp. 74 f. and note). We

[1] see above, Ch. I, § iii, last par. but three.

must therefore notice that the only NT instance of ἀποκαθίστημι outside the Synoptics and Acts is in Hebrews 13[19] where the author asks for his readers' prayers 'that I may be *restored* to you the sooner'. At the conclusion of their note (*op. cit.* Vol. iv, p. 38) LC cite Mark 9[12] and Matt. 17[11] in support of their theory. The difference here between the two evangelists is interesting and perhaps significant. In Matthew's version our Lord repeats the actual tense of Mal. 4[5] LXX (ἀποκαταστήσει). 'Restore all things' then would mean re-integrate Israel into wholeness of social life as LXX *ad loc.* clearly indicates. On the other hand Mark changes the future tense of LXX into a present; and this appears to agree with his symbolic treatment of the Baptist (for which see my Vol. I; p. 222, note 2). 'Elias' came and was martyred. But the restoration of all things goes forward in the mission of the Son of Man who, as 'the Servant', has identity with his forerunner.

Are we to conclude that the two renderings of Acts 3[21] are mutually incompatible? I do not think so. Nothing is more likely than that St Luke so framed his sentence as to make it bear a double meaning. Here we may quote the happily worded statement with which the authors of *Beginnings I*, Vol. ii., conclude an opening section already cited above: 'the editors of this book are anxious to state as emphatically as possible their conviction that much more can be done by considering how far Luke was Greek and how far Jewish in his methods of writing. *The foundation of all wisdom on this subject must be a consideration of the use made by Luke of the Septuagint, of the Gospel of Mark, and of the Greek language in general*' (*op, cit.*, p. 29). Of this wise counsel the two former parts have received careful attention in the first chapter of the present volume. The third part would provide an endless task concerning which others must form their judgements. In conclusion, however, it must be affirmed that a matter of this kind cannot be adequately decided by a statistical survey of linguistic habits. There is a theological issue involved concerning the unity of Scripture and the relation of the OT to the NT, an issue which was fully discussed in our first volume.

One last consideration is worth mentioning. There are instances where the Greek noun under discussion, or its verb, mean 'restitution' or 'payment of a debt'. The earliest instance in LXX is Abraham's payment to Ephron (Gen. 23[16]). Here the Hebrew picture of money being weighed out is replaced in the Greek by the notion of 'paying what is due' in recompense for value received. So right relations are 'established' by 'restoring' to a person what is due to him. In their Vocabulary MM cite several examples of such payments which they appear to understand as acts of 'restoration', whereas LC would probably classify them as 'the establishment of what is due'. Similarly the Hebrew word which Driver-Gray render 'restore' in Job 8^{6} (see above) occurs in Job 21^{19}, 41^{3} (EVV 41^{11}) with the meaning: 'recompense' or 'repay'. Lastly in Amos 5^{15} the prophetic injunction to 'establish judgement in the gate' may well have seemed to the translators centuries later a summons to 'restore' the true order of life; and they so rendered it. The theological issue may make room for both meanings, if the 'establishment of prophecy' in Christ involves 'a restoration of creation' as it was 'in the Beginning'. If *ἀποκατάστασις* in Acts 3^{21} were allowed in this sense to carry both meanings, it would become practically a synonym of *ἀνακεφαλαίωσις* as understood by St Irenaeus.

CHAPTER II

RETURN TO THE BEGINNING

i

The connexion between 'healing' and 'restored inheritance' further illustrated. 'Return to a former condition' may be a change for the worse (Hosea's threat of doom), or for the better, as when the Exodus discipline is repeated. This 'return' fulfilled in the Form of the Servant, which binds both Testaments into one.

In the latter part of the preceding chapter (§§ iii and iv) we were examining the biblical theme of 'restoration to wholeness', and that too mainly as it is represented under the symbolism of healing. But we also took note of 'restoration' under another of its scriptural aspects. The question of the disciples in Acts 1 6 took us back to those prophetic passages which promise a return of Israel from captivity to dwell once more in the holy land. At certain points a connexion between the two forms of speech became manifest. For the figure of a sick person restored to health could and did symbolize a recovery of the body politic, and so too a re-establishment of the people of God in their own proper place, where they might fulfil their true destiny as the sphere within which the rule of God is to be manifested here on earth. In his report of St Peter's speech in Acts 3 St Luke employs a word which could have conveyed precisely this double meaning. For the word rendered 'perfect soundness' in Acts 3 16 (*holokleria*) might well have suggested to a Greek-speaking Jew the idea of a 'whole inheritance' (*holos kleros*); and this in turn would have recalled to mind the original apportionment of the holy land to the twelve tribes by Joshua, each tribe receiving its due share of the newly-conquered territory.[1]

[1] Josh. Chs. 12–21. In LXX this sequel to Joshua's victories shews a dominant interest in the theme of κλῆρος and μερίς which culminates in the addition to Josh. 21 40: 'Jesus made an end of dividing the land' (διαμερίσας τὴν γῆν). In Acts there is a corresponding sequel to the victory of a new

There is another sense in which these two forms of speech are comparable. Restoration to health means a *return* of the physical organism *to a former condition* which existed before the sickness supervened. So too the political restoration of Israel depicted by prophecy implied a return from captivity and exile to the original homeland of the chosen people, from subjugation, moreover, to relative independence. In both these series of images what is envisaged is a return to an earlier, more natural and more desirable state of things. Running through these biblical themes there is, also, another noticeable feature to which attention must be drawn. Return to health is inevitably also a return to something more like what the sufferer was in his youth. The recovered cripple who followed Peter and John into the temple, 'walking and leaping and praising God', had a new vitality which must have made him seem decidedly younger in appearance to those who had known him before this great transformation. So too in the prophecies of Israel's 'return' there is a recurring reference to the days of the nation's youth.

At this point, however, we must notice that the bare notion of 'return to a former condition' is capable of very varied application. In itself it does not necessarily imply a change for the better, a fact which can be illustrated from some of the prophetic oracles where this form of expression is employed. Thus, in Isaiah $23^{17(16)}$ an oracle of uncertain date concerning the city of Tyre declares that after so many years she 'shall return to her hire'. This is explained to mean that after a period of desolation that famous city will recover her function of world-wide trade to the lasting benefit of her neighbour Israel. Indirectly, then, this secular recovery will serve the divine purpose. So, whereas the context likens Tyre to an old harlot returning to her 'profession', in the Greek version we read that 'God will make a visitation of Tyre, and she shall be restored again to her ancient state'.[1] The language here employed seems to be conformed, perhaps unconsciously, to similar descriptions

Jesus who 'gave lots to' his chosen ones (1^{26}; contrast 8^{21}). Moreover he made an end of 'division' (Gen. 10^{25}) by 'dividing' tongues of fire in distribution to all (2^{3}; cp. 2^{45}). Thus the agelong *διαμερισμός* of Babel was reversed in the *ὁλοκληρία* of a new *κοινωνία* (2^{42ff}, 4^{32ff}).

[1] *πάλιν ἀποκαταστήσεται εἰς τὸ ἀρχαῖον.*

in which a restoration of the Hebrew theocracy is depicted. Moreover there is one further detail in the parallel which has special significance.

The return of Israel to *her* 'ancient state' is often, in such descriptions, combined with, and complicated by, that other prophetic image of Jahveh's bride turned harlot. In one instance the grim parallel which we are considering is actually complete. In Ezekiel 23^{19-21} unfaithful Israel is threatened with the terrors of a Babylonian conquest because she is 'repeating' the idolatries of a more ancient bondage at the dawn of her history, '*remembering the days of her youth* wherein she had played the harlot in the land of Egypt'. In the phrase just quoted there sounds a profoundly ironical note. For elsewhere the prophet has used precisely this phrase in an opposite sense. If Israel now hankers after the sins of a mis-spent youth[1] that backsliding tendency corresponds to the fact of her *not* remembering the love and care bestowed upon her in the helplessness of her childhood days ($16^{22, 43}$; cp. 16^{60}).[2] Before we go further into that, however, we must glance at yet one more instance of 'return to the beginning' which has nothing joyous or glorious about it.

The second chapter of Hosea is in some ways the most important, as also the most striking, of the group of prophecies which we are now examining. In its present shape it provides a link between the two forms of return to the past, the one dark and sombre, the other lit with rays of light; and upon any view it is the historical starting point of an extended sequence. It is, however, considered to be certain that the original prophecy offered no comfort at all to guilty Israel. What Hosea wrote was, according to this view, an oracle of doom which contained no hope of recovery. The comforting verses in this chapter were inserted by later editors on a model drawn from elsewhere in the corpus of 'writing' prophets.[3] If this conclusion is correct, there is

[1] cp. the divine complaint in Jer. 22^{21}: 'This hath been thy manner from thy youth, that thou hearkenedst not to my voice'.

[2] In such passages LXX appears to make a distinction, not present in the Hebrew, between νηπιότης ('childhood', Hos. 2^{15}, Ezek. 16) and νεότης ('youth', Jer, 2^{2}, 3^{25}, 22^{21}, $38(31)^{19}$, $39(32)^{30}$, Ezek. 23). The difference of language does bring out a real distinction between the two notes of helplessness and wayward adolescence alternately struck.

[3] The crucial section is to be found in Hos. 2^{4-19} (H), which becomes 2^{2-17} in LXX and EVV.

no reason why it should be thought disturbing for faith. It would mean, simply, that the scriptures were the work of many more inspired persons than appear on the surface. It would also illustrate the truth that the full form of revelation developed only through a slow-moving process in a series of stages.

The sentence of judgement comes at the beginning of the section (EVV., $2^{2,3}$). The opening words are a despairing cry to the Israelites: 'Plead with your mother that she put away her adulteries lest. . . .' Repentance, however, is not expected, and judgement will take effect. The threat is five-fold, and in its original form it reads thus:

> Lest I strip her naked,
> And set her as in the day that she was born,
> And make her as the wilderness,
> And set her like a desert land,
> And slay her with thirst.

For the full understanding of these words two facts must be borne in mind: (1) With the Hebrews, apparently, as with other peoples, an adulterous wife was liable to be shamed by stripping and exposure; (2) in the Semitic world a people was commonly identified with the land in which it dwelt. Accordingly, the first two lines of the threat indicate a grim sort of 'return to the beginning'. The unfaithful wife will find herself reduced to the condition of a new-born infant. We may compare the saying of Job, when suddenly stripped of everything: Naked came I out of my mother's womb, and naked shall I return thither' (Job 1^{21}).[1] But secondly, the idiom of identification suddenly changes the picture, and the threat of stripping takes a new form. Israel is the unholy bride who deserves to be shamed; but also, Israel is the land which has suffered defilement. It must therefore become like that wilderness where Israel's story began.[2]

The passage with which we are dealing is the earliest of a series in the prophetical writings. The theme is elaborated by

[1] It is to be noticed that this saying illustrates the idiom of identity. The woman who bore Job is identified with mother-earth to which he will eventually return. See further below, Ch. V, § iv, par. 5.

[2] The *Soncino* Comm. finds here a further parallel; as the harlot belongs to no husband, so the wilderness with which she is identified is 'ownerless property to which anybody could lay claim' (*The Twelve Prophets*, ed. A. Cohen, p. 7).

Jeremiah and Ezekiel; and, according to the view here accepted, the later elaborations have modified the original picture. But certain common assumptions appear to underlie the sequence as a whole. Thus the story of the Exodus is accepted as the starting-point of Israel's history. The history, then, is by its very inception *redemptive history*, and, further, it was cradled in the covenant of Sinai. Secondly the prophets agree in the assumption that Israel began life as a nomadic people, and, as we shall see, they often set store by that fact. Here, however, another point of view presents itself. The threat which Hosea hears is something worse than a decree that the chosen people shall return to nomadic wanderings in the wilderness. For the holy land itself is to become completely barren. As a bestial man is lower than a beast, so urbanized Israel will be worse off in the day of judgement than her primitive ancestors. A wilderness provides for its inhabitants, however sparingly. But Israel is to become a desert land with no green coverings; and a landless peasantry without a drop of rain will die of starvation.[1]

The conclusion of the threat is devastating. Yet the opening phrases contain in their actual form the germ of a most fruitful idea, one which became prominent in the main stream of later prophecy. For the threat identifies a new-born child with wilderness conditions. This association of words could and did suggest a return to childhood days and to the desirable simplicity of an earlier period in the nation's history. Reduction to a 'wilderness' way of life might be an inevitable punishment for apostasy; but it might also be a profitable discipline opening a way to national re-birth. This thought is clearly expressed in Hos. $2^{16,17b}$ (H) where Israel is allured into the wilderness to renew the experience of Sinai-Horeb.[2] The various strata of prophecy which bear the names of Hosea, Jeremiah and Ezekiel exhibit this particular conception of 'return to the beginning' in a variety of ways. Sometimes the prophets are content to draw idyllic pictures of the past, pictures which contain an implicit summons to return to 'the old paths' so described.[3] Sometimes, again, they plead with Israel to 'return' from the sins of wayward youth,[4] or reaffirm the divine remembrance of former intimacies.[5]

[1] For a similar vision of doom see Jer. 4^{23-28} (below, § ii, par. 1).

[2] Presumed to be one of the later additions.

[3] Jer. 6^{16}.

[4] Jer. 3^{19-25}, 22^{21}.

[5] Jer, 31^{19}, Ezek. 16^{60}.

The pictures also oscillate between two forms of family love. Hosea describes Israel as a small boy being taught by his father to walk.[1] Jeremiah shows Israel as a young bride bravely following her divine spouse out of Egypt into the unknown perils of the wilderness.[2] Ezekiel elaborates this picture by tracing the bride's story back to infancy. Jahveh found a new-born waif 'cast out into the open field' and nursed her through childhood until she was old enough to become his wife.[3] Sometimes the prophet summons Israel to remember 'the days of her childhood' or reproaches her for forgetting it.[4] Finally the Greek version of Hosea's five-fold threat introduces a significant change which goes far towards a reversal of its original meaning. In this version the second line becomes: 'I will *restore* her as the day of her birth'. The introduction of the key-word 'restore'[5] reflects the influence of the main 'restoration' sequence with its predominantly hopeful associations. The infant, naked and helpless, will none the less experience once more the healthy process of learning to know the mind of her loving Father.

Such a return to childhood's early schooling will be against the grain of a humanity grown sophisticated. Here once more the Septuagint interprets the message of hope in its own way.[6] In the original the sentence runs: 'She shall *respond* there as in the days of her *youth*, and as in the day when she came up out of the land of Egypt'. This belongs to the allegory of the young wife returning to her true husband. The 'response' is precisely that which is so beautifully described in Jeremiah 2^2. Another Jewish tradition connects the word with Israel's songs of triumph, as at the Red sea,[7] and the same Hebrew word carries a third meaning which the translators preferred: 'She shall be *humbled* there as in the days of her *childhood* etc.' Here the bride has been

[1] Hos. 11^3; cp. Jer. 31^{19}.
[2] Jer. 2^2.
[3] Ezek. 16^{3ff}.
[4] Ezek. $16^{22, 43}$.
[5] ἀποκαταστήσω. LC do not cite this instance for their thesis (Addit. Note A). To do so would involve overlooking the critical theory of a doom-oracle transformed into welcome discipline. This transformation is further accentuated by changes in LXX (see next par. above in the text). Thus the Greek version of Hos. 2 is more clearly linked with the main sequence of 'restoration' passages.
[6] Hos. 2^{15b} (=H. 2^{17}).
[7] Exod. 15^{21}; cp. 1 Sam. 18^7 (the *answer* in antiphonal singing). So Kimchi.

put back to school and finds it a humiliating experience. In all of these three versions there is 'repetition' of past history, such as we have learnt to expect in the bible way of thinking. The two former renderings, however, emphasize the joyful aspect of the Exodus, that which might seem to render repetition attractive, whereas the Septuagint reminds us that there is a price to be paid for such a return.

There are passages in the Septuagint where a divine over-ruling seems to be moulding the Greek language into forms of speech which are soon to become characteristic of the revelation in Jesus Christ. Such a passage is the one at which we have just now glanced. The conjunction of 'humiliation' with 're-birth' through a 'return to childhood'[1] sounds like a dramatic foreshadowing of that new birth of the world which was first manifested in a Holy Childhood, when the Son of God 'took the form of a servant and humbled himself' (Phil. $2^{7, 8}$), thereby fulfilling a principle enunciated in one of his own sayings (Matt. 23^{12}). For her self-exaltation Israel 'shall be humbled' (the prophetic word and tense are repeated in the Gospel); and so too for his self-humiliation the Holy Child who is the true Israel shall be exalted. In this sense the dominical saying covers both Testaments and binds them into one. In this sense, too, the second chapter of Hosea, with its joyful conclusion, comes near to being an epitome of divine revelation.

If, however, we are justified in thus 'reading back' the New Testament into the Old Testament we must go further. If 'restoration' is repeated from prophecy to the gospel and from Jesus to his church in the sense in which such a repetition was outlined in the preceding chapter, then what may here be found epitomized in prophecy is a way of 'return' to our lost inheritance once for all enacted in Jesus and now in process of reproduction in his mystical body as a whole. For a more detailed picture of that way we may turn with advantage to the prophecies of Ezekiel, from which indeed the Greek version of Hosea may well have drawn some of its special insights. There are two passages in particular to which attention must be directed. The first of these is the latter part of chapter 16 which appends to the prophetic allegory of the unfaithful wife a further allegory concerning Judah, Samaria and Sodom. It is

[1] *ταπεινόω* with *νηπιότης* in Hos. $2^{15(17)}$; cp. *γένεσις* in $2^{3(5)}$.

this picture of three 'sisters' which may possibly have inspired the Septuagint emphasis upon 'humiliation' in Hosea. The second passage is the prophecy of *return through the wilderness* in chapter 20.

In the former of these sections there are two points for consideration, namely, first the extent of the humiliation suffered by Judah, and secondly the nature of the restoration which she is to share with her two sisters. On the first point the prophecy insists that Judah was the greatest sinner of the three. She ranks lower than Sodom! Moreover, in the restoration she will have to acknowledge Sodom whom she has treated with contempt. For they will share together in the new covenant on equal terms. We are reminded of the similar use which our Lord made of Sodom as an extreme type of wickedness, when he set her above some of his own contemporaries.[1] Finally Sodom here typifies a return from the dead after total extinction. By so much then is Judah's humiliation also intensified. We are inevitably reminded of the fact that in the Greek version of Hosea's doom-oracle death by thirst and restoration as though by a new birth are set side by side as if they were parts of one process.[2] This brings us to the second point for consideration. The Hebrew text of Ezekiel 16^{55} prophecies a return of the sisters, each to her 'former estate', that is to an earlier condition of prosperity before disaster overtook them. The Septuagint, however, has a variant which deserves attention: 'They shall be restored as they were from the beginning.'

Such a change of expression might be thought insignificant. On the other hand it may have seemed to be required by the context. For in the final section (verses 59–63), which may come from a later hand,[3] Sodom is given to Judah as a daughter in 'an everlasting covenant'. This is not a return to any 'former estate' recorded in history.[4] It is something new to history, although it might have belonged to a divine plan which was 'from the beginning'. Whether some such idea was behind the

[1] Matt. 11^{24}, in a context to which we shall presently return.

[2] Hos. $2^{3(5)}$.

[3] So G. A. Cooke in ICC, *ad loc.*, p. 180.

[4] And so there is no real parallel with Ezek. 36^{11}, where 'your former estate' is identified with 'your beginnings' in H. This sentence, however, provided a certain justification for the LXX rendering in 16^{55} (see above).

Greek phrase or not is of no great importance. What matters here is, once more, the forging of a significant expression which, for early Christian thought, might seem to form part of a biblical pattern concerning 'return to the beginning'. Its place in such a pattern cannot, therefore, become fully manifest at this stage of our survey. Here we can do no more than point out that 'restoration to wholeness' in its ultimate meaning must have a significance far transcending a return to the historical past. The symbolism of healing with which we have been so much occupied implies rather *a return to the true order of creation.*

Here we have resumed the topic of the Two Creations with which the present volume opened. It was pointed out in the first section of Chapter I (pars. 7 ff.) that God's plan for creation is to be interpreted through insight into his plan for the redeemed community. The key to the former is in the latter, although each throws light upon the other. Similarly, what I have called 'the plan for the redeemed community' is spread out through both Testaments in such a manner that it can be rightly understood only through an insight which sees each of these two 'parts' in terms of the other. Two conclusions follow. First of all, our present section, occupied as it largely is with Hebrew prophecy, provides nonetheless an essential link in the argument concerning *Christ and Creation.* Secondly, the theme of 'return through the wilderness' occupies an important place in that scheme of historical redemption which culminates in Jesus and his church. The theme in question is most fully set forth in the twentieth chapter of Ezekiel, to which accordingly we now turn.

There are many passages in the prophets which foretell a return to the Holy Land. But Ezekiel's treatment of this subject is unique in several respects. Here we confine ourselves to chapter 20 where the thesis of 'return *to* the wilderness' (Hosea 2) is developed into a detailed programme of 'return *through* the wilderness'. Moreover, a precise analogy is made out between this exodus of the future and that which took place at the beginning of Israel's story. The idea of 'repetition' in redemptive history was never more elaborately expressed than in this particular prophecy. It is, of course, true that the notion of a second exodus comparable to the first occurs elsewhere in Hebrew prophecy. Indeed, Jeremiah goes so far as to say that the second will be the more memorable ($16^{14,15}$); and some of the 'restoration' passages suggest parallels to the miracles of the wilderness wanderings.[1] Ezekiel, however, has something much more definite in view. About half of his chapter is devoted to a resumé of Israelite history 'from Egypt to Babylon', as we might say. This is followed by a statement concerning the new exodus which shows repetition and correspondence at each stage.[2] Thus (1) to idolatry in Egypt there corresponds idolatry in Canaan and in Babylon. Then in each part of the analogy follow (2) divine fury, (3) exodus to a wilderness discipline, (4) a sifting out of idolaters and rebels who are excluded from the Holy Land. At the last stage the former story has warnings of future exclusions, whereas the new exodus terminates soberly in a return of the Remnant, a procession of shame-faced penitents (verses 40–44).[3]

In the preceding chapter (end of § iii) it was remarked that Jesus identifies himself 'with his foreshadowing types in the Old Testament' and 'with his disciples under the new covenant'. This was connected with a parallel drawn between the prophet Jeremiah and our Lord's first disciples in respect of penitential or sacrificial discipline. What was there traced in the experience of representative individuals has here been set forth on a broader canvas. In scripture, however, individuals often stand for the whole community; and in our reading of scripture Israel and the Church are united in Jesus under one pattern of Return. Of that return we wrote: 'every step towards the End is also and equally a movement back to the Beginning' (end of § ii in Chapter I). For Christ is both of these, as he is also the whole path of that pilgrimage along which we move, treading still in the steps of the true Remnant of both covenants.

But if he is the Way he is also the pioneer,[4] who, as our leader, undergoes in his own person the whole discipline of the

[1] e.g. Jer. 31^{8}; but notably Isa. 35, 41^{14-20}, 43^{14-21}, 49^{8-13}.

[2] The kernel of the new exodus story is given in verses 33–39.

[3] One of the most striking features of the analogy is to be seen in the parallel drawn between 'the wilderness of the peoples' (that is the desert which must be crossed on the journey from Babylon to Jerusalem) and the original 'wilderness of Egypt', i.e. the Sinai desert.

[4] ἀρχηγός (Acts 3^{15}, 5^{21}; Heb. 2^{10}, 12^{2}).

new exodus.[1] There is, however, this difference; what was foreshadowed in prophecy ideally is repeated in us mystically, whereas it was enacted in our Saviour historically, and that too at a depth to which we cannot reach down, in a mystery which we can scarcely begin to plumb. Herein lies some part of the significance attaching to the editorial treatment of Hosea's second chapter, a significance which we had in mind in referring to it as in some measure 'an epitome of divine revelation'. The doom which the prophet pronounced could not be the last word for the Israel of God. For *we* must advance through the wilderness to the holy land of a paradise regained. Yet for all that the original oracle in all its horror was fulfilled at Calvary when Israel was stripped and exposed to die of thirst. In that event moreover the whole of the new exodus was included. For in the return of that human spirit to the Father of spirits Israel the bride was restored again to her Beginning. There and then she found 'the Day of her Genesis' in the true Adam.

ii

The harmonies of creation restored through acts of redemption. This 'Genesis-Exodus mystery' of 'return' elucidated in the plan of Matthew 11 and 12 by comparison with Mark and Luke. The restoration of created sonship by return to a child-like condition (Job 33^{14-30}).

We have been surveying an Old Testament topic which appeared, on the surface at least, to present Israel's destiny under two contrasted alternatives. One of these might fairly be described as a return to primitive chaos; and if we think in biblical terms the corresponding alternative could be appropriately defined as a restoration of creation's harmonies. In speaking of a 'return to chaos' I am not thinking solely of Hosea's five-fold threat. The prophet Jeremiah has left to his readers a vivid picture of the lifeless chaos which would instantly supervene if the Creator withdrew his providential activity from this earthly sphere within which human history is enacted. Moreover the description is not hypothetical; for

[1] In this section the term 'exodus' covers the discipline of the Sinai wilderness as well as the exit from Egypt. This enlarged sense is suggested by the LXX version of Exod. 19^1.

cosmic chaos is there expected to occur at the climax of approaching judgement. In the midst of this scene of desolation is set the ruin of Israel the unfaithful wife. The prophet is unable to distinguish a final collapse of redemptive history from universal desolation.[1] Similarly, in the Book of Isaiah and in the Wisdom of Solomon we are shown nature co-operating with her Creator in the redemption of Israel from captivity.[2] Again, Psalm 74^{12-19} describes the events of the Red sea crossing in terms of the old creation-myth, Jahveh smiting the dragons as Marduk smote Tiamat.[3]

This conflation of redemptive history with the creation-cycle of imagery is thoroughly typical. So too, if prophecy makes it clear that only by way of an 'exodus discipline' can we hope to return to our lost inheritance, it also hints, poetically but not obscurely, that the new exodus, like the old, is itself an act of new creation. In other words a Return to the Beginning is a return to Genesis as well as to Exodus, or perhaps we should say: a return to a mystery which might be called 'Genesis-Exodus'. For if we were right in supposing that 'restoration to wholeness must have a significance far transcending a return to the historical past' then (in a kindred sense of the word) Hebrew 'wholeness' of thought-idioms itself forbids us to regard a return to the exodus-discipline as simply a stage on the way back to Genesis. It will surely be more true to the biblical way of thinking to say that the six days of creation are renewed in all the redemptive events of history. Thus 'the Day of her Genesis' recurs in the whole story of Israel's re-making, alike at the Red sea and at Sinai-Horeb. This striking Septuagint phrase[4] is itself an appropriate by-product of that entire tradition of religious culture which we been considering. So too in the new exodus the Christian neophyte is re-born through identification with the divine Bridegroom and his bride in 'the

[1] Jer. 4^{23-28} should therefore be read in the context of the chapter as a whole.

[2] For the former see the refs. under the first note to the last par. but two of § i above.

[3] On this aspect of the Exodus see J. Pedersen's important appendix to *Israel III–IV*, p. 729.

[4] From Hos. $2^{3(5)}$. The double meaning of 'genesis', with its applicability both to the cosmos and to the human individual, is a good example of the way in which the biblical idioms take effect. Cp. I. VI; p. 157.

Day of her Genesis' which covers the death, entombment and resurrection of Jesus.[1]

What I have just called the 'Genesis-Exodus' mystery will be the main theme of the present section; and we shall approach it through a return to that gospel healing-miracle upon which a 'restoration' mark was, so to speak, imprinted by three evangelists. We have not yet considered St Matthew's treatment of that incident, although a hint was dropped that this evangelist places it in a context which is peculiarly his own.[2] This is certainly true; although in making his unique contribution he also shows cross-connexions with the other synoptists at several points, over and above the bare fact of recording, as they do, two selected incidents connected with the sabbath controversy in the symbolic manner already described. This seems an appropriate point at which to remark that the diversities both of matter and of arrangement which characterize the four gospels by comparison with each other can be fully appreciated only if we are able to see those diversities as occurring within a wider frame of unities opening out in successive strata until they are found to cover the whole of the Scriptures.[3]

There are signs that Matthew's chapters 11 and 12, like other parts of the first gospel, are very carefully constructed; and we shall have to examine in some detail the bearing of this fact upon our main theme. We may begin by noticing points of contact with the other two Synoptists. The 'restoration' of the withered hand (12^{13}) is followed by Pharisaic hostility and consequent withdrawal from publicity in which the evangelist sees a fulfilment of the Servant prophecy (Isaiah 42^{1-3}). Then there follows a healing of one who is 'blind and deaf' (12^{22}); and this may perhaps signify that Matthew wishes to bring together Mark's two 'restoration' incidents (Mark 3^{5}, 8^{25}). The whole Marcan sequence from 'deaf' to 'blind' (7^{32}–8^{25}) and its connexion with Isaiah 35 might even have been present to the mind of the first evangelist. Moreover in this gospel, alone of the

[1] In these two paragraphs a thesis concerning creation and redemption in scripture has been repeated in a fresh context from an earlier statement in Ch. I. § iii, par. 5.

[2] see above, Ch. I, § iii, par. 6, note.

[3] This observation has in part been elicited by the very searching review of Vol. I in this series contributed to *Sobornost* (series 3: No. 9) by Fr G. Florovsky.

three, the echoes of Isaiah 35 in our Lord's own description of his works occur at the beginning of the context which we are now examining (Matthew 11^{5}). There it is 'the blind, the lame and the deaf'. We noticed that 'the lame' was missing in the Marcan sequence. But 'the blind and the lame' are found together at Matthew 21^{13} in a Davidic context to which we shall return later in the present volume.

In view of that later collocation, however, we must not fail to notice that, as in Mark also, the Davidic nuance of the first sabbath incident (12^{1-8}) is once more in evidence immediately after the two healings and the prophetic quotation which falls between them (12^{13-23}). As David slew Goliath and was persecuted by Saul, so Jesus expelled the demons and yet his victories were discounted by the Pharisees (12^{23-28}). If we look back in this gospel behind the story of David eating the showbread ($12^{3,4}$) we come to our Lord's promise of that messianic 'rest' which was originally offered by the deity to David himself (2 Sam. 7^{11}; cp. Matt. 11^{28}), and with the same phrase.[1] Also, the first instalment of a fulfilment was acknowledged by Solomon in his prayer at the dedication of the temple (i Kings 8^{56}). Thus in Matthew 11^{28}–12^{8} the messianic rest, surrounded as it is by theocratic and regal associations of a great epoch in redemptive history, is connected with the true meaning of the sabbath-rest as in Hebrews 4^{1-11}.[2] These passages support the conclusion, already reached, that the title 'Son of Man' is, in this context, messianic.[3] Moreover here, as in the argument of Hebrews (and in the saying of John 5^{17}), Jesus is 'Lord of the Sabbath' because the Messiah shares the cosmic functions of the Creator. Once again the author of the Epistle to the Hebrews interprets the saying recorded by all three evangelists.[4]

In Hebrews 4^{10} a comparison is made which must, in the first instance, refer to our Lord himself: 'As God (after the six days of creation) rested from his works, so he who entered into his rest (that is Jesus, at his ascension) likewise rested from his'. Here we have another instance of that mysterious conjunction which I referred to as 'the Genesis-Exodus mystery'. The author

[1] ἀναπαύσω in 2 Reg. 7^{11}, as in Matt. 11^{28}.

[2] On which see *The Common Life*, p. 382 and nn.

[3] see above, Ch. I, § iii, par. 7 and note.

[4] Matt. 12^{8} and parallels.

clearly conceives the ascension of our Lord to be the climax of a 'new creation' series. The Exodus of a new Israel from the bondage of sin, which was completed by the heavenly session of the priest-king, is also a repetition of the works completed in the original six days of creation. The messianic rest, therefore, which Jesus inaugurates has identity with the Sabbath-rest which the Creator enjoys in the unending seventh-day of heavenly life. Thus the epistle agrees with the first gospel in fusing together the functions of the Messiah and the Creator; and if we look once more at the gospel context we find here, as so often in the New Testament, a coming together of several biblical types. We encountered similar phenomena in our examination of Acts 2 and 3.[1]

If all acts of redemption are liable to be regarded as acts of new creation, that fact will in itself make for a fusion of types. Thus, in Isaiah 11 the messianic reign is described in terms which suggest a restoration of the earthly paradise. Again, Ezekiel declares that the holy land restored is to 'become like the garden of Eden' (36^{35}) with 'my servant David' as the shepherd-ruler of a well-watered land (34^{23-31}). Once more, in deutero-Isaiah the acts of new creation which characterized the Exodus are expected to recur.[2] Moreover, in that group of prophecies a renewal of 'the sure mercies of David' (55^{3}) is closely associated with the Servant's mission. It is not surprising, therefore, if a repetition of David's trials and conflicts is conceived to have occurred in the earthly ministry of him who took the form of the Servant, the evangelists feeling at liberty to pass backwards and forwards between one type and another. This occurs in the section of St Matthew's Gospel which we are examining. Thus it is that the victories of David's Son over the demons follow close upon a citation of the Servant prophecy. So too in St Mark the second 'restoration' healing introduces the revelation of a Messiah who is to suffer (8^{22-38}).[3]

[1] see above, Ch. I, § iv, later pars.

[2] see above, Ch. II, § i, last par. but two and note.

[3] A further examination of the 'Genesis-Exodus' complex in its Matthean context will be found below in Addit. Note B. What has been said in the text about a fusion of types requires to be completed by the introduction of a type not yet examined namely, 'Son of Adam' (for which see Ch. III ff.). I agree with Dr Farrer that this is already present in Mark 2^{10} and 2^{28}. See also below on Luke 14^{5} and on Matt. 11^{16ff}.

We now turn to a point of contact between the first and third evangelists. For this purpose we must pay attention to some variations which occur in the story of the 'restoration' healing in the synagogue as told by the three evangelists. In all three there is a dramatic clash between our Lord and the Pharisees, an encounter in which these latter have the worst of it. But in his account of the incident Matthew has a somewhat fuller version of this particular feature. The other two evangelists represent our Lord as taking the initiative by asking a formal question: 'Is it lawful on the sabbath . . . ?' St Mark alone records that the Pharisaic observers 'were silent' (a point to which we shall return later), while St Luke makes the question slightly more rhetorical and leaves the silence to be inferred. In the first gospel, however, there occurs a little dialogue in which the Pharisees take the initiative. It is they who ask the question: 'Is it lawful . . . ?' and our Lord replies with a counter-question, posing a particular case:

> What man of you shall there be who shall have a sheep, and if it fall on the sabbath into a pit will he not take hold of it and raise it up? Of how much more value then is a man than a sheep? So that it is lawful to do good on the sabbath. (Matt. $12^{11,12}$).

In this version, as in St Luke's account, it is assumed that the critics are silenced, but here by force of an argument to which it may be supposed that they can find no answer. Now the peculiar Matthean interlude just recorded is very similar in character to a corresponding encounter between Jesus and the Pharisees as told by the third evangelist at a much later point in his gospel. In Luke 14^{1-6} the setting of the incident is not in the synagogue but in the home of a Pharisee to which our Lord is invited for a meal. Once again it is the sabbath-day, and a man stands before the Saviour waiting to be healed of his dropsy. Once more, as in chapter 6, our Lord asks the question: 'Is it lawful . . . ?' On this occasion we are told that 'they held their peace'. Jesus then healed the man and proceeded to ask another question. I will give it in the form in which I think that the evangelist recorded it:[1]

> Which of you shall have a son or an ox which shall fall into a well, and will he not immediately pull him out on the sabbath day?

[1] For a discussion of the correct text in Luke 14^5 see Addit. Note C.

To this question the evangelist appends the comment: 'they could not make answer to these things'.

Difficult questions arise both with regard to the exact form of the saying last quoted and in respect of its relation to the similar saying in Matthew $12^{11,12}$ cited above. The problem is touched upon in an Additional Note. Here we must confine ourselves to a bare indication of the attitude concerning these problems which is here presupposed. The fact that two gospels record in two quite different contexts sayings of a similar character is no adequate ground for supposing that one of the two evangelists must have misplaced the saying. For nothing is more probable than that Jesus in fact said the same sort of thing on different occasions. It is also possible that in two parallel lines of tradition the same saying diverged into two different forms as it was unconsciously reshaped through the interpreting mind of the apostolic church. This is simply to recognize that the teaching of Jesus is mediated to us through church tradition within the New Testament as well as outside it. We may speculate as to the exact form of the *ipsissima verba;* but what is given to us in the gospels is the revealed Word of God, whether verbally identical with Christ's spoken words or not.[1] In the example before us it may well be that Luke 14^5 represents an elaboration upon that which Jesus said. This possibility will be borne in mind in what follows.

If both these sayings go back to a common original, it seems highly probable that the *sense* of our Lord's words is most clearly brought out by the first evangelist. The argument is *a fortiori.* If an animal can be lifted out of a hole on the sabbath, how much more is one justified in healing a man on the holy day. By contrast, in the version of Luke 14^5 which we are here following[2] the saying has two noticeable differences: (1) the 'man' has been transferred to the beginning where he is now an alternative to the animal; (2) the tragedy here envisaged is a much more personal affair. For it may be a son of the house who has fallen into the well or cistern. What would St Luke have in mind if he actually reported the saying in this peculiar form?

[1] This question concerning the status of Christian interpretations of revelation within the New Testament was dealt with in Vol. I in various contexts. See especially I. III. i, pp. 60–62.

[2] The Greek text of which is printed in WH.

Peculiar it certainly is. For on the one hand man and animal are now grouped together, just as though they were being thought of as two live creatures belonging to one owner. On the other hand there is a vast difference between them. For one of the two is a son in his father's house. The theological implication here lies very near the surface. For in the Old Testament man is constantly classed with the lower creation as one of the creatures. Yet by virtue of the divine image imprinted upon him he is God's son.[1]

To these biblical associations we shall presently turn. For the moment, however, let us ask ourselves whether the 'theological implication' just now mentioned would be congenial to this evangelist's way of thinking. We know, from the parables in his fifteenth chapter that he thought of the human sinner both as a lost animal rescued by his shepherd and as a lost son returning to his father. But it is also likely enough that he knew our Lord to be the Lamb of God as well as the Beloved Son. Like his fellow-evangelists he records the utterance of this latter title by the voice from heaven at the baptism. Unlike them, however, he inserts a version of Christ's legal genealogy between the baptism and the temptation. This traces the messianic line back to 'Adam the son of God'. What was the reason for this? Was not Jesus the promised seed, the son of Adam who was to bruise the serpent's head? And does not the evangelist immediately show this promise coming to fulfilment in the incident which follows? For the Son of God became son of Adam *in order that he might fulfil Adam's destiny as son of God by creation.*

It is from this point of view that St Luke emphasizes equally our Lord's heavenly origin and his human development through childhood. It is as the human son that the boy Jesus speaks of himself in the incident at the temple (2^{49}). This evangelist would have agreed with St Paul that 'the second man is from heaven' (1 Cor. 15^{47}). But he is the second *man*, who must take up Adam's burden (Ecclesiasticus 40^{1}) and do battle with the serpent as God's son by virtue of the imprinted image (4^{3}). Let us now return to the incident in chapter 14. The word used for a cistern or artificial well in verse 5 is used in the Revelation of St John for the pit of hell, that is the lowest part of Sheol (Rev. $9^{1,2}$). So now we can perhaps read St Luke's

[1] The reader is referred back to Vol I. (Addit. Note B), pp. 254 ff.

thoughts. This is a parable of the new creation, a 'Genesis-Exodus mystery'. The 'son' has fallen into the pit of Sheol,[1] and the brute creation shares his fate. But he is drawn out of the pit on the seventh day of creation when Jesus (*Iêsous*) bestows healing (*iâsis*) and so 'finishes' the works (Genesis 2^2). In order to effect this the Son of God must go down into the pit. He must become like a lost son in order that all lost sons may return to their heavenly Father.

A fuller explication of these two similar sayings in Matthew and Luke must be deferred for the present until we have first delved more deeply into their biblical background and context. At present we will concentrate our attention upon a single passage in the Old Testament which provides a significant foreshadowing of this whole parable of the 'son' and the 'pit'. In Job 33^{14-30} Elihu elaborates a thesis first sketched in outline by Eliphaz (5^{8ff}). The earlier speaker in turn followed the traditional teaching of Proverbs $3^{11,12}$ concerning the chastening which God, as a father, administered to his son.[2] 'Whom the Lord loveth he chasteneth' is the true solution of Job's problem. 'Blessed is the man whom the Lord reproved . . . for he puts a man in pain and then *restores* him; he smote, and his hands *healed*'.[3] This forms the text of Elihu's discourse; but his elaboration, besides presenting the whole picture of divine chastisement in a most vivid fashion, contains two new features of which we must take notice. In the Hebrew original and in at least two English versions we are told five times over that the object of the divine chastisement is to deliver the sufferer from going down into 'the pit'.[4] The other new feature is a striking description of the effects of divine healing upon the human frame of the disciplined man. This last is for our present purpose the most important detail in the whole passage.

In the story of Naaman the Syrian whom Elisha recovered

[1] This meaning of φρέαρ occurs in LXX. See Pss. 54 $(55)^{24}$, 68 $(69)^{16}$, and Grimm-Thayer, p. 657.

[2] Quoted in Heb. $12^{5, 6}$.

[3] Job $5^{17,18}$ LXX, with two of our key-words italicized.

[4] So RV and AJV. AV spoils the sequence characteristically by substituting 'grave' for 'pit' in verse 22. M prefers to follow LXX in reading 'death' for 'pit'; and the Vulgate takes the Hebrew word to mean 'corruption', as LXX does, e.g., in Ps 15 $(16)^{10}$. Cp. above, Ch. I, § iv, last par. but two, second note.

from his leprosy we read that when Naaman dipped seven times in Jordan 'his flesh came again like unto the flesh of a little child' (2 Kings 5^{14}). This picturesque phrase was clearly in the mind of whoever composed the Elihu speech, when he described the healing of the man under divine chastisement in almost identical terms. But this outward transformation is effected only after the sufferer, under the guidance of an angel, makes a genuine repentance. In other words the theme of Elihu repeats the experience of Jeremiah, where, it will be remembered, God says to the prophet 'If thou art converted, I will restore thee'.[1] Previously the flesh of the sufferer in Job 33 was consumed away and his bones obtruded in unsightly fashion (verse 21); but now 'his flesh is tenderer than a child's; he returneth to the days of his youth' (verse 25).[2] In itself this picture is typical of the Old Testament where health of body and a righteous life are expected to be normally concomitant. Nevertheless, it not only adds one more ingredient to the complex of biblical healing images which we are considering. It also links repentance to the notion of return to a childlike condition,[3] and so prepares the way for the dominical saying which occurs in Matthew 18^{3}: 'Except ye be converted and become as little children, ye shall not enter into the kingdom of heaven'.

iii

The higher unities of revelation can be illustrated by an exegesis of Matthew 11, to which the 'Wisdom Christology' provides a master-key. Himself '*the Beginning* of God's ways' in creation's order, Jesus offers to beginners the Servant's discipline as the way of filial response which leads to Wholeness of life.

The gospel sayings about 'little children' will be considered in our next chapter. There is, however, one such saying which must be taken to some extent by itself, because it occurs within the context which we are at present examining. The saying just

[1] Jer. 15^{19} (LXX); see above, Ch. I, § iii, last par. but three and note.

[2] As rendered by AJV, while LXX has: 'he will make his flesh as tender as a babe's (νηπίου), and he will *restore* him among men with the strength of a man'.

[3] cp. in this chapter § i, par. 2.

now quoted from Matthew 18[3] is in a sense anticipated in our Lord's thanksgiving to the Father (Matt. 11[25,26]). This, in turn, is a prelude to other great utterances including that offer of messianic rest which we have already found to be connected with the sabbath incidents following (11[28]–12[14]). There is, I believe, a close sequence of thought running through Matthew 11[25–30]. The inner nature of this sequence, however, can be penetrated, only if it is rightly connected with its background in the Old Testament. So far we have examined that background mainly in connexion with the promises of 'restoration to wholeness' and their relation to 'new creation' ideas. In this way it became clear that redemptive history is, in scripture, interwoven with the divine plan of creation in such a way that the two themes cannot be torn apart. So far then we have provided some detailed justification for a thesis drawn from the teaching of St Irenaeus in the previous volume concerning what was there entitled 'the three-fold structure of orthodoxy'.[1]

That particular phrase does not mean quite the same thing as what in this chapter I have called 'the Genesis-Exodus mystery'. But it is obvious that both phrases are concerned with the higher unities of revelation, including the unity between the two Testaments as well as the unity between creation and redemption. In this volume, as in its predecessor, we are occupied inevitably with the cross-connexions between these two last-mentioned unities; and in the present chapter we have been engaged in tracing out these cross-connexions along the line of one particular theme to which I have given the title: 'return to the beginning'. Thus far the foundations of this notion in the old covenant have been traced out mainly in a prophetic cycle of teaching concerning 'restoration'. Yet within that cycle we found ourselves driven back from an 'Exodus-return' to a 'creation-return'; and this fact, in itself, suggests that there are other parts of the Old Testament to which we must now pay attention. In particular, our examination of Matthew 11 cannot proceed further without some consideration of its relation to the Wisdom literature.

There are several indications of such a connexion. For example, the statement in Matt. 11[19] that 'Wisdom is justified from her works' is a direct reference to the cosmic functions of

[1] I. IV. vi, p. 125.

Wisdom as the co-partner of deity in creation, a thesis first laid down in Proverbs 8 and taken up by a succession of writers in later 'Wisdom' literature. Secondly there is the paradox of our Lord's preference for the 'babes' over the wise and prudent in his thanksgiving to the Father (11^{25}). Thirdly, 'the great invitation' (11^{28-30}), both in form and in subject-matter, corresponds to Wisdom's 'invitations' to mankind in the writings already mentioned, and likewise to the wise man's exhortations to his disciples. At this point, however, we must remember that the typical wise man of the Old Testament is Solomon who is also in certain respects (notwithstanding serious faults) a type of the messianic king. He enjoys this position in biblical thought because his reign seemed to subsequent generations to be the golden age of unity, peace and prosperity, in short, all that the Hebrew people meant by *shâlom*, a concept vastly more significant than is suggested by the English word 'peace'.[1] Solomon, whose name means 'peaceful', might be regarded as the Hebrew counterpart to Plato's conception of the philosopher-king.

As such he is a messianic figure; and it is an idealized Solomon who is depicted in the messianic prophecy of Isaiah 11. Like Solomon he is endowed with wisdom, as a gift received from God which enables him to bestow the messianic rest and restoration for which Israel longs, and which, when bestowed, carries with it a transformation of creation's order. As the brute creation shared the son's fall into the pit, so also it will share in that 'restoration of wholeness' which belongs to the sabbath-rest of the new creation. It will be observed that the characteristic features of Matthew 11 which point to a 'Wisdom' background have actually led us back into the prophetic visions of idealized redemptive history, once more demonstrating the irrefragible unity between the cosmic background and the redeemed community in the foreground of the scriptural revelation.[2] For the deeper source of such unities the reader may be reminded of a statement made in Volume I. In the divinely composed historical drama of revelation 'Jesus is not

[1] As Pedersen has said in his admirable account of this concept: '*shâlom* designates . . . the fact of being whole', 'consists in complete harmony', is 'comprehensive and positive', 'comprises all that the Israelite understands by "good"'. 'It expresses every form of happiness and free expansion, but the kernel in it is the community with others' (*Israel I–II*, pp. 311–13).

[2] see above, Ch. I, § i, pars. 8 ff.

simply the principal actor; he is the whole action in which each of the actors in turn plays his part'.[1]

With these thoughts in our minds let us hold up Matthew's eleventh chapter before us like a mirror and see what elements of scripture we may find reflected there. In verses 2–15 we have the visit of John's disciples with their master's question: 'Art thou the Coming One?' There are reasons for thinking that this title is (in the tradition represented by our gospels) intended to identify Jesus with 'the angel of the covenant' of whom it is said in Malachi's prophecy: 'behold he cometh'.[2] Jesus replies in language which suggests a fulfilment in himself of 'restoration' prophecies such as Isaiah 35. But afterwards he refers to John in language which seems to effect something like an 'interchange of properties' between the Forerunner and the Messiah. For example, in his concluding statement about John he says: 'he is Elias who is to come'.[3] The composite quotation in verse 10 (= Mark 1^2) is even more complicated. For its first line is taken from Exodus 23^{20} and its second represents a version of the second clause in Malachi 3^1. Thus the Baptist is identified first with 'my messenger' who is sent before Moses, and then with 'my messenger' who goes before the Lord. But thirdly 'thy face' (from Exodus) has replaced 'my face' (from Malachi), so that in effect Jesus is identified both with Moses and with the Lord Jahveh.[4]

The preceding paragraph with its footnotes may perhaps

[1] I. VII. v., p. 221.

[2] Mal. 3^{1b}. Cp. I. VIII. iv, especially the notes on pp. 245 and 247.

[3] Verse 14. With this cp. the last two notes of Ch. I, § iii above. The title of Jesus covers his forerunner, because they are 'identified' in the mission of the Servant.

[4] In Mark 1^2 Jesus is identified with Moses only. But in the next verse 'thy way' becomes 'the way of the Lord'. On the other hand in Matt. 11^{10} 'before my face' (Mal. 3^1) has become 'before thee', an unmistakable identification of Jesus with Jahveh. The similarity in the opening clauses of Exod. 23^{20} and Mal. 3^1 has also brought about an identification of the two persons designated as 'my messenger'. But further, 'my messenger' in Exodus is superior to Moses, who must obey him (23^{21}), whereas in Mal. 3^1 'my messenger' is the subordinate of him whom he precedes, namely 'the Lord', who in turn is identified with the 'angel of the covenant'; and the latter title clearly refers to the superior 'messenger' of Exodus! In this way the new Elijah, identified in NT with 'my messenger' of Mal. 3^1 also acquires identity with 'the angel of the covenant' (Exod. 23^{20}). As such he prepares the

have made clearer the meaning of the statement that Jesus 'is the whole action in which each of the actors in turn plays his part'. This statement, just now quoted from Volume I of this series, was originally made in connexion with the Christian identification of our Lord with the personified figure of Wisdom which first appears in Proverbs 8. In that context it was also pointed out that in the Christian interpretation of Isaiah 53 'Jesus is the Servant of the Lord in whose mission the true *torah*-wisdom is enacted so that "the many" are thereby justified'. In short Jesus is both the Servant and Holy Wisdom (I, pp. 219–221). This agrees well with the conclusion of our last paragraph in the present section. Jesus as Wisdom incarnate has identity both with Moses, the human author of the old *torah*-wisdom, and also with Jahveh, its divine author. These widespread phenomena of identification can be correctly estimated only by a patient study of those idioms of Hebrew psychology which were explained in Volume I. Meanwhile, enough has been said to show how the Jewish-Christian Wisdom-Christology could include within itself the entire substance of the Old Testament revelation. This fact is an all-important clue to the correct exegesis of Matthew 11.

Let us apply the clue, then, to the next two sections of the chapter (11^{16-24}). The parable concerning the children in the market-place might seem to have little to do with the prophetic doom pronounced upon the cities of Galilee. Yet they are linked together (verse 19) by the saying about wisdom which we have already connected with Proverbs 8. When we look into that chapter we find that it begins and ends with Wisdom's appeal to mankind (literally 'the sons of Adam', verses 4, 31). But there is a difference of tone in these two parts. The first half of the chapter shows Wisdom as mistress of the moral order denouncing the folly of wickedness in public life, whereas at the conclusion she is most probably represented as a child gathering children round her to share her pleasures (vv. 30–32). It looks as if the early part corresponds to the doom upon the cities.

way of the new Moses (Jesus) who fulfils the prophecy of Deut. 18^{15ff}. That may help to explain a phenomenon observable in Acts 3^{21-23} which was noticed above in Ch. I, § iv, par. 6 and notes. The Baptist is in effect identified with Jesus in his function as 'angel of the covenant' as well as in the mission of the Servant (see above, last two notes).

For Wisdom denounces pride and arrogancy (Prov. 8^{13}), just as our Lord denounces Capernaum for imitating the builders of Babel—'Shalt thou be exalted unto heaven?' (Matt. 11^{23}). Similarly in the parable of the children our Lord pillories 'this generation' because the secret of harmonious response to leadership has been lost. If the game of life is no longer to be frustrated Wisdom must show how it is to be played.

If we are on the right track the two parts of Matt. 11^{16-24} have already been drawn closer together. Both parts are saying that the true happiness of human life (*shâlom*) has its source in Holy Wisdom. The connecting link, however, is all-important. In Proverbs 8 the moral order is one with the plan of creation of which Wisdom is the mistress because she was present at the six days work of creation and learnt all its secrets. She alone, therefore, can pass those secrets on to the sons of Adam to whom the stewardship of creation's order has been committed. That stewardship, our Lord might be represented as saying, is now being restored in the mission of the Servant; and in this the Forerunner shared with the true Wise Man who is both Moses and Solomon. For divine Wisdom and her human agent are at last united in one Person, that is in One who became a son of Adam in order that he might teach the sons of Adam what are the true delights of creation's order. If we will accept his leadership in the game of life we shall find that 'Wisdom's delights are once more with the progeny of Adam' (Prov. 8^{31}).[1]

[1] The two renderings in Prov. 8^{30}—'nursling-child' and 'master-workman' —are not necessarily to be regarded as mutually exclusive. For the Hebrew mind loved words to have more than one meaning. The author of the poem may have intended his picture-story to be understood in this way. Wisdom is the small child watching her father building a castle of bricks. She is so fascinated by the operation that she takes a hand in the game herself. Guided by father's hand she builds the edifice; and then in an ecstasy of delight she gathers round her the other children and imparts to them the secrets of her father's skill. A clever child could thus become the leader of a new game. In Luke 7^{35} we read: 'Wisdom is justified from all her children' and this reading has strong support also in Matt. 11^{19}. If, however, Matthew wrote 'works' he probably wished to avoid the suggestion that Jesus who *is* Wisdom could be classified with the Baptist as one of Wisdom's children. On the other hand, if Luke saw Wisdom as the Holy Child whose boyhood he describes he would have no difficulty in making Jesus play the part of the divine 'nursling' who is teaching the game of life to all God's children in the new creation.

We must now show the connexion of Matt. 11^{16-24} with what follows (11^{25ff}). That there is a connexion is made plain by our Lord's reference in verse 25 to 'these things' of which he has been speaking. He has just been comparing the cities of Galilee, first to Tyre and Sidon and then to Sodom. A key phrase, already noticed for its affinity with Proverbs 8^{13}, now comes into clearer light. The words addressed to Capernaum should be connected, *in the first place*, with the preceding reference to Tyre and Sidon. A doom upon these two cities was pronounced in Ezekiel, chs. 26–28; and the lament over the prince of Tyre (28^{1-19}) has close affinity with our Lord's warning to Capernaum. The prince's heart was 'lifted up' by his wisdom and wealth; but he will go down to the pit (verses 2–8). His 'wisdom' proves to be a snare; and it is this kind of wisdom to which Jesus refers in Matt. 11^{25}. Secondly the reference to Sodom also has its background in Ezekiel (ch. 16^{44-63}). In Matt. $11^{23, 24}$ Capernaum is to Sodom as in Ezekiel Judah is to Sodom. The analogy is exact. Very well, then, Ezekiel promises that Judah and Sodom alike shall return to their former estate, or, as the Septuagint has it, 'shall be restored as they were from the beginning'.[1] The worldly wisdom of sophisticated city life has brought ruin. But a 'return to the beginning' (typified in Ezekiel by the new-born infant of 16^{1ff}) will bring salvation. No wonder that our Lord speaks next of a revelation to babes which the 'wise' cannot know!

But secondly, the actual words addressed to Capernaum are a quotation, not from Ezekiel 28 but from Isaiah 14, where they form part of a dirge over the king of Babylon for the collapse of his empire (see especially verses 3–8, 12–15). What is of special interest, for our present purpose, however, is the fact that in this chapter as a whole there recur certain words which reappear in our Lord's great invitation. Israel is promised that 'in that day shall the Lord give thee rest' because 'the Lord broke the yoke of the sinners, the yoke of the rulers', and 'having smitten . . . he rested'.[2] The breaking of the hostile yoke, more-

[1] see above, Ch. II, § i, the two pars. which precede the last four pars.

[2] Isa. 14^{3-6} LXX. In this chapter, which includes a shorter doom over Assyria, ἀναπαύειν occurs six times (twice ironically of the enemy in v. 4); and the breaking of the foreign ζυγός is mentioned four times. Cp. Isa. $9^{4(3)}$.

over, is in Isaiah 9^{3-6} attributed to, or connected with, the birth of the messianic child: 'unto us a Son is given'. In contrast to the yoke of slavery (Isaiah 14^{3}), which Israel had endured in the past, Jesus offers the messianic rest to which prophecy had pointed. But he couples this offer with the acceptance of his own yoke by his disciples. As in Proverbs 8 the kingdoms of this world are superseded by a Wisdom which has access to divine mysteries, so it is here. God reveals his secrets to those who accept the yoke of Wisdom incarnate. That we are still in the orbit of 'Wisdom Christology' is clear from a whole series of 'Wisdom' passages, notably Ecclesiasticus 6^{18-33} and $51^{13-\text{end}}$. Lastly, the 'heavy yoke' which 'is upon the sons of Adam' (mentioned in 40^{1ff} of the same work) was borne by Jesus himself on his journey to Calvary.

Now in Proverbs 8^{22} Wisdom declares that 'the Lord possessed me as *the beginning* of his way before his works of old'; and this became a foundation text of apostolic thought about the person of Christ. 'In the beginning God created . . .' (Genesis 1^{1}) was understood to mean that all things were created in God the Son. Obviously Matthew 11^{25-27} is another cardinal passage for this apostolic way of thinking. For, if we have correctly estimated the background, the relation of Wisdom to the sons of Adam in Proverb $8^{30, 31}$ has for its counterpart here the relation of Jesus to those whom he calls 'the babes'. Jesus, as 'the Son', is that Wisdom which alone has access to the Father's mind. He alone can impart to his disciples the secrets of deity as reflected in creation's order.[1] He became a Child for this purpose. He who is 'the Beginning of God's way' became a 'beginner' that he might impart to those who would share the beginner's attitude the way of 'return to the beginning'. Accordingly, as we said before,[2] 'every step forward towards the End is also and equally a movement back to the Beginning'. For the way of 'return to the beginning' is nothing else than the way of the Son's response to the Father. In so far as we are taken into that response which is the very *locus* of revelation,[3] we are returning in the Son to the Father whose children we are.

To embrace that filial attitude is part of what Jesus meant by

[1] Note the Creator's title in Matt. 11^{25}.
[2] Ch. I § ii, last two sentences.
[3] I. II. § i.

his reference to 'the babes'; and this conception will have to be explored more fully at the next stage. For the present we may be content to take note of the fact that the childlike condition which our Lord associated with his own filial relation to the Father is also an attitude of self-committal to all that is implied in that filial relation. To be 'sons in the Son' involves a sharing of the Son's obedience, 'the obedience of the Christ', as St Paul calls it (2 Corinthians 10^{5});—in other words 'the babes' who receive our Lord's revelations are also those who accept his yoke of discipline. At this point we can perhaps begin to see how crucial the concluding verses of Matthew 11 are for the main themes of this Book on *Christ and Creation*. The preceding section (Matthew 11^{16-24}) shows our Lord looking out upon human life and finding in it a dislocation of creation's plan through the pride and folly of our fallen nature. The false wisdom of the world is here seen to be an outrage upon the Creator's purpose; and so, in close accord with the spirit of the wisdom books, the invitation to an acceptance of filial discipline is seen to have a cosmic significance. For, as we pointed out at an earlier stage in the argument, the whole scheme of creation's order is instrumental to a revelation of divine fatherhood and its corollary of predestined human sonship.[1]

Similarly the connexion between sonship and discipline has its roots in the theme of discipleship as unfolded by the wise men of Israel. The constant interlocking of revelation and new creation in what I have called 'the Genesis-Exodus mystery' corresponds to what was said in Volume I concerning the identity of the teacher-disciple relation and the father-son relation in Jewish tradition, or again the identity of life and light, of illumination and regeneration in Christian initiation *praxis* and the ideas to which it gives expression.[2] The discipleship of the learner corresponds to the dependent attitude of child to parent. So we see in a new context the theme of an Exodus discipline which involves a return to the conditions of childhood. Lastly we have found as a recurring motif of scripture the notion that restoration to wholeness of life involves humiliation in its

[1] Above, Ch. I, § i, middle pars. and notes.

[2] I. VII. iii and IX. v. The 'mystery' is now seen to be threefold, divine creativity being both revelational and redemptive. cp. again in Vol. I 'the structure of orthodoxy'. See further below, Addit. Note B.

two forms, namely that repentance for sin which the prophets call a 'return' to God, and secondly an acceptance of the Servant's mission, with its sacrificial quality, as an indispensable factor in the way of discipleship. We have still to explore the scriptural pattern which links these two modes of humiliation to the dominical sayings about children and their theological background.

Additional Note B.

Exodus 31^{12-18} *in relation to Matthew* 11 *and* 12

In the preceding chapter (§§ ii and iii) two successive steps were taken with regard to the recognition of interrelationship between biblical concepts. (1) In the earlier part of § ii a fusion of redemptive acts with the creation-cycle of images was emphasized; and an illustration was given, in which the messianic rest (Matt. 11^{28-30}) was eventually identified with the sabbath-rest of the Creator. This illustration was designed to reinforce the 'Genesis-Exodus' fusion of historical 'return' with a more fundamental return to the true order of human life. But (2) in the second paragraph of § iii and also in the concluding paragraph of the same section a further step was taken. The unity of creation and redemption was linked up with the unity of scripture in accordance with principles laid down in Vol. I. In that volume it was also shewn that the combination of images into patterns persisting through repetition is often assisted through the varied associations of particular words and phrases. In the present note a further illustration of this kind of thing will be attempted, in which the triadic relationship of creation, revelation and redemption will be again exemplified.

As the title of this note indicates, our illustration is taken from Exod. 31^{12-18}; and we shall pay particular attention (*a*) to the language used about the sabbath in verses 12–17, and (*b*) to the character of the connexion between verses 17 and 18, although these two matters cannot be kept altogether apart. We begin by noticing that in this short section two quite distinct reasons are given for the ordinance of sabbath observance. The first reason is given in verse 13. Here it is affirmed that the sabbath is a 'sign' between Israel and their God 'unto your generations, that ye may know that I am the Lord who sanctify you'. This covenant-sign between Jahveh and his people is re-affirmed even more strongly in verse 17; for both sign and covenant are to be age-long. Then, however, there follows a second reason; the sabbath observance of Israel commemorates (and corresponds to) the sabbath-rest of the Creator after the six days of creation. It must also be pointed out that the second reason is introduced in a way which suggests that it is all one with the first reason. Thus RV renders the verse as follows:

It is a sign between me and the children of Israel for ever: for in six days the Lord made heaven and earth, and on the seventh day he rested, and was refreshed.

In both the Hebrew text and LXX the covenant-sign of redemptive revelation is here associated indissolubly with the sabbath-rest of creation. Moreover the connexion between the two aspects of sabbath-observance is also emphasized in another way. In verse 15 there is an implicit parallel between the seventh day rest of the Creator and the weekly rest of his people. Further, the Hebrew phrase: 'a sabbath-observance, holy to the Lord' is here changed in LXX to: 'sabbath, a holy rest (ἀναπαύσις) to the Lord'. Thus the word used by our Lord in his promise of messianic rest (Matt. 11[29]) is in Exod. 31 connected with the weekly memorial of the creation story. This use of ἀναπαύσις is by no means isolated. Although it is not the word used in the creation-narrative (where we read κατέπαυσεν twice in Gen. 2[2,3]), yet other instances can be cited. Thus, whereas the Decalogue repeats κατέπαυσεν from Genesis (Exod. 20[11]), the weekly memorial is described as follows in Exod. 23[12]: 'Six days shalt thou do thy works, and on the seventh day ἀνάπαυσις. There follows an explanation that animals and servants are to be given an opportunity of 'resting' (the corresponding verb); and this sequence is repeated precisely in the Deuteronomic version of the Decalogue (Deut. 5[14]).

In scripture, then, the meaning of κατάπαυσις and its verb is-primarily associated with the creation narrative; but it also has a messianic reference of which full use is made in Hebrews 3, 4 (cp above, Ch. II, § ii, pars. 5 and 6 with ref. to *The Common Life*). The verb can also mean simply 'to cease from' doing something, a fact of which we shall presently take cognisance, whereas ἀνάπαυσις and its verb seem to refer primarily to 'rest' (or recreation) as such. These latter words, also, can refer both to the sabbath-rest (as we have just seen) and to the messianic condition of *shâlom*. This second meaning is well brought out in 1 Chron. 22[9], where the Hebrew text connects *shâlom* with *Shĕlômoh* (Solomon's name); and the accompanying promise reads in LXX: 'He shall be a man of ἀνάπαυσις, and I will give him rest (ἀναπαύσω) from all his enemies round about'. In Exod. 35[2] both nouns occur together with a subtle difference: 'six days shalt thou do works, but on the seventh day is a *cessation* (κατάπαυσις), holy, a sabbath *rest* (ἀνάπαυσις) to the Lord.

Lastly, here is a parallel which has meant much in typology: (1) Gen. 8^{9}—'The dove found no rest (ἀνάπαυσιν) for her feet and returned . . . into the ark'; (2) Isa. 11^{2-10}—The Spirit of God shall rest (ἀναπαύσεται) upon him (the Messiah), so inaugurating messianic *shâlom* until, in a final reference to 'the root of Jesse', it is said that 'his rest (ἀνάπαυσις) shall be honourable'.

In the LXX version of Exod. $31^{17,18}$ the word κατέπαυσεν occurs twice in two different senses. In verse 17 it represents the 'resting' of the Creator after the six days; and (as in Gen. $2^{2,3}$) it renders a Hebrew root from which comes the word 'sabbath'. In verse 18, on the other hand, it is said that 'when God *finished* (κατέπαυσεν) speaking to Moses on Mt Sinai he gave him the two tables of testimony, tables of stone written with the finger of God'. There are several points worth noticing about this statement. In the first place, in an English rendering of these two verses there can be no hint of a close verbal connexion between them. Verse 18 may, in fact, read like an editorial conclusion to a series of ritual directions. In LXX, however, the two verses contain a suggestion of parallelism, because the standard way of describing the inauguration of the Creator's sabbath-rest is followed by a 'repetition' of the same keyword (κατέπαυσεν) in connexion with another divine act of obvious importance. As the Creator *ceased* from his work of creation so also he now *ceased* from his work of revelation. Moreover, the parallel may be put more strongly; for creation was inaugurated by the divine words: 'let there be light'; and revelation (the giving of light) is now terminated by the ending of the divine words.

There is also in the Hebrew text a verbal connexion with the story of creation. In Gen. 2^{2} it is said that 'God *finished* on the seventh day his work which he made, and *rested* on the seventh day'. In Exod. $31^{17,18}$ it is said that God '*rested* on the seventh day, and . . . *finished* speaking'. In these two quotations the words in italics are respectively the same in Hebrew, as indicated in my rendering. The phenomena here noticed, moreover, are possibly more than verbal. For in Volume I it was shown that in biblical thought creation is always revealing, while revelation is always creative (e.g. I. VII. iv). There are also two other details to be taken unto account. The first may be put in this way: In 31^{12-17} the sabbath is given as a covenant-sign which commemorates the completed work of creation. In 31^{18}, likewise, the 'two tables of the testimony' might be regarded as a covenant-sign, a perpetual reminder of the completed work of revelation. Finally these 'tables of stone' are said to have been 'written with the finger of God'; and this creative act has its counterpart in other scriptural statements, which refer in similar language both to the work of the six days and also to a typical act of redeeming power.

There are apparently only four certain references to 'the finger(s) of God' in the Old Testament (Daniel 5^5 might refer to an angel). They are as follows: (1) Exod. 8^{19} (the plague of lice)—'The magicians said unto Pharaoh, This is the finger of God'; (2) Exod. 31^{18}—'tables of stone written with the finger of God'; (3) Deut. 9^{10}, referring back to (2)—'The Lord gave me two tables of stone written with the finger of God'; (4) Ps. $8^{3(4)}$—'When I consider thy heavens, the work of thy fingers, the moon and the stars which thou hast ordained'. Of these, (3) repeats (2); but the context indicates that the tables contain the whole *torah*-revelation. Thus we may reduce the number to three and re-arrange them thus: (1) The works of God in creation; (2) a typical act of redeeming power in the Exodus story; (3) the completed work of revelation. Or, if we prefer it, we may say that by this typically anthropomorphic expression the acts of God in redemption and in revelation are declared to be creative. In whatever way we put it, however, the story of the Exodus is once more seen to be a revelation of the Creator which comes to its fulfilment in the giving of the *torah* to the people of God. Moreover Exodus 31^{18} is represented as a conclusion to what precedes, namely the completed works of the divinely appointed cultus, as given in revelation, *with the precept of the sabbath as its climax*. This corresponds to the order of the creation-cycle, and seems to imply that the founding of the theocracy is itself a work of new creation.

In I. VI. § iii (pp. 170, 171, note 4) the OT texts concerning the finger of God were connected with Matt. 12^{28} (=Luke 11^{20}). Here Luke's version has Exod. 8^{19} as background. As Moses defeated the magicians, so Jesus cast out demons, and by the same weapon, namely 'the finger of God'. It must be presumed, then, that in Matt. 12^{28} 'the Spirit of God' has the same meaning; and the Spirit is active in creation (Gen. 1^2, Ps. 33^6). Here we have another indication that our Lord's works of power are correspondingly acts of new creation. Nevertheless it is natural to ask whether anything lies behind the difference thus exhibited as between the two evangelists. Now we have seen reason for thinking that the third evangelist regards our Lord as the new Moses whose way is prepared by the new Elijah, See above, Ch. II, § iii, par. 5, final note, with ref. to Ch. I, § iv. See also I. VIII. § i, p. 227 with note 1, where the new Elijah is said to take precedence over Moses in the gospels; an additional reason for this fact is the tendency to identify the Baptist with the 'angel of the covenant' in Exod. 23^{20}, a tendency which we attributed to the similarity of that text to Mal. 3^1. It seems, then, that in Luke 11^{20} the type presented in Exod. 8^{19} finds its antitype, and that too in general accord with the Lucan typology.

On the other hand in Matt. 12^{22-28} Jesus is the Son of David, who, like his royal ancestor, is anointed with the Spirit. Pedersen has shown how the whole conflict between Saul and David is dominated by the transfer of 'blessing' from the former to the latter (*Israel I–II*, pp. 184 ff.). But the scriptural way of putting the matter is to be found in the juxtaposition of two facts (1 Sam. $16^{13,14}$): When Samuel anointed David 'the Spirit of the Lord came mightily upon David from that day forward. . . . Now the Spirit of the Lord had departed from Saul'. So in the fulfilment a new David has been anointed with the Spirit. He gives *shâlom;* he is greater than the temple and Lord of the sabbath; he restores Israel to wholeness; he conquers the demons. Yet the official rulers cannot recognize his mission of 'restoration' because the Spirit has been transferred from them to him (Matt. 11^{25}–12^{28}).

Additional Note C.

The text of Luke 14^5

In Luke 14^5 the textual authorities are divided in a way which makes it difficult to say whether our Lord is represented as referring to an 'ass' or a 'son' before the 'ox'. In *An Aramaic approach to the Gospels and Acts* (Oxford, 1946) Dr Black pointed out that the text as printed by WH contained a pun on three words in the Aramaic which may be presumed to lie behind the Greek:

Which of you shall have a son (*bera*) or an ox (*be'ira*) fallen into a pit (*bēra*). See *op. cit.*, p. 126.

In JTS (NS), April 1950 (Vol. I. Part I) Dr Black revised his earlier conclusions, and offered the following suggestions:

'The original first line of the simple Aramaic couplet at Luke 14^5' read: 'Which of you shall have a *beast* (*be'ira*) fallen into a pit (*bēra*).' The word rendered 'beast' has a generic meaning, and the variations in the text (*βοῦς, ὄνος, πρόβατον*), 'are Greek explications' of a single Aramaic word. *υἱός* is due to a misunderstanding. 'With the falling away of the gutteral' we get 'a sound (and a written word) closely resembling *bera*' (=son).

Dr Black does not consider the possibility of a difference between the original form of the dominical saying and the form eventually adopted by the third evangelist. One need not therefore hesitate to recognize the value of his revised reconstruction. As a conjecture concerning the original form of our Lord's saying it must be acknowledged to have a high degree of probability. In Chapter II, however, we were concerned with probabilities which pertain to St Luke's use of a traditional form of the saying. In all such instances there are psychological factors to be borne in mind. Some of these may concern the traditional development of a saying (oral or written); others may concern the theological outlook of the evangelist himself. Thus one may suppose that the 'striking word-play' which impressed Dr Black, when in his book he considered the Aramaic possibilities of Luke 14^5, may also have influenced the traditional development of the saying into a longer form, that is a form closely approximating to what one may call 'the WH text' of this Lucan verse.

On a purely linguistic basis the word 'son' may seem 'incongruous', as Dr Black suggests. But from other points of view this is not necessarily the last word. For example the Mishnah, in its section on 'damages', considers the possibility of 'a boy or a girl' falling into a pit, as well as 'an ox or an ass' (*Baba Kamma*, 5. 6). Moreover *υἱός* is the more difficult reading on any showing; and for that reason alone a linguistic explanation may seem too simple. When, however, we try to read the evangelist's mind further possibilities present themselves. In Dr Black's book word-play takes a very prominent place. Whether, then, the evangelist knew Aramaic or not, his considerable sojourn in Palestine (Acts 24^{27}) might qualify him to appreciate the additional force of a triple *paronomasia*. In such cases there would be no conscious or deliberate alteration of a dominical saying. What is here suggested is an unconscious elaboration in tradition which the evangelist accepted as expressing a truth, vital in itself, and harmonious with his own theological outlook.

CHAPTER III

THE KINGDOM OF CHRIST

i

***Its child-like character* exemplified in our Lord's sayings about little children. In the lowliness of Jesus the two creations meet; and 'to enter the kingdom' involves participation in that lowliness. The spiritual adults are those who have become 'little ones'.**

In our Lord's sayings concerning children and 'little ones' we can distinguish three types of teaching. In the first type the child is regarded as a pattern of the true disciple; for he is eager for knowledge and has a fresh outlook which is unspoilt by prejudice, disillusionment or sophistication. The fullest statement along these lines occurs in Matthew 11^{25-27} and in Luke $10^{21,22}$. As we have already glanced at St Matthew's report of this saying it will be sufficient, at this stage, to take note of the paradox preserved in both versions. Inasmuch as the Son has perfect communion with the Father the mystery of his sonship transcends human understanding. Yet this transcendent mystery is the very *locus* of revelation in which access to the Father is bestowed upon one whose faith is childlike in its character. Secondly, our Lord once took a child into his arms and said: 'Whosoever shall receive one of such children in my name receiveth me; and whosoever receiveth me, receiveth not me but him who sent me' (Mark 9^{37}). One who performs such an act receives a representative of Christ, and so receives unto his life (whether he knows it or not) the mystery of God in Christ.[1]

Up to a point there is an obvious connexion between these two types of saying. For in both Jesus shows a way of access to divine mysteries, a way of discipleship. In the second saying we learn that the child is the test of the childlike. In some sense this is a fact confirmed by ordinary human experience. For

[1] We may recall here what was said in Ch. I, near the end of § ii concerning the saying in Matt. 25^{40}.

children are quick to discern character; and he who wins their confidence must in some measure share their qualities. Moreover the context shows that the child in Christ's arms typifies humility; so, he who receives the child 'as Christ' is himself a humble person. The saying, therefore, indicates an attitude of mind the very reverse of that which our Lord condemned in the cities of Galilee (Matthew 11[23]), namely the self-exaltation so fitly symbolized by the tower of Babel. So far we are still well within the orbit of what I have called the first type of saying. The dictum in Mark 9[37], however, was accompanied by an action which shows us another facet of its many-sided truth. Christ himself received the child. The lowly received the lowly.

This act was our Lord's answer to the strife of the disciples over the question; 'Who is the greater?' They acknowledged Jesus as the greatest; yet they disputed for the title of 'the greater' among his followers. What then did greatness mean for him? Before taking the child he had told them: 'If anyone will be first he shall be last of all and servant of all'; and a little later in St Mark's story Jesus brought this truth into connexion with his own acceptance of death as the one who gave his life 'a ransom for many '(Mark 10[45]). This interpretation of 'service' was of one piece with the condescension exhibited by the incarnate Son. He showed himself to be lowly of heart when, in taking our nature, he took the lowliest place. Here we may notice St Luke's version of the incident which we are considering. The question: 'Who is the greater?' is answered thus: 'He who is the lesser among you all, he is great'. This *follows* the taking of the child by Christ. So the child, the lesser or smaller member in their midst, represents greatness (Luke 9[46–48]).

Now Christ himself deigned to become a child. He showed his greatness by becoming a helpless infant, one of the smallest and lowliest members of the human race. But further, in so doing he took into his embrace the lowliest member in the created hierarchy of God's children, namely man. For Jesus and his disciples acknowledged in the angelic host the many higher ranks of God's children. Yet 'he taketh not hold of angels, but of the seed of Abraham' (Hebrews 2[16]), whose lineage is traced back to the man whom 'the Lord God formed out of the dust of the ground' (Genesis 2[7]). The child, therefore, may be held to typify man's lowly place in creation and, further, his lowly origin in contrast to the heavenly origin of the Saviour who takes him into his arms. In this acted parable of human nature, then, the child stands for the greatness of God's condescension in the Incarnation. Thus were fulfilled some words of a psalm, quoted (according to one evangelist) by our Lord himself on another occasion: 'Out of the mouth of babes and sucklings hast thou established strength'.[1]

The psalm continues:

When I consider thy heavens, the work of thy fingers,
The moon and the stars which thou hast ordained;
What is man, that thou art mindful of him?
And the son of man that thou visitest him?
For thou hast made him but little lower than the angels[2]
And crownest him with glory and honour.
Thou madest him to have dominion over the works of thy hands;
Thou hast put all things under his feet.

(Psalm 8^{2-6}.)

In the psalmist's thought the speech of little children is a manifestation of the Creator's power. In the Septuagint version (exemplified in Matthew 21) the emphasis falls upon the fact that the praises of creation for its Creator become vocal in the human race, whenever a child is old enough to frame the words. I am suggesting that in our Lord's sayings little children aptly symbolize both the prerogative and the lowliness of man as set forth in the rest of the psalm. Amid the splendours of creation and the awful majesty of the heavenly court God has honoured in us the very babes and sucklings of his family. For in giving to man the dominion over the earth and its contents he has staked all upon our stewardship of his created works. So too, the child in Christ's arms typifies every man in his true significance as God's child, a lowly being with a lofty destiny, having a corresponding value in God's sight. The two aspects of man are implied in the two sayings of our Lord about sick humanity (Matt. 12^{11}, Luke 14^{5}) which we previously compared.

[1] Or 'perfected praise' (LXX). cp. Matt. 21^{16}. To that quotation we shall return later.

[2] So RV margin and LXX. cp. Heb. 2^{6ff}. Briggs suggested: 'superhuman, divine beings, including God and angels' (ICC. *ad loc.* p. 66). But A. R. Johnson's theory of 'plurality' in the traditional Hebrew conception of God is, perhaps, near the mark. If so, LXX gives a justifiable paraphrase from the later Jewish standpoint. See I. IX., note to last par. but one.

But if we accept his estimate of every 'man' as a 'son' in need of restoration, we do so because the Son of God identified himself with all the children of men.

In his next chapter St Mark tells the story of the children brought to receive Christ's blessing. 'Of such is the kingdom of heaven' said our Saviour, and continued: 'Whosoever shall not receive the kingdom of God as a little child, he shall not enter therein' (Mark 10^{13-16}). In the first gospel, however, this saying is taken into the context of the other Marcan incident which we have been considering (Matt. 18^{1-5}). The effect of this re-arrangement is to give startling clarity to yet a third type of teaching which brings to the front another implication of the whole group of sayings. Throughout this part of the gospel story the disciples are convicted of failing to understand the mind of Christ. They have been brought within the new Israel of which he is the nucleus; but they are as yet scarcely penetrated by his spirit. They need to undergo a radical change of mind, if they are to 'enter into the kingdom of heaven'. They must 'turn and become as the little children'. These words recall the name of Isaiah's little son, *Sheär-yashûb*—that is, 'a remnant shall return'—, with whom the prophet went forth to confront the worldly policies of king and people.[1] As the prophet's child symbolized Israel returning to God, so the child in the arms of Jesus symbolizes the new birth which Jesus inaugurated and the new life which all must enter when taken into his embrace.

In the preceding paragraph conversion and regeneration have been treated as two aspects of one vital transformation. In such treatment we do not overlook the important distinction between these two aspects nor the difficult problems which confront us when we seek to adjust their relations, not least in the sacramental practice of the Church. Here, however, we are concerned with a much larger issue within which all such particular problems are presumed to fall. For in this inquiry we are occupied with the theme of the two creations, the old and the new. Their mutual relationship may be indicated if we say that the two creations already meet in Christ, with a promise of final unification in him. What this implies we have still to con-

[1] Isa. 7^{3ff}. This parallel gives significance to Heb. 2^{13}, which quotes from Isa. $8^{17,8}$. Here the prophet and his sons become a type of Jesus and his new family. See also below, pars. 2 and 3 in section iii.

sider. St Matthew's interpretation makes the child to be manifestly a symbol of the Christian neophyte, who is like a child newly born in the new creation. To enter the kingdom of heaven is like going back to the first lowly beginning of our life. Moreover, the next verse (Matt. 18^{4}) declares that greatness in the kingdom depends upon the possession of that lowly character which is signified by this 'return to the beginning'. Regeneration is not only an event, but also a condition of the soul. The spiritually mature (the 'great' ones) are those in whom the lowliness of the new beginning has become an essential feature of their life, as they in turn have become permanent participators in the lowliness of the Christ.[1]

ii

***Its servant-form* fuses the types of the old covenant into unity. The lowliness of Jesus restores the dominion of Adam. Treatment of this subject in early Christian thought. Agreement of the Epistle to the Hebrews with St Augustine and St Paul.**

At this point the third aspect of Christ's teaching brings us back to the first type of saying which we found fully stated in Matthew 11^{25-30}. Here we enter upon a new stage of our investigation into the relation between the two creations. In that section of the first gospel two sayings of Jesus are brought into close connexion. In the prayer which St Luke also records our Lord says: 'All things were delivered to me by my Father'.[2] In the invitation which follows in Matthew only Jesus says: 'I am meek and lowly in heart.' Here once more we are confronted with a conjunction of greatness and lowliness. The Matthean collocation of sayings implies an interpretation which enters into the heart of the gospel. This evangelist's arrangement, however, also implies a fusion of Old Testament types of a kind which is familiar enough in the New Testament. Moreover, the example of such fusion which occurs in this passage is of central importance in the rich variety of the vistas which it seems to

[1] Thus the 'adults' of the new creation may be contrasted with the adult Israelites who were destroyed in the wilderness, while their 'little ones' were destined to 'inherit the land' (Num. $14^{4,31}$).

[2] Matt. 11^{27}, Luke 10^{22}.

open up. We have already heard creative Wisdom speaking here with messianic authority, and have also found the Servant's mission wrapped up in the gracious invitation. There is yet one more type implicit in these pregnant verses which now calls for serious consideration.

In the lowliness of his incarnate state Jesus thinks and speaks as man. When, therefore, he says: 'All things were delivered to me by my Father' it would seem that, in the first instance at least, the saying should be understood to refer to his historical mission, even though it be also true that for Christian faith no purely human reference can exhaust the mystery of such a claim. In its *primâ facie* meaning, then, this utterance should be connected with our Lord's messianic mission to fulfil the promises of God. We cannot, however, isolate the messianic theme from other factors in the scriptural imagery. For one thing, the fusion of types to which reference has just been made is already fully operative in the Old Testament. A good example is to be seen in the description of the messianic king in Zechariah 9, where clearly the earlier prophetic pictures such as Isaiah 9 and 11 have been profoundly modified under the influence of the Servant songs.[1] In other instances the fusion is prepared for by similarities of thought and expression only, the final identification being effected in the New Testament. An example of the latter kind must now engage our attention.

The example in question is one which shows a certain affinity of language between things said concerning the dominion over creation assigned to Adam in the Genesis-cycle and things said elsewhere in contexts which receive messianic application in the New Testament.[2] In other words here, as elsewhere, we are in

[1] cp. H. G. Mitchell in ICC. *ad loc.*, pp. 272–276; see especially his observations on the Hebrew word in 9^{9} which LXX renders by πραΰς. This, in turn, is appropriated to himself by Jesus in Matt. 11^{29}.

[2] The following details will illustrate: (1) In Gen. $1^{26,28}$ two Hebrew words indicate the dominion of Adam (roots: *rdh* and *kbsh*). Of these the former is rendered in LXX *ad loc.* by ἄρχειν (twice), but also in two messianic psalms 72 $(71)^{8}$ and 110 $(109)^{2}$, by κατακυριεύειν. This second Greek word, in turn, renders *kbsh* in Gen. 1^{28}, and again in Num. $32^{22,29}$, where it refers to the conquest of the Holy Land. (2) In Ps. 8^{7} the 'dominion' doctrine of Gen. 1^{28} is expressed by *mshl;* and in 1 Kings 5^{1} the same word indicates the suzerainty of Solomon over an area corresponding to the promise made to Abraham (Gen. 15^{18}). (3) (*a*) 'Thou didst put all things under the feet'

the presence of a 'Genesis-Exodus' mystery. The function of Adam in the first creation is carried over into the functions of the Redeemer in the new creation. But it is to be observed that in the fulfilment there is, as always, a transformation. In the gospels this stands out noticeably in our Lord's comments upon the ambitious request of James and John (Mark 10^{42ff}, Matt. 20^{25ff}).[1] Moreover, the transformation which associates universal dominion with lowliness is everywhere present in the apostolic writings; and just as the Servant-form transforms the messianic idea so it also throws a flood of light upon the 'Adam' typology as handled in the New Testament. We shall have to proceed by slow stages in this matter; and our next step will be to consider the treatment of Psalm 8 which is set before us in the Epistle to the Hebrews. Later we shall find a connexion between this psalm of creation and other strands of the biblical pattern which are vitally relevant to our argument.

In Hebrews 2^{6-9} the author quotes the central section of the psalm, beginning with the words 'What is man...?' and continuing to the statement: 'Thou didst put all things under his feet'.[2] This is a statement about man's place in the plan of creation; and some comment is necessary upon the expression 'son of man' which occurs in the second line of the quotation. There are several points to be noted: (1) The idiom of parallelism in Hebrew poetry shows that in this verse 'man' and 'son of man' have the same meaning; 'son of man' means 'man'. But (2) in the Hebrew text the expression is 'son of Adam'. This is rightly rendered, in translation, as 'son of man' because 'Adam' in Hebrew is a generic word for 'man'. Nevertheless it also carries a reference to the 'Adam' of the creation narratives in Genesis, and this double nuance of the word could not be carried over in translation. The psalmist, then, was referring

of the son of man (Ps. 8^7) is fulfilled (*b*) in Dan. 7^{27}. This refers in (*a*) to 'the son of Adam' (Heb.) and in (*b*) to Israel. In both LXX has ὑποτάσσειν. Finally the expression 'footstool of thy feet' in Ps. 110 (109)[1] is in LXX very like the conclusion of Ps. 8^7 (in EVV 8^6).

[1] In both passages our Lord is represented as repudiating the current associations of κατακυριεύειν (see last note), and in this respect his teaching is echoed in 1 Pet. 5^3, notwithstanding the benevolent promise of Jer. 3^{14} (LXX).

[2] From 8^{5-7} (LXX), corresponding to 8^{4-6} in EVV. The numbering of verses in LXX is identical with that of the Hebrew text.

here to 'the dominion of Adam' over the lower creation; and the psalm as a whole is clearly a meditation upon that theme. (3) We cannot say how much of this was in the mind of the apostolic author; but we may be sure of one thing. For this Christian writer the term 'son of man' had acquired a new meaning as the title which Jesus chose for himself. In Hebrews 2, therefore, we have a typical statement of the way in which the new creation is related to the Creator's original plan.

Here we must observe that the writer to the Hebrews shows traces of an acquaintance with the theology of St Paul as well as special affinity with the mind of St Luke. It will be in order, therefore, at this point to recall what was said in the preceding chapter concerning the Lucan thesis that 'the Son of God became son of Adam in order that he might fulfil Adam's destiny as son of God by creation'.[1] The connexion with St Paul will be considered presently. But the Adam typology is sufficiently widespread to serve our purpose.[2] We have only to add that in Hebrews 2^{14} the serpent's head is duly bruised by a son of Adam who fulfills the psalm of creation. Returning now to this author's use of the psalm, we read as follows: We do not yet see the fulfilment of the poet's vision in which all creation is subject to man. But we do see in Jesus the beginning of its fulfilment. For we see him who was 'made a little lower than the angels' 'on account of the sufferings of death crowned with glory and honour'. The last phrase could be understood in two ways. It may indicate the familiar sequence of glory *following* suffering. It might, however, refer to the event of the Transfiguration in which Jesus was crowned *before* his passion to fulfil the sequence of Isaiah $52^{13\,ff}$.[3]

This possibility arises from the clause which *follows* after: 'that by the grace of God he should taste death for every man'. But whether the author had in mind the mystery of Jesus transfigured upon the mount or not it certainly looks as if his applica-

[1] See above, Ch. II, § ii, two pars. near the end. For agreement with St Paul on 'Adam' see also my essay in *The Apostolic Ministry*, p. 87, note 4.

[2] Even Dan. 7, which does not employ 'son of Adam' phraseology, looks back to the dominion over the beasts in Gen. 2. cp. I. VIII. p. 251 note. The connexion of Matt. 11^{29} with Ecclus. 40^{1} *et al.* is also again relevant.

[3] cp. *The Apostolic Ministry*, p. 61 and note. There was also a Jewish belief, doubtless based on Ps. 8, that *before* the fall Adam had a halo of glory. See further below, § v, pars. 3 ff.

tion of the psalm is coloured by a typical fusion of two images, namely Adam and the Servant of the Lord. The doubt about the meaning of verse 9 referred to at the end of the last paragraph need not prevent us from going forward; for on any showing the curious sequence: 'death, glory, death' demands explanation, and the suggested fusion of images may provide a clue. The 'glory' of Adam[1] was *followed* by sin and sentence of death. The prophetic counterpart of this appears in the sequence of the Servant song where glory is first assigned to the Servant, to be *followed* by a sin-bearing which involves death. Thus the death-sentence upon Adam with its entail of suffering for all mankind finds its remedy in the glory of the Servant; and this in turn is manifested in and through the Servant's surrender to a death for all.[2] In Jesus, however, the two scriptural images are not merely arranged in a double sequence with points of similarity recurring in the pattern. For he is the whole in which both these fragmentary parts find their fulfilment.

Let us, then, seek the whole through the parts by seeing the parts in the setting of the whole. Psalm 8 agrees with Genesis in placing man at the head of creation while laying equal emphasis upon the fact that he is also a creature of earth and not a celestial being. There is here a combination of greatness with lowliness corresponding exactly to our Lord's teachings. God is the only true king of the world which he has created. The dominion of Adam, therefore, is a delegated sovereignty, rightly exercised under obedience; and its effectual exercise was lost through disobedience. When man treats the world as his own property he loses the mysterious secret of its control which was originally granted to him. This is precisely what we see happening to-day. Without ceasing to be the appointed viceroy of this earth, the human steward of its treasures has by false independence lost control. For he has changed his stewardship into a usurpation. Thus the *grande latrocinium* of which St

[1] see the last note.

[2] Superficially this makes τὸ πάθημα τοῦ θανάτου refer to the total consequences of Adam's sin. But there may well be a deeper thought. *One* of the consequences was the passion and death of Jesus, in which he made himself one with all Adam's progeny. This thought would tend to effect a mystic identity between the two 'death' references in this verse.

Augustine wrote[1] leaves its blight everywhere and continues to mar the divine plan. Yet this is not the end of the story. For the first Adam's act of spoliation[2] has already been surpassed and superseded by the second or 'last' Adam's act of obedience.

In Christ the dominion of Adam is once more restored. In their handling of this topic St Paul and the writer to the Hebrews are in close agreement. Both connect the very similar phrases in psalms 8 and 110. Both interpret the messianic sovereignty of the latter in terms of the headship over creation in the former. Lastly, both find in these oracles a double truth. The reign of Jesus had begun; yet he still waits until all his enemies are put under his feet.[3] The messianic glory of Jesus is complete; yet our human destiny in creation still awaits fulfilment. Fastening upon the phrase of psalm $8^{7(6)}$ ('subject all things') in Hebrews 2^{8} the author observes that we do not yet see this consummation. That is one half of the truth. The other half is attested by St Paul in Philippians 3^{21}, where, quoting the same phrase from the psalm, he affirms the present glory of the risen Christ to be the pledge of our final share in the psalm's fulfilment. This pledge, indeed, over-arches all those elements of our experience which seems to negate its reality.

iii

The Child and the Servant. **Their interrelation in scripture examined. The typology of Hebrews 2 leads us through Psalm 8 to the language of the Second Isaiah. The Servant as a 'young child' is a theme which foreshadows the gospel picture of the Holy Child.**

In the course of the preceding section we passed from our Lord's sayings about little children to a number of scriptural

[1] *De civitate dei*, IV, 6, where the reference is to the founding of Babel by Nimrod (Gen. 10^{10}; cp. 11^{1-9}).

[2] By his use of ἁρπαγμόν in Phil. 2^{6}, to describe Adam's sin St Paul anticipated the thought contained in St Augustine's phrase. Cp. the description of faithless Israel in Ezek. 22^{25-29}, where LXX has a threefold repetition of ἁρπάζοντες ἁρπάγματα following upon the twofold use of this phrase in $19^{3,6}$. The ruling classes in Ch. 22 follow the lead given by their kings in Ch. 19. So too in his great reversal the Christ king is followed by his loyal subjects who share his lowliness.

[3] 1 Cor. 15^{20-28}, Eph. 1^{20-22}, Heb. 1^{13}, 2^{6-9}.

images drawn from the Old Testament. The link between these two topics was formed by the dominical paradox concerning greatness and lowliness. The paradox lay in the union of these two things; and this, in turn, determined the course of the ensuing argument. For at the centre of our discussion concerning certain scriptural images lay the transforming influence of one particular image, namely that of the Servant of the Lord. The union of greatness and lowliness, symbolized by the child in Christ's arms, is also manifested in the fusion of images. For it is only within the orbit of that majestic revelation that the various images can be so interpreted that they blend together into one whole. That they do so blend in the gospel revelation is an undoubted fact. How they do so is a matter which will repay further consideration. For this our method of procedure has already, in principle, been laid down. The paradox of our Lord's teaching, it has been suggested, appeared in two forms; these are quite literally the form of the child and the form of the Servant.[1] It seems possible, then, that there will be a scriptural connexion between the two 'forms' in question; if so, this further link might bring to us fresh illumination.

There are quite a number of indications in scripture which point towards such a connexion. It will be simplest, however, to begin our investigation by selecting from the New Testament a passage where the connexion is already becoming clear. The second chapter of the Epistle to the Hebrews, which has engaged our attention in the preceding section, contains the very characteristics for which we are looking. The argument begins at verse 5 with the declaration: 'Not unto angels did he subject the world to come whereof we speak'. This indicates that the psalm of creation which is next quoted is being regarded as a prophecy of the new creation. As the argument proceeds we see both the creation-cycle and the story of redemptive history being brought to their fruition in the dominion of Christ, and that too by virtue of his accepting the Servant's vocation 'to taste death for every man' (2^{9}). By this act he bruises the serpent's head and reverses Adam's fall (2^{14}). Before this point has

[1] I hold it to be certain that our Lord's human mind was deeply influenced by the Servant prophecies. But the statement in the text does not depend upon the truth of this supposition. It is quite sufficient that his teaching as a whole is massively congruous with the 'Servant' idea.

been reached, however, two quotations from the Old Testament have been introduced which reveal the author's thoughts concerning the story of redemption. The first is from Psalm 22, for Christians a classic picture of the divine sufferer which we associate with Calvary. The second is from the symbolic story of Isaiah's children and repeats the key-word of our Lord's child-sayings. Thus the servant-form and the child-form are introduced together, in the closest conjunction, into this exposition of Adam's restored dominion.[1]

The main thesis of Hebrews 1 and 2 is that the only Son of God who is superior to the angels was made to occupy a place beneath them in order that he might be made one with us men in our creaturely destiny and thus restore us to that destiny. This identification with us is affirmed three times over under three distinct images: (1) The Son brings many sons to glory. For this he became a 'son of Adam', identifying himself with us in origin as well as in destiny. By this he also took upon him the discipline of filial obedience which, in a fallen world, involves suffering as the necessary path to perfection. (2) By his identification with us in sonship he also made us his brethren to whom he becomes 'leader' in the school of suffering. Thus he initiates us into the '*ecclesia*' of the true worshippers. (3) The filial attitude learnt in the school of suffering is the trustful dependence which is a characteristic of children. In this, too, Jesus (like Isaiah of old) identifies himself with his children, whose flesh and blood he took (Hebrews 2^{10-14}). At this point, perhaps, we can begin to see in detail precisely how the psalm of creation fits the situation which the apostolic author is unfolding. By identifying himself with 'the children' the Son of Man enables praise to be perfected from their mouths through the destruction of the 'enemy'.[2] Thus the opening phase of the psalm ($8^{2,3}$ in LXX) is fulfilled in the manner described in Hebrews 2^{9-16}.

[1] The argument thus outlined begins in verse 9. The keyword referred to in the text is, of course, παιδία (v. 13), repeated emphatically in v. 14. The quotations are from LXX (Ps. 21^{23} and Isa. $8^{17,18}$). cp. above § i, last par. but one and note.

[2] In the psalm the babes are instrumental to the enemy's defeat. In Hebrews the Son of Man 'putting all things under his feet' is at the centre of the picture. But 'the children' share his triumph (2^{15}).

From the preceding analysis it has become clear that the identification of our Lord with his people is stated in terms of three Old Testament images, namely (1) Adam's seed bruising the serpent, (2) Isaiah's messianic remnant, (3) Israel the Servant whose mission involves suffering. Of these the third may well be, historically, a later development of the idea contained in the second. We have now to consider, however, the possibility of a further connexion between the first and the third. The connexion which I have in mind is in itself purely linguistic, and therefore (in a sense) quite fortuitous. Accidental coincidences of language are, nevertheless, not infrequently the starting-point of scriptural patterns which became significant for the first Christian age. In the present instance there is a verbal link between the psalm of creation, part of which is quoted in Hebrews 2^{6-8}, and the song of the Servant which begins at Isaiah 52^{13}. Such a connexion, if in any sense valid, would once more bring the creation-cycle into the plan of redemptive history. More important for our present purpose is the fact that the linguistic phenomena which we are to consider bring the child-form into fusion with the servant-form.

In the Hebrew text of Psalm 8^3 (EVV. 8^2) the word rendered 'sucklings' is *yônekim*, and its singular form (*yônek*) occurs in Isaiah 53^2 where it is rendered 'tender plant'. The context in both passages shows these renderings to be correct. The picture in Isaiah makes the Servant to be like a young plant in poor soil. Israel in captivity is like 'a root out of dry ground', insignificant and without future prospects. The word *yônek*, however, can mean any living object which is young and tender, whether plant, animal or human child. This range of meaning gives significance to the picture of the 'lamb led to the slaughter' a little further on in the prophecy (53^7). But it also helps to explain the peculiar rendering of Isaiah 53^2 in the Septuagint. Here the 'tender plant' has become a 'young child' (*paidion*); but also two other changes have altered the whole meaning of the sentence. A literal rendering would run thus: 'We announced as a child before him, as a root in a thirsty land'. *Yônek* can certainly mean 'a child'; and 'we announced' picks up and repeats a word from the preceding verses (52^{15}). But why has 'my servant' (*pais*), who is the subject of the poem (52^{13}), suddenly been 'announced as a child' (*paidion*)?

If we look at the sentence as a whole we see that with the disappearance of the growing plant the 'root out of a dry ground' has also changed its character. It is no longer growing 'out of' the ground. It is now simply said to be 'in a thirsty land'. Thus the last trace of *growing* vegetation has vanished from the picture. The translators have, in fact, substituted a new picture; and we naturally ask what it means. I think the clue to an answer lies in the collocation of the two words, 'child' and 'root'; for both are messianic by virtue of their use in the prophecies attributed to the original 'Isaiah' in the earlier chapters of the composite work which now bears his name.

In the Greek version of Isaiah *paidion* is used of the 'Immanuel' child in 7^{16}, and again in the Christmas lection: 'unto us a child is born' (9^{6}). It is also applied significantly to one or both of Isaiah's children.[1] In chapter 11 the messianic king is called 'a rod from the root of Jesse' (11^{1}); and in verses 6–10 the two words for 'child' and 'root' are brought together as in 53^{2}. In the transformation of creation which accompanies the messianic age wild beasts will be so tame that 'a little child shall lead them' (as though they were cattle or farm-horses). Moreover the 'children' of ox and bear shall be together, and an 'infant child' shall play with asps unharmed.[2] Two verses later (11^{10}) the messianic king is called 'the root of Jesse' whose rule will bring 'rest'.[3] It would seem then that the Greek version of Isaiah 53 identifies the Servant, in some sense, with the messianic king. This would agree well with the renewal of the Davidic covenant in 55^{3}. Moreover the preceding invitation: 'Ho every one that thirsteth, come ye to the waters' (55^{1}) follows aptly upon the picture of Jesse's 'Root' giving refreshment in a thirsty land (11^{10} and 53^{2}).[4]

[1] In 8^{4} Isaiah's second son is referred to in a manner analogous to what is said of 'Immanuel' in 7^{16}. In 10^{19} (LXX) the remnant of Israel will be a small number which 'a child shall write'. Cp. Luke $10^{20, 21}$ (=Matt. 11^{25}), where the remnant are 'babes' whose names are written in heaven.

[2] The conjunction of παιδίον νήπιον here unites two of our key-words. For the νήπιοι of Ps. 8^{3} reappears in Matt. 11^{25} and in Luke 10^{21}. See last note.

[3] Thus νήπιος and ἀνάπαυσις occur in close association as in Matt. 11^{25-30}. Cp. above, Addit. Note B, conclusion of par. 4.

[4] The fourth Servant-song could be (and sometimes was) interpreted messianically by Jews until the controversy of the Synagogue with the Christian Church rendered this inexpedient.

This survey of linguistic connexions which started from the Hebrew text of Psalm 8 and Isaiah 53 has incidentally brought to light a further point concerning the expression: 'babes and sucklings'. For the 'babes' of Psalm 8 (in its Greek form) recur significantly in the gospels (note 2 on p. 84). This adds something to our previous analysis of Matthew 11. For there we found the 'babes' of the new creation set upon a cosmic background; and it may well be that the first evangelist had in mind here 'the psalm of creation' as well as the Wisdom literature. We have not yet wholly exhausted the literary affinities between the psalm and the prophecy. But at present we must keep to the 'child' motif introduced into the Greek version of the prophecy at 53^2; and first let us consider the connection of this motif with the language used about the Servant in the same Greek version. Here we must take note of another curious detail of language. In the second half of the book which bears Isaiah's name the word commonly used by the translators for 'servant' is *pais*, a word which can also mean 'a child'. This double meaning of the word corresponds closely to our English use of the word 'boy' in certain parts of the world to indicate a male native servant. The point of similarity lies in the fact that in both idioms the word refers not so much to youthfulness as to a subordinate status and perhaps also to a simple, unsophisticated mind.[1]

At the conclusion of chapter II we found in our Lord's 'great invitation' (Matt. 11^{28-30}) a gospel renewal of the prophetic theme concerning 'an Exodus discipline which involves a return to the conditions of childhood'. In deutero-Isaiah the expectation of an impending 'exodus' from Babylon is expressed in terms of an analogy with the original exodus from Egypt. We have already noticed one application of this idea, namely the co-operation of creation with the redemptive plan of the Creator. A further application may well be intended in the demand for a disciplined co-operation of Israel the Servant, a demand which runs right through the prophecies of the Second Isaiah. At one or two points, moreover, the notion of an 'exodus discipline' comes into prominence. The question may therefore be raised: does this also involve 'a return to the

[1] In Gal. 4^1 St Paul remarks that an heir who is still a child in pupilage 'differs in nothing from a slave'.

conditions of childhood'? For answer we may turn to Isaiah 50^{4ff}, the passage which is considered to be the third of the four Servant songs. The picture of the Servant here set forth is in an 'exodus' setting; for at verse 2 there is an obvious reference to the drying up of the Red sea. Also, the passage as a whole was for the first Christians a foreshadowing of our Lord's passion in view of verse 6: 'I gave my back to the smiters' etc.[1]

Before we reach the Servant's 'passion', however, we get a glimpse of his training by which he was prepared for his mission. In verse 4 he becomes a learner who is taught how to speak appropriate words to the 'weary'. So our Lord in summoning 'the weary' to 'learn of me' is himself the perfect disciple who 'knows the Father' (Matt. 11^{27ff}). In the Greek version of verse 4 'the tongue of them that are taught' becomes 'the tongue of discipline'; and in verse 5 we read that 'the discipline of the Lord God openeth my ears'. The word here rendered 'discipline' is *paidia*, which is in form identical with the plural of *paidion*. 'Discipline' is in some sense appropriate for 'children'; and in Isaiah 53^{5} the word is once more introduced in application to the Servant who has here just been called a child (verse 2)! These verbal details will repay fuller consideration. Let us first notice the difference of tone between the two Servant-songs to which reference is here being made. In Isaiah 50 the servant is a young disciple learning to face the difficult path marked out for him, whereas in the later poem we have a retrospect upon a mission finally accomplished.

In the former song the Servant himself describes how the 'discipline' affects his sense-organs. He is given a trained tongue, to know how to speak; and the same process opens his ears to hear the divine Word which he must utter. At this point we are inevitably reminded of the story of King Solomon's equipment for his office at the beginning of his reign (1 Kings 3^{5-15}). The young king is overawed by his responsibilities. He feels himself to be a 'little child'. So he asks for a 'hearing heart'; and his request is granted. Earlier still the child Samuel had been

[1] The expression in v. 7: 'set my face like a flint', which may be based upon Ezek. $3^{8,9}$, seems to lie behind the similar phrase in Luke 9^{51}, where Jesus 'set his face to go to Jerusalem' on his final visit. Again, v. 8 is quoted in Rom. 8^{33} where it is applied to the members of Christ who share with him the Servant's vocation.

taught to say: 'Speak, Lord; for thy servant heareth' (1 Sam. $3^{9,10}$).[1] So also in the fourth gospel Jesus says of his Father: 'What I heard from him I speak' and 'all that I heard from my Father I made known unto you' (John 8^{26}, 15^{15}). This preparatory discipline of hearing and speaking, however, issues, for the suffering Servant, in a sterner and more exacting ordeal. 'The chastisement' which was laid upon him was afterwards seen to be not his but 'ours'. It was the vicarious '*paidia* of our peace'; and so 'by his stripes we were healed'. Thus the messianic 'child' was led to the slaughter; and in his passion the discipline of speech was changed into a holy silence. In the Greek version it is the young lamb which is dumb before its shearer. 'So he openeth not his mouth' ($53^{5,7}$).

iv

St Matthew's picture of 'the young child' as a king who fulfils the Servant prophecy and 'repeats' the Exodus is unique in the gospel records. Traces of such imagery in Luke and John. The typology of Philippians 2 to be correlated with the child-like character of the kingdom.

Our Lord's words about children and their symbolic significance have led us to a consideration of their wider biblical context. The threads of connexion thus traced were of different kinds. Some were purely verbal, whereas by contrast others seemed to enter into the pattern through that fusion of types which is already perceptible in the Old Testament. Sometimes, however, an interweaving of different threads affects the whole pattern. An example will make this point clearer. The occurrence of *paidion* (young child) as a designation of the Servant in Isaiah 53^2 may seem to be an accident of translation due to the wide range of meaning in the original Hebrew word. In fact, however, it would probably not have been employed in that way unless the translators were already disposed to see messianic significance in the Servant. For with that thought in their minds

[1] In 1 Sam. 1 LXX has παιδίον four times in reference to Hannah's childlessness. Afterwards (1^{21-28}, $2^{11,18ff}$, $3^{1,8}$) Samuel is repeatedly referred to as the παιδάριον; this is the word which Solomon applies to himself on the occasion mentioned in the text.

they would quite naturally render the Hebrew word in a manner which suggested a continuity between the Servant's mission and that of the messianic child (Isaiah 7–11). Such a connexion between the two themes might be all the more easily made when the two groups of prophecies were ascribed to a single author.

Once made, the connexion was bound to have a powerful influence upon the thought of the first Christians. A striking example of this appears in St Matthew's Gospel. In his second chapter he records two incidents from the life-story of the Holy Child, the visit of the Magi to Bethlehem and the flight of the Holy Family into Egypt to escape from the murderous sword of King Herod. The story begins and ends with messianic prophecy. The oracle of Micah is cited in full for the expectation that a Davidic messiah will be born at Bethlehem;[1] and at the end of the chapter the settlement at Nazareth is regarded as a further fulfilment of prophecy. Most probably Isaiah 11^1 is the passage to which the evangelist here refers.[2] It is clear then that when the evangelist designates Jesus as 'the young child' he sees in him the messianic child of prophecy. But it seems that he also sees something else. It is significant that, as the evangelist tells the story covering this group of incidents, he introduces the word *paidion* (always with the definite article) no less than nine times in fourteen verses! Moreover the child of whom he writes is, in the narrative, first honoured as a king and then hunted as a fugitive, first glorified and then humiliated.

This sequence corresponds exactly to that of the principal Servant-song where the Servant is first uplifted and exalted and then led as a lamb to the slaughter. In the Greek version the Servant is first 'glorified' (Isaiah 52^{13}) and then 'announced as a young child' before he goes to his passion. So the evangelist 'announces' Jesus 'as the young child' of messianic prophecy who is glorified by the worshipping Magi; and he then goes on to show how, in accordance with scripture, the child begins at once to fulfil the vocation of the suffering Servant. The flight into Egypt is, of course, only a beginning; but it is also a

[1] Matt. 2^6 = Micah 5^2 (H.5^1). But the gospel version does not correspond exactly either to the Hebrew or to LXX.

[2] Connecting 'Nazareth' with *nêtzer*, the Hebrew word rendered 'branch' in EVV.

foreshadowing of greater woes to come. It is, indeed, symbolical of the Servant's entire mission. For the Servant is the true Israel which must 'repeat' the Exodus from Egypt. In the prophetic cycle this was envisaged as a flight from Babylon to the Holy Land. In the fulfilment the evangelist sees paradoxically a flight from the Holy Land to Egypt before the genuine Exodus can take place.[1] For the land of Israel has become a place where the true Israel is an outlaw. We have already had occasion to notice how this notion is further developed through the medium of David's story at a later point in the gospel history.[2]

In this prelude to the new Exodus there is a slaughter of babes parallel to that which occurred in the first Exodus. But in the 'repetition' the incident has a very different significance. The innocent victims are not now, as then, the first-born of old Israel's enemies. On the contrary, they are the first-fruits of new Israel's martyred hosts. They are also contrasted with 'the young child' as 'children' (*paides*). We have already noticed the double meaning of this word.[3] It is frequently employed in the Septuagint for the servants of a king or other magnate. In the singular, however, it could mean '*the* Servant'; and these children are proto-types of all those who are destined to be participators in the Servant's passion. It is perhaps worth mentioning that, whereas the first evangelist reserves the *paidion* title to the Christ in his story of the holy childhood, he later follows St Mark in the plural use of this word when he records the dominical sayings about little children. On the other hand, in St Luke's story of the infancy it is scarcely possible to trace any such peculiarity as we have found in his fellow-evangelist. The most that can be said is this, that the word *paidion* is applied several times both to Jesus and to his forerunner, and in such a way as to develop the parallel between them.[4]

[1] And in the greatest possible contrast to the honourable descent of old Israel in circumstances of almost royal splendour (Gen. 45^{9}–47^{12}).

[2] see above, Ch. I. § iii, par. 7 and the conclusion of Addit. Note B.

[3] see above, § iii, par. 8.

[4] cp. Luke 1^{66} with 2^{17}, and 1^{80} with 2^{40}. It must be remembered that παιδίον was the natural word to use of any child. On the other hand in 2^{43} the boy Jesus is called ὁ παῖς at the point where sorrow and perplexity begin to manifest themselves in the Holy Family. The sword of which old Simeon spoke (2^{35}) begins to pierce as soon as Jesus takes upon him the yoke

In the story of Genesis 22, where Abraham is bidden to offer his son Isaac in sacrifice, the Greek version makes the lad a 'young child' (verse 5) and then a 'little boy' (verse 12). This sacrificial story of an 'only son' has been thought to lie behind the incident in John 1^{29-34}, where the Baptist first calls Jesus 'the Lamb of God' and then bears witness that 'this is the Son of God'. The lamb 'which God provides' is thus the true fulfilment of the Genesis story.[1] Now, quite apart from the speculation which finds an Aramaic background for the connexion between 'lamb' and 'son',[2] we have already found such a connexion in the Hebrew text of Isaiah 53^2, which for the fourth evangelist would receive further illumination from the Septuagint. For we are assuming that the *paidion* of the translators in Isaiah 53^2 was connected by their early Christian readers with 'Unto us a child is born, unto us a son is given' (Isaiah 9^6). Moreover the word which means 'lamb' in John $1^{29,36}$ is the word employed in the Septuagint of Isaiah 53^7, although throughout the other great Johannine book another word was preferred.[3]

It will be noticed that in this section examples have been cited from three gospels for a fresh stage in that fusion of type-images which is already apparent in the Old Testament. The evidence is cumulative, and for that reason we cannot safely ignore the slighter indications which have been cited from St Luke and St John. The three main types which have recurred in the present chapter are Adam, the messianic king and the suffering servant; and our handling of these themes has shown them to be very variously blended in the unfolding process of revelation. One further example of this phenomenon shall now

of the law, and so becomes 'subject to them' (2^{51}). As though in anticipation of St Luke's story, St Paul provides an eloquent comment upon this situation in Gal. 4^{1-5}.

[1] In Gen. $22^{13,14}$ 'the Lord provides' a ram to take the place of the only son.

[2] Burney suggested that the actual word employed by the Baptist was *talya'* (cp. *talitha* in Mark 5^{41}, which that evangelist seems to regard as an equivalent of παιδίον in verses 39, 40). This word would, in the Baptist's mouth, have the same wide range of meaning as *yonêk* in Isa. 53^2.

[3] ἀρνίον (Rev. 5^6 *et al.*), which comes from Jer. 11^{19}, the nearest OT parallel to Isa 53^7. The paschal lamb was ἀρήν (Exod. 12^5), as also the 'sucking lamb' offered by Samuel (1 Reg. 7^9).

be submitted to inspection, in some ways the most complex of them all. It is to be found in the well-known Christological hymn of Philippians 2^{5-11}. Evidence for its complexity is to be seen in the literature which it has called into being and in the extent to which it has baffled the commentators. I believe that the difficulties found in this passage will tend to disappear just so far as we can correctly apply to it the principles of biblical interpretation which we have been following. If this hope should be justified, the resultant integration of parts in the whole will appropriately introduce some final thoughts about the childlike character of the kingdom.

V

Philippians 2^{5-11} examined in detail. The Adam of the creation-cycle seen in the light of Ezekiel's vision and the Servant prophecy. The language of Philippians concerning the *kenosis* determined by Hebrew idioms of thought.

The Christological statement in Philippians 2^{5-11} has the appearance of being very carefully worded. Every phrase employed is clearly important for determining the precise meaning of the whole. Again, if our main supposition is correct, the blending of types which is contained in the statement has the effect of expressing each type in a form which is not precisely that exhibited in the Old Testament. For each tends to bend the others to itself; but, even more, the actual fulfilment in Christ is richer than anything contained in the types, regarded severally or collectively. For these reasons it seems desirable to begin by setting down a literal rendering of verses 5–8, which contain the more complex part of the statement. The whole is also divided into three main parts; and some biblical references are provided which indicate the background:

Have this mind in you which you also have in Christ Jesus,

(1) Who, being in the form of God, did not count it a thing to be grasped at (*res rapienda*) to be equal with God, Gen. $3^{5, 6}$

(2) but *poured himself out*, Isa. 53^{12}
having taken the form of a slave, Mark 10^{44}
having become in the likeness of men; Ezek. 1^{26-28}

(3) and being found in fashion as a man,
he humbled himself, Hos. 2^{15b} (LXX)
having become obedient Rom. 5^{19}
unto death, even the death of
the cross. Isa. 53^{12}.

The opening clause, as rendered, has the effect of bringing the Christian readers right into the main picture. It has the same significance as the quotation from Isaiah 8 in Hebrews 2^{13}: 'Behold, I and the children which God gave to me'. What is true of the Christ is to become true of his members; for they are inseparable from him. In terms of our Lord's own symbolism 'the children' are signified in 'the Child'. We come next to the first main affirmation (1). Happily, its interpretation has registered a maximum amount of agreement. The serpent said 'Ye shall be as gods', and the specious promise was eagerly grasped at. The typology here follows the model set up in Romans 5^{12-21}. Adam 'is a type of the coming One', but in a manner which involves contrast at every point. The contrast would be complete if it were expressed thus: 'Adam, the man, grasped at equality with God, whereas Jesus who was in the form of God took the form of a man.' In fact the contrast is not made with this verbal simplicity. The generous condescension of him who came 'from heaven' as 'the last Adam' or 'the second man' (1 Cor. 15^{45-47}) is more elaborately stated in the series of clauses which are cited above under (2) and (3).

Perhaps the most curious feature of the contrast as stated lies in the twofold description of the Incarnation under (2). Instead of 'the form of a man' we have 'the form of a slave' and 'the likeness of men'. Why the double phrase? Why 'slave'? These two questions press for answers. Also, the contrast between God and a slave renders all the more remarkable the application of the word rendered 'form' to both sides of the contrast. For light on these problems we turn first to the passage from the prophet Ezekiel cited in the margin above. The prophet saw a vision of cherubim supporting on a throne a manifestation of the deity in human form. In this description (1^4–2^1) the word rendered 'likeness' in our text occurs repeatedly in the Septuagint version. Moreover in that version verse 5 appears to anticipate the theophany of vv. 26 ff. It concludes with these words: 'the likeness of a man upon them' (that is, 'upon the cherubim') anticipating the actual vision of deity in verse 26 where we read 'a likeness as a form of a man'.[1] In the Hebrew text, however, both expressions refer to a 'likeness of Adam'; and it seems clear that Ezekiel's vision is a source of the statements in Genesis concerning the creation of Adam 'in the image and likeness of God'. Now the theophany appeared to the prophet as a human form surrounded by a halo or garment of light. Moreover in Psalm 8 the 'son of Adam' is said to have been 'crowned with glory and honour'.

These expressions suggested to Jewish teachers that Adam originally shared the glorious form of the deity, at least to the extent of a crown or halo of light, or according to another tradition a complete 'body-garment' of light.[2] The latter view was widely accepted in the early Church and must have been known to St Paul.[3] In this Jewish (and Christian) conception Adam lost his share in the outward glory of the divine likeness when he fell. Thus his descendent, Ezekiel, although himself a 'son of Adam', did not share that radiant garment of light which he saw surrounding the deity-in-Adam's form. We can now begin to see what is signified by 'the form of a slave'. Adam prior to the fall is a partner of deity in the stewardship of creation's order. In a derivative and creaturely sense he might even be described as having been 'in the form of God' by virtue of his share in the divine likeness. Moreover his outward appearance corresponded to that fact. Herein, perhaps, lies the significance of the word rendered 'form' in the Pauline text. For we are told that this word (*morphé*), 'always signifies a form

[1] In Ezek. 1^{5} LXX has ὁμοίωμα ἀνθρώπου, in 1^{26} ὁμοίωμα ὡς εἶδος ἀνθρώπου. In 2^{1} ὁμοίωμα occurs again ('likeness of the glory of the Lord'). In all three expressions ὁμοίωμα renders *demûth*, the word which means 'likeness' in Gen. 1^{26} and again in Gen. $5^{1,3}$ (twice). But further, in Ezek. 1^{5} and 1^{26} ἀνθρώπου renders *adham*. What the prophet saw was 'a likeness as an appearance of Adam' sitting upon a throne; and this vision is surely the basis of the statements in Gen. 1^{26} and $5^{1,3}$. The author of the 'P' sections in Genesis drew from Ezekiel the following deductions: (1) God exists in the form of a glorified man (cp. Ezek. $1^{27,28}$). (2) This 'form' was conferred upon Adam, and (3) transmitted to the *bené adham*. In Ezek. 2^{1ff} the prophet is addressed as *ben adham* (Son of Adam).

[2] For the latter opinion see the Introduction to Rendel Harris's edition of *The Odes and Psalms of Solomon*, pp. 67 ff.

[3] As Burkitt pointed out, it is probably the background of 2 Cor. 5^{1} (*Early Eastern Christianity*, p. 215, quoted by Rendel Harris, p. 68).

which truly and fully expresses the being that underlies it'.[1] What follows, then? Shall we say that Adam, without ceasing to possess 'the image' of God was, after his fall, in 'the form of a slave'?[2]

The language of the New Testament on this subject is paradoxical. In 1 Corinthians 11[7] St Paul affirms that a man (as such) 'is the image and glory of God'.[3] Yet because 'all sinned' 'they lack' or 'fall short of the glory of God'. The image is still there and is still *capax gloriae;* yet our sinful condition frustrates the fulfilment of this possibility (Romans 3[23]). In Romans 6–8 the apostle unfolds the consequences of this situation. Fallen man is a slave of sin, and his only path of recovery lies in becoming a slave of God (6[16–22]). The way of recovery was made possible by the act of Jesus Christ who, 'being in the form of God', stepped down into Adam's place and 'took the form of a slave'. He took that very form which had once been glorious, yet was so no longer. He had 'no form nor comeliness'. At this point the Adam type passes inevitably into the type of the suffering servant. The word rendered 'comeliness' in Isaiah 53[2] is the word which occurs in Psalm 8 to describe the 'honour' with which the son of Adam is crowned. Yet *this* Son of Adam (cp. Luke 3[38]), to whom it belonged by right, stripped himself of that honour. In order to enter upon the slave status of our fallen humanity he 'emptied himself'. This word (*ekenosen*) has been a storm centre of theological discussion and controversy for centuries. We have now to see how it fits into the preceding argument.

The phrase which we are about to consider is apt to provoke the question: 'Of what did he empty himself?' This question is

[1] Kennedy in EGT, quoted with approval by MM, p. 417[2], in reference to NT usage. It is at least doubtful whether the special instance of Mark 16[12] ('in another form') is really an exception to this rule.

[2] It is noteworthy that the writer of Gen. 5[1–3] does not affirm that the *demûth* which Adam passed on to his son was in all respects the same as that which he, Adam, had received. There is every probability that he knew the story now set out in Gen. 3.

[3] This corresponds to the language of Isa. 5[13,14] where the chief men of Israel are described successively as 'their glory' and 'their honour'. These two words are used in Ps. 8[6] and the latter in Isa. 53[2]. Also in Mic. 2[9] the probable rendering: 'From their babes ye take away my glory for ever' refers to acts of social injustice by which fathers are wrongly separated from their children (J.M.P. Smith in ICC *ad loc.*).

certain to prove misleading unless we take account of the relevant idioms presented to us in Hebrew thought. Pedersen has described them fully in his great work (*Israel I–II*, pp. 149 ff.). Two quotations will give the leading idea: 'The anguished soul is *empty*'; and again (since 'soul' renders *nephesh*) 'the miserable has poured out his *nephesh*, i.e. emptied it of its fulness and strength' (*ib.*, p. 149). That might lead to death; so in 2 Sam. 14^{14} we read: 'We must needs die, and are as water spilt upon the ground'. This, however, presents the imagery in an involuntary form. In Isaiah 53^{12} the Servant's voluntary sacrifice is described in these words: 'he poured out his soul unto death'. The idiom seems to be the same in Philippians 2^{7}. Moreover, if we glance down our quotation of this passage from the beginning of (2) to the end of (3) we find something that looks like an echo. I have indicated this by placing the two relevant phrases in italics: 'he *poured himself out . . . unto death*'. Regarded from that point of view the whole of Philippians $2^{7,8}$ might be understood as a paraphrase of the brief but vivid word-picture in the concluding verse of the great prophecy.[1]

[1] For the crucial phrase in Isa. 53^{12} LXX substituted an alternative image which became even more important in the terminology of NT. St Paul, therefore, had to render the Hebrew idiom with a word of his own choosing. κενόω actually occurs only twice in LXX (Jer. 14^{2}, 15^{9}). Why, then, was it selected by the apostle? I offer the following suggestions. In Isa. 53^{12} the word rendered 'he poured out' (*'ârah*) can mean 'to make bare' as well as 'to pour out'. (A pitcher is made bare by emptying out its contents; cp. Gen. 24^{20}). Moreover the former rendering (also in *hiphil* mood) is used of sexual offences which might give the word a nuance of humiliation. On the cross Jesus was actually 'exposed' in this sense (see above, Ch. II, end of § i). Similarly κενόω in Hellenistic use, had two meanings: (1) 'to empty out', and (2) 'to make void' (MM., p. 340^{2}). The two meanings are both comprised in the Hebrew idiom. A soul 'poured out' becomes weakened to the point of exhaustion. So in Jer. 15^{9} a prolific mother 'languished' (ἐκενώθη) so that she was no longer capable of child-bearing. Thus the double meanings of the two verbs employed in Isaiah and Philippians are not far apart. By voluntary self-giving Jesus reduced his strength to zero (ἐκένωσεν); and further, the suggestion of shameful humiliation which might attach to the Hebrew word is fully brought out by St Paul's next main verb: ἐταπείνωσεν. One final comment.—In 1 Cor. 1^{17}, 9^{15}, 2 Cor. 9^{3}, Rom. 4^{14} κενόω has the secondary sense: 'to make void'. In Phil. 2^{7}, however, the primary sense of the word is required, if the Pauline resistance to all 'voiding' of the gospel is to retain any significance whatever.

vi

The Hebrew idioms more fully explained. Weakness, smallness and poverty in the *kenosis* of the Servant. The messianic concept transformed in our Lord's teaching. The song of 'little' David and the praises of babes. Receiving the kingdom as a little child.

We have now fixed the main lines for our interpretation of the passage in Philippians. But there are still several points to be cleared up before we can see this great statement in its relation to the prevailing theme of the present chapter. The first problem which arises at this stage of our investigation concerns the temporal relation of the expression: 'he emptied himself' to the two participial clauses which follow. In other words did the Son of God make an act of self-abnegation with a view to taking the form of the slave, or did he take the slave-form in order to 'pour out his soul unto death'? Or, thirdly, should the second and third clauses of verse 7, which we have numbered (2), be regarded as the method by which the *kenosis* took effect? If the third alternative be adopted we should, I think, be obliged to bring into 'the method' of self-emptying all the clauses of verse 8 as well, that is the whole of (3) in our enumeration. The third suggestion has the advantage of bringing together the two echoes of Isaiah 53[12] without narrowing the range of the 'kenotic' idea unduly. The first two suggestions are not necessarily untrue in themselves. But the first seems to miss the Hebrew idiom, whereas the second might appear to confine the *kenosis* to the passion and death.[1]

The problem posed in the last paragraph is largely forced upon us by our habit of thinking in terms of a causal sequence of events. When, however, we think our way back into the Hebrew idioms, and just so far as we do so, problems of that sort cease to be relevant. For we are now in a pictorial world of thought where several relevant features of the picture *may be* simultaneous.[2] For this reason the phrase 'poured himself out' was deliberately

[1] The problem thus posed does not seem to be greatly affected by the question whether St Paul was here adopting an earlier Jewish-Christian hymn, written in Hebrew or Aramaic. For in any case the Christian Rabbi was thinking as a Jew, for whom the three clauses of verse 7 would not constitute primarily a causal sequence, but rather a complex piece of imagery.

[2] On this point see Vol. I, especially pp. 152, 153.

employed in our rendering of verse 7 in order to avoid a host of 'kenotic problems' which have infested the theological debates about St Paul's words. What is described in these mysterious sentences is a sacrificial act of a heavenly person; but the form of the description is drawn from human analogy as conceived by the Hebrew mind. 'As the happy soul is wide, so the anguished soul is narrow';[1] here is another facet of that same analogy. The form of the slave was like a 'straight waistcoat' into which the Son of God entered, and within which he restricted himself, thus narrowing his scope of action and making himself small. We are again reminded of the remarkable passage in Galatians where the apostle likens a child in tutelage to a slave; and then passes at once from this description of Israel under the old covenant to its 'repetition' in Jesus made subject to the Law.[2]

Two aspects of the Hebrew idiom have thus entered into the picture. The soul poured out shows strength reduced to weakness; the soul in anguish is reduced in size. In 2 Corinthians 8⁹ we have the parallel conception of riches reduced to poverty. Although the idiom there is different, the parallel is useful, because it clarifies a truth common to all these conceptions in the apostle's thought. By a surpassing paradox the strength, greatness and wealth persist after a new fashion under the grim realities of weakness, smallness and poverty. Finally, at the zero-point of death life in its fulness is inaugurated in a new form. This brings us to a fresh stage in our investigation. Thus far 'the form of a slave' has been contemplated in its contrast to 'the form of God'. We have now to look at the same phrase in its contrast with what followed 'the death of the cross'. The exaltation of the Servant gives to him the divine honours which in that section of the second Isaiah are ascribed to the deity. The quotation from Isaiah 45^{23} in verse 10 of the Philippian text makes it clear that the Lordship ascribed to Jesus in the final clause is the universal sovereignty of deity over all orders of creation. But with equal certainty it is a messianic sovereignty of the Son of Man over a restored dominion of Adam.

Now we have previously traced an interweaving of messianic sovereignty on the one hand with the dominion of Adam and on

[1] *Israel I–II*, p. 149.

[2] Gal. 4^{1-5}. The heir is at once νήπιος, δοῦλος and κύριος πάντων a significant conjunction of terms for the thesis of this chapter.

the other hand (through the Greek version of Isaiah 53^{2}) with the Servant prophecy. Moreover, we recall that in our Lord's own teaching a transformation of the concept of messianic authority occurs which involved a verbal repudiation of language used in the creation-cycle concerning the dominion of Adam (above, § ii, par. 3 and notes). Jesus had accepted the form of 'the slave'; and after the ambitious request of James and John his discourse on true sovereignty culminates in this word: 'Whosoever will be first among you shall be slave of all'. The principle thus enunciated is then illustrated in its supreme fulfilment. Jesus, the 'slave of all' will 'give his life, a ransom for many' (Mark $10^{44,45}$). The last two words are an echo of Isaiah 53^{11}. Thus the evangelist reports our Lord's saying, as though he had given his own rendering of the Hebrew word '*ebedh* (servant) in defining his own concept of the messianic kingdom.[1]

In this dominical rendering of the 'Servant' idea (Mark 10^{43-45}) the phrase 'slave of all' is in parallelism with another word, *diakonos*, a general term for a 'minister', from which comes our word for the order of 'deacons'. The corresponding verb for 'ministering' provides a connecting link between this passage and a section peculiar to St Luke in his account of the last supper. The occasion was also similar,—a contention between the disciples as to which of them was to be accounted 'greater' (Luke 22^{24ff}). Here, immediately after an unmistakable reference to the Servant prophecy[2] and directly before a verbal quotation from the same source, the Lucan parallel to the Marcan 'slave of all' pronouncement occurs. Here we find the same transformation of the messianic idea in a setting which gives new content to the old title: 'David, my servant'. The Davidic background is unmistakable, quite apart from the 'thrones' promised in verse 30. This appears from verse 26 where Jesus defines the 'ethos' of his kingdom thus: 'Let the

[1] If we place beside Mark 10^{44} (Matt. 20^{27}) the Pauline and Johannine uses of δοῦλος we have clear evidence for an apostolic conviction that, notwithstanding the predominance of παῖς in deutero-Isaiah, the gospel fulfilment was more adequately represented by the harsher word. Moreover, whereas the two words are all but synonymous in LXX, δοῦλος is more frequently used of David as the representive king of Israel.

[2] παραδίδωμι twice in verses 21–23, from Isa. 53^{12}; cp. the actual quotation from the same verse of Isaiah in Luke 22^{37}.

greater among you be as *the younger*, and *he that is chief* as he that serveth'. The biblical associations of the two italicised phrases will repay careful scrutiny.

The latter phrase corresponds to Hebrew words meaning ruler, prince, captain or leader. It is frequently applied to kings, and has special associations with David and his royal house.[1] It is cited in Matthew 2^{6} as occurring in the messianic prophecy of Micah 5^{2}. The former phrase brings us back to the childlike character of the kingdom. It is used by Jeremiah on the occasion of his call to be a prophet. He applies it to himself in protesting his immaturity and unfitness.[2] But it also has Davidic associations, as will appear from the Greek version of 1 Samuel 17^{14} ('David was the youngest')[3] and from the additional psalm (151) appended to the psalter in the Septuagint. The latter is liberally sprinkled with words which have special significance in the New Testament. The little poem is put into the mouth of David after his victory over Goliath. We will confine our attention here to the opening words and to one other phrase in the psalm. David says:

> 'I was *little* among my brethren and *youngest* in my father's house.'

'Little' comes from the Greek version of 1 Samuel 16^{11}, where Jesse tells the prophet about his youngest son, David: 'There is yet the little one'. We are reminded of our Lord's words in Luke 9^{48}, where the comparative form of the same word occurs. We may render the saying thus: 'He who is least among you all, he is great'.

There are also sayings of Jesus about the 'little ones', the weaker members of the messianic community, which are relevant (cp. Mark 9^{42}, Matthew 10^{42}), because throughout the New Testament Jesus is inseparable from his 'children', the members of that body of which he is the head. This brings us to the other phrase in David's little song. In verse 5 we read: 'My brethren were handsome and tall; but the Lord was not well-pleased with them'. The Lord's adverse attitude to the

[1] This title, *ὁ ἡγούμενος*, appears in the 'messianic' oracle of Gen. 49^{10}. It is applied to David significantly in such texts as 1 Reg. 22^{2}, 25^{30}, 2 Reg. 5^{2}, 6^{21}, 7^{8}; again, to Solomon in 3 Reg. 1^{35}, 9^{5}. Cp. also the parallel passages in 1, 2 Chron.

[2] *νεώτερος ἐγώ εἰμι*, repeated in the divine reply (Jer. $1^{6, 7}$).

[3] From codex A.

brethren is described as the contrary of that which, in the New Testament, designates Jesus as the Servant 'in whom I am well-pleased'.[1] By contrast David is a type of the future Saviour, as had already been indicated in the Greek version of an earlier 'Psalm of David'.[2] Lastly the 'handsome' brethren are unlike the Servant in another respect. For in Isaiah 53^{2} the Servant as messianic 'child' is without 'comeliness'.[3] We see, then, that in making himself 'little' in the form of a slave Jesus fulfilled the Davidic type.[4] The shepherd-boy's 'rod' had messianic potency to the enemy's undoing;[5] and this was the first step to kingship. So the evangelist saw the regal glory of the Servant in a hunted child;[6] and praise shall be perfected out of the mouths of babes and sucklings when the universal lordship of a Son of Adam is once more acknowledged to the glory of God the Father.[7]

We must now recall to mind the purpose with which St Paul embarked upon his great Christological statement. 'Have this mind in *you* . . .'; 'the children' are signified in 'the Child'. We are still occupied with *our* return to him who is 'the Beginning', the true source of our being. The child taken up into Christ's arms signifies the return of man to the very site of his creation, —to the place where, in his Wisdom, the Father conceived the design of our common humanity,[8] that secret place of filial being which is in the Only-begotten Son. But secondly, the saying which accompanied that symbolic act of Jesus (Mark 9^{37}) should be connected with the similar, yet different saying in the next chapter: 'Verily I say unto you, whosoever shall not receive the kingdom of God as a little child, he shall not enter therein' (Mark 10^{15}). The situation in the two contexts is simi-

[1] Matt. 12^{18}, where εὐδόκησεν is the key-word. Moreover in Mark 1^{11} and parallels this quality of the Servant is applied to 'the beloved Son', that is the Messiah.

[2] 2 Reg. 22^{20}: εὐδόκησεν ἐν ἐμοί.

[3] The brethren are καλά; but the Servant, ὡς παιδίον, has no κάλλος.

[4] Some of the key-words of the present argument recur together in Ps. $118^{124-141}$ (LXX). The psalmist repeatedly calls himself δοῦλος, places himself among the νήπιοι (130) and affirms that he is νεώτερος (141).

[5] 1 Reg. $17^{42,43}$; cp. Ps. 2^{9}. When St Paul threatened to come to Corinth ἐν ῥάβδῳ (1 Cor. 4^{21}) had he these antecedents in mind?

[6] see above, § iv, pars. 2–4.

[7] Ps. 8^{3-7} (LXX), Matt. $21^{15,16}$, Phil. 2^{9-11}.

[8] cp. βουληθεὶς ἀπεκύησεν in James 1^{18}.

lar; for here too Jesus takes children into his arms after rebuking the disciples. This rebuke suggests the Matthean theme of conversion and new birth. Following that line of thought Mark 10[15] could then mean that we must receive the kingdom in a childlike spirit. The connexion with Mark 9[37], however, offers a more profound, and therefore more inclusive, interpretation of this saying. The child is now identified, not with the convert, but with the kingdom.

The kingdom of God is like a child. Its characteristics are simplicity and lowliness, trustful love and ready response; and these are the qualities of Jesus himself, who in his humble and loving response to the Father embodies the eternal newness of the kingdom. The connexion between the two sayings in St Mark (9[37], 10[15]) now becomes clear. For the child symbolizes the kingdom which is embodied in Christ. So then, 'to receive the child in Christ's name' is to receive him as representing this kingdom messianically embodied in the incarnate Saviour. The two sayings are complementary. To receive the mystery of lowliness revealed in Christ is to receive Jesus as Lord together with a whole world of unexpected resources, new vistas and fresh opportunities which his humble obedience places at our disposal. St Matthew's interpretation (18[1–5]) is here implicit. For the childlike character of the disciple is conditioned by the childlike character of the kingdom. The concluding words of the first evangelist, however, introduce a further point of great importance. In 18[5] we read: 'Whosoever receiveth one such little child in my name receiveth me'. As we have already seen, the child here symbolizes the believer, defined in the next sentence as 'one of these little ones who believe in me'. To receive the child is to receive Christ; for the believer has mystical identity with Christ in his Body (cp. Matthew 25[40]).

If, then, a child can symbolize the believer in so high a degree, this fact discloses a radical analogy between the first creation and the second. If we employed western terminology we should say that in those qualities of the child which are 'natural' we could trace the outline form of higher qualities which are 'supernatural'. The child, for example, accepts his position as a 'little one' who lives in simple dependence upon others. This fact is not only symbolic of Christian humility but also significant of the divine image in man.[1] The child enters a fallen world; but he enters it bearing traces of his origin. In particular his capacity for dependence upon God is his highest heritage. It is like a seed which carries the potentiality of holiness and the promise of all its fruits. Man's capacity for response to that which lies above him is the hall-mark of his greatness. These marks of the divine image Jesus discerned in those who responded to his message; in them he traced bonds of kinship with his sinless humanity. In them he read the original design of creation restored by his own action. For the two creations (old and new) are truly integrated only in the perfections of the divine humanity.

So far we travel with St Matthew. Returning to St Mark we find that the crucial phrase about receiving the child in Christ's name concludes thus: 'Whosoever receiveth me, receiveth not me but him that sent me' (9^{37}). To receive the child is to receive not only Christ but the Father. This detail is omitted by Matthew, because he is referring the saying to the organism of the new creation. In receiving a believer we receive the Christ of whom both he and we are members. For St Mark, however, this truth concerning the Body of Christ belongs to a yet vaster mystery. For him, to receive the child means receiving the kingdom embodied in Jesus. It is, therefore, to partake in the loving response of the Son to the Father. The context interprets this loving response in terms of the lowly mission of the Servant. These sayings belong to the last procession to the Passion. *Vexilla regis prodeunt.* Through the Passion we enter the secret place of sonship in which both creations have their being.[2]

[1] For the childlike innocence of Adam in the teaching of the Greek fathers see the evidence collected by N.P. Williams in Lecture IV of his *The Ideas of the Fall and of Original Sin.*

[2] We might perhaps say that Mark 9^{37} is the Marcan counterpart to Matt. 11^{25-30}.

BOOK II

CONFLICT AND VICTORY

CHAPTER IV

THE DIVINE CONFLICT: (1) IN THE CREATION-CYCLE

i

The conflict between two orders of being in ourselves and in the world intensified by the gospel. Through union with Christ we are involved in his victorious struggle with the powers of darkness. A return to the Johannine version of this theme.

It will be remembered that in the first chapter of this book reference was made to two orders of created being, which, in our present experience, are always contrasted and often in actual conflict.[1] The tension lies within ourselves; and it might be said that, in one sense, the conflicting elements are, on the one hand, that which man is by virtue of his fallen condition, and, on the other hand, that which he is by creation in the divine image. If the image were perfectly restored there would no more be any conflict. In its place there would be the harmony or peace of an integral nature, no longer divided against itself either inwardly or outwardly. That, again, could occur only through the complete restoration of man to the original relationship with God in which and for which he was created. Now this conflict within man is intensified and deepened by the gospel, and that in two ways. For, first the revelation given in Christ shows us the full integrity of human nature. In him we see the New Man fulfilling the destiny for which we were created. In him we see the harmony and simplicity for which our divided nature craves. But secondly, in the New Man there is a new creation to which we belong, in which, therefore, we cannot be neutral spectators. For in this new order of being new life radiates forth from Christ to us recreating our nature in his own likeness.

[1] Ch. I, § i, last two pars.

The gospel, then, implies two things; and first, that there is in all of us something to which Christ can appeal, a capacity to recognize what he offers—in short, the divine image not wholly effaced. But secondly, the image, if not effaced, has been defaced, and so needs that very restoration which our Lord came to give. The light of Christ discloses the good imparted to us at creation, but also exposes the evil with which the good has been overlaid. The rays of the Sun of righteousness cause the trees of God's planting to blossom forth like flowers in spring. But the same rays which quicken the life of growing things will also hasten the corruption of decay. So the advent of Christ as the Light of the world was the crisis both of salvation and of judgement. In the plan of creation man was 'crowned with glory and honour', and despite his fallen condition he is still 'the image and glory of God'. There is no other place in this world where God's image can be seen and his glory effectually manifested save only in this nature of ours. The image, however, is disfigured. In Adam crowned with glory we see the priest-king of creation through whom the rule of the Creator over his creatures is to be effectually manifested. In fallen man, on the other hand, the vindication of the divine purpose in creation is frustrated.

Yet the full import of this disaster was disclosed only when the restoration was effected in Christ. For he *is* the image of God, uncreated, but also incarnate. For that very reason there is in him a new creative act of God like that which took place in the beginning. Since he is the stainless image he has also the fulness of the glory; and we who are re-created in him are thereby illuminated with the uncreated light of 'the glory of God in the face of Jesus Christ'. But, as the apostle points out, those who are made new creatures in Christ not only receive and reflect the glory of the New Man; they are also transformed by its entry into their lives.[1] This re-entry of the divine glory into human life in Christ is the key which unlocks to us the secrets alike of creation and of our fallen state. In Christ, then, is the clue to the riddle of our present conflict. But since we are in Christ the clue is also present in us in whom the two creations meet. The conflict within us was not ended when we became new creatures. It was, on the contrary, intensified. It was, in

[1] 2 Cor. 3^{12}–6^{11}.

an altogether new sense, begun. For we then became sharers in the cosmic battle between light and darkness, between God and the devil, between the Lamb and the dragon, the battle of the ages which has its centre in Jesus and his church.

The Christian leaven is at work upon our fallen nature, undermining the smooth surface of its proud self-sufficiency and destroying its complacency. When, therefore, we look out upon the tortured writhings of our world, we recognize there on a vaster scale those same disintegrating effects of sin which we have found in ourselves. We know that these things have not happened by chance, by ephemeral stupidity, by mere mismanagement, or again by the abnormal wickedness of this or that group or section in human society. These are but the outward signs of a much vaster and more mysterious cataclysm which has overtaken God's creation. But that is not all. We may also see in those same tortured writhings indications that the effectual power of God's creative plan is still present amongst us and still at work in the world. For the new creation is in fact a new revolution, the greatest of all revolutions. The coming of Christ has (in Barth's phrase) effected 'the great disturbance'. It was the unforseeable event which shook the kingdom of Satan to its foundations; and the repercussions of that event echo down the Christian centuries. The presence of Christ, operating in that new order of being which he inaugurated, has had the effect of a new magnetic centre of disturbance.

In human experience the path of creative advance lies through conflict. This fact may perhaps make intelligible to us an ancient belief that the creation of the world was actually the sequel to a superhuman conflict between good and evil powers. This idea is also reflected here and there in holy scripture; and the New Testament teaches that the new creation in Christ was effected through his victorious struggle with the powers of darkness. Nevertheless, neither the new creation nor the messianic conflict is an episode of past history. If we belong to the one we are involved in the other, even as our Lord himself was. In fact we cannot limit the scope of either the one or the other. All men, whether they know it or not, are involved in the disturbing effects of our Lord's incarnation and in its renewal and deepening of the cosmic strife. All this is clearly set forth in the New Testament, and perhaps with special clarity in the Johannine writings. St John's Gospel brings to its fullest development both the doctrine of the new creation and its integral relation to the divine conflict. In what follows, therefore, we shall take that Gospel as our main guide, paying special attention to the prologue because it epitomizes the main thought of the evangelist upon this double theme.

In the previous volume of this series some consideration was given to the plan of the fourth evangelist in his opening section (I. VIII. §§ iii–v). The subject must now be further developed in accordance with principles there unfolded. In particular it will be well to bear in mind the conception of a pattern woven from several strands and repeating itself in fresh phases (I, p. 242). To this corresponds also what was said earlier in the present volume concerning those scriptural combinations of 'new creation' phenomena and redemptive history which were referred to as 'Genesis-Exodus' mysteries. For in such combinations the pattern is woven out of images drawn respectively from the creation-cycle and from the story of Israel.[1] Finally it must be remembered that the prologue to St John's Gospel requires elucidation from the body of that Gospel and from the other Johannine books as well as from Scripture as a whole. In fact, there is a certain correspondence between the unity of Scripture which transcends all its manifestations and again the unity of a biblical 'mystery' which transcends all the scriptural ingredients of which it appears to be composed. In both we can discern the Hebrew wholeness of revelation.

ii

In the Johannine writings there is a parallel between the end of the Apocalypse and the beginning of the Gospel; and this implies an identification. For the light of the Creator-Word is essentially sacrificial. So in the conflict of light and darkness Wisdom prevailed over guile, because God had provided a Lamb to conquer the serpent.

In the poem of the first creation the divine Word summons the light to appear. God then 'divides the light from the

[1] e.g. Ch. II, § ii, pars. 1 and 2.

darkness'. Henceforth the darkness, which previously existed, is known by contrast with the light which 'God saw to be good'. There is a suggestion here that the divine Word caused the light to overcome the darkness, thereby opening the way for further creative activity. In St John's prologue, however, the contrast between light and darkness reveals a conflict which is not the prelude but the sequel to creation. As he proceeds he traces both creations to their source in the divine Word in whom they are perfectly integrated. On the other hand, and with equal emphasis, he points to a divine conflict in history. This, however, is to anticipate. In scripture the Word of God is light and gives light (Psalm $119^{105,130}$); and in the first creation the self-imparting act of the Word diffused his rays throughout his created works. So, before ever the conflict between light and darkness was joined, the light of the Creator-Word was sufficiently manifested to men through the witness of his life-giving activity in the living organism of his creation.[1] By his gift of light to man there was also introduced a momentous alternative. Men might prefer the darkness to the light.[2]

Our exegesis of the prologue has now brought us to the middle of verse 5. Before proceeding further, however, we must recall certain details of verse 4 previously considered, and a certain contrast which those details suggest.[3] The second clause of verse 4 runs thus: 'the life was the light of men'. There is here a definite parallel with the concluding vision of the Apocalypse.[4] There the city-bride, the New Jerusalem, is a vast luminary which, by virtue of its brilliant light, serves as a magnet to draw mankind into itself. Here on the other hand it is the living organism of creation which fulfils a similar function. Two further points of difference between the two pictures must be noticed. Whereas in both scenes the created object is suffused with rays of light, the source of these rays is, in each case, differently described; and again the mutual relations between source of light and illuminated object are, physically speaking,

[1] For the significance of this expression the reader is referred to Vol. I, pp. 239–241. For the sentence as a whole cp. Rom. 1^{18-20}.

[2] John 3^{19-21}.

[3] For this see I. VIII; for what follows the reader is referred to § iv of that chapter (I, pp. 243 ff.).

[4] The relevant details of the vision are to be found in Rev. $21^{10,11}$ and 21^{22-27}.

in complete contrast. As to the first point, in the Gospel the source of light is the Creator-Word,[1] whereas in the Apocalypse it is the Lamb of God (that is, the incarnate Lord, victorious through death and resurrection). The second point of contrast can best be seen in a diagram:[2]

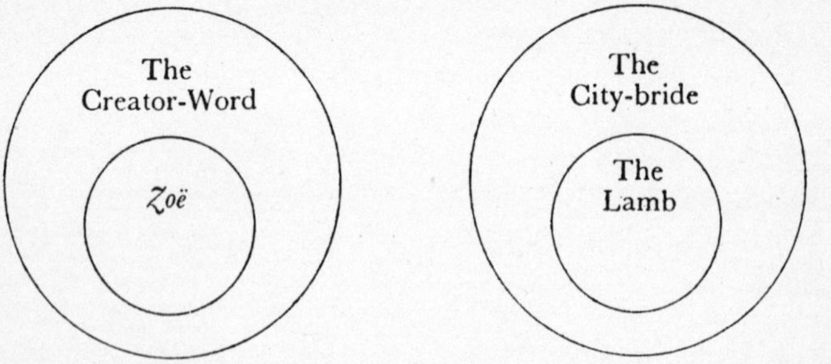

A B

In the Apocalypse the outer luminary, that is the New Jerusalem, has within it a temple which is identified with God and the Lamb. Then it is said that 'the glory of God gave her light, and her lamp was the Lamb'. Thus it appears that the incarnate and glorified Saviour, situated at the centre of the city like a radiant temple, serves as a lamp in which are focussed the rays of uncreated light proceeding from deity. The Shekinah of the Father, present in the Son, thus radiates forth into the city, making it in turn to be a luminary. In the other figure the situation is the reverse. The Creator-Word is *the site* 'in whom all things were created' (Col. 1^{16}); thus St Paul agrees with St John.[3] For the evangelist 'that which hath been made was Zoë

[1] This is further clarified in verses 9 ff.

[2] As explained in I. VIII. § iii, the reader is reminded that *Zoë* (=life) is in LXX (Gen. 3^{20}) a rendering of Eve's name as 'the mother of all that lives', and that John 1^{4} identifies her with the created universe as the cosmic bride of the Logos.

[3] For St Paul Jesus is the ἀρχή of both creations; and in both of these spheres it is true that 'in him all things hold together' (Col. $1^{17,18}$). Our Lord is thus 'the Beginning' in which 'God created the heaven and the earth' (Gen. 1^{1}. LXX). St John does not use ἀρχή in this way, unless the question in 8^{25} is a punning reference to it. On the other hand 'the Only-Begotten in the bosom of the Father' (1^{18}) may be equated with 'In the beginning was the Word' (1^{1}), the Father being the underived ἀρχή. Cp. 17^{21}: 'I in thee, that they also may be in us'.

in him', that is in the Logos. It follows from the next sentence that the cosmic bride is also a luminary; and we must conclude from verses 9 ff. that she 'is the light of men' because she is suffused with rays of light proceeding from the divine Logos in whom she is situated. It is difficult to believe that there is no literary connexion between these two images. Moreover, if Dr Farrer is right in holding that the Apocalypse was written before the Gospel, it will seem to follow that the evangelist had the earlier picture in mind, when he drafted his prologue.

We shall find reason presently for thinking that the connexion between the two images is best understood in that way. Meanwhile let us return to verse 5. Here we have a vivid description of the cosmic conflict in language which could in fact apply equally well to both creations; 'the light shines in the darkness, and the darkness did not overcome it'.[1] The evangelist, doubtless, has in mind the concluding lines of a famous passage in praise of Wisdom:

She is fairer than the sun, and above all the constellations of the stars:
Being compared with light, she is found to be before it;
For to this light succeedeth night; but against Wisdom evil doth not prevail;
But she reacheth from end unto end mightily, and ordereth all things well.

(Wisdom of Solomon, 7^{29}–8^{1}.)

It will be noticed that the concluding phrase implies a connexion between creative Wisdom and the *order* of creation. The conflict between heavenly light and abysmal darkness is a battle for *cosmos* against chaos.[2] Remembering that St John transfers the attributes of Wisdom to the Word we may here recall a sentence from our earlier volume: 'The creative Word of God . . . in one and the same movement of creativity . . . brings into existence an ordered cosmos and also illuminates that given order with his own rays of uncreated light that thus it may serve as a mirror of deity'.[3]

'To *this* light succeedeth night.' The poet here fastens upon a limitation which is characteristic of finite creaturehood. The

[1] RV margin.
[2] cp. above, Ch. II, § ii, par. 1.
[3] I. VIII. i, pp. 226 f. For Wisdom and Logos see also *ib.* pp. 230–232 and notes.

same contrast is made in the Epistle of James (1^{17}), where the author speaks of 'the Father of the heavenly lights, who knows no change of rising and setting, who casts no shadow on the earth' (Moffatt). When light inaugurated the works of creation, darkness was not banished; it was made subservient to cosmic order. Night follows day, but never prevents the dawn of another day. Darkness follows light, like a shadow following a moving object. But unless it *overtakes* the light, it cannot master it. This happens at sunset when the shadows lengthen and the traveller too may be 'overtaken' by night. So Jesus said: 'Walk while ye have the light, that the darkness overtake you not'.[1] In the last two sentences we have introduced a new factor. In Jewish-Christian idiom 'walking' (*halakah*) constantly carries a spiritual significance: 'walk in love' or 'in the Spirit'; 'walk while ye have the light'. So the traveller overtaken by 'darkness' on that journey has himself to blame for not using the light that he had. In a world which includes freedom there is a 'darkness' which can subserve cosmic order only in the sense that it is a permanent possibility of free choice, freedom being what it is. For it is only out of the mouths of his children that God can 'establish strength' and so 'cause the enemy to cease'.[2]

So darkness followed light into the earthly paradise. Yet it did not overcome. For the serpent's guile was met by a promise of victory to the woman's seed; and that promise was fulfilled in the gospel history. Appropriately, therefore, at this point the evangelist introduces the figure of the Baptist, giving to St John a position in the prologue analogous to his function in the gospel as a whole. There is nothing fortuitous about this arrangement. For with the entry of the Baptist we begin to see more clearly the connexion between the two images illustrated in the diagram, the one taken from the Apocalypse and the other from the Gospel prologue. In the narrative which follows in this Gospel the Baptist identifies Jesus as the Lamb of God, the predestined victim who fulfils the scriptures. In the Old Testa-

[1] John 12^{35}, a characteristic repetition of the image in 1^{5}, where, however, κατέλαβεν is more diversified in its connotation. The word could mean 'overtake' and also 'hold down', and so here perhaps 'extinguish'. The two RV renderings correspond to the second and third of these meanings.

[2] Ps. 8^{3} (H; EVV. 8^{2}). This rendering of the psalm is illustrated in the Book of Job. God can silence Satan only out of the mouth of his sorely tried servant.

ment prophecy bears continuous witness to the sacrificial mission of Israel, the key to the inner meaning of history. In the Gospel the Baptist is the finger of prophecy pointing to Jesus as the fulfilment of that mission. Accordingly, the introduction of John in the prologue as preëminently *the* historical witness to the light of the divine Word has the effect of identifying the Lamb of God by anticipation with that Word through whom and in whom all things were made. We may well pause to consider what bearing this identification has upon our interpretation of the prologue as a whole.[1]

Here, as in the Apocalypse, the Lamb is the torch or lamp of divine revelation, to which John, the lesser lamp, directed men's steps (cp. John 1^{6-8} with 5^{33ff}). But here, also, the predestined victim (cp. 1 Peter 1^{19}) is the source and site of creation. The light of the Word which illuminates the world proceeds from a sacrificial flame in the heart of God. Creation was designed in terms of sacrificial love; and in the appointed sacrifice the whole purpose of the Creator comes to its fruition. The witness of the Baptist to the Light of the world so understood justifies the triumphant statement, by which it is immediately preceded, concerning the failure of the darkness to overcome the light. The guile of the serpent was no match for the Wisdom of God; for 'against Wisdom evil doth not prevail'. So at the outset of his narrative the evangelist, through the mouth of the Baptist, shows that God had provided a Lamb to conquer the serpent. Indeed the victory had already begun, as is shown in the testimony that even now 'the Lamb of God taketh away the sin of the world'. Thus the end of the Apocalypse enters into the beginning of the Gospel, because Jesus is both the Beginning and the End. The Lamb is the final Word of revelation; but also the creative Word is, in his creativity, the preordained Sacrifice.

iii

The penetration of the Word into the world intensifies the clash between light and darkness, and lays bare its significance. The Incarnation, as the focal point of penetration, includes within its range all redemptive history. Dependence of new birth

[1] For what follows see also I. VII., pp. 222–224, I. VIII, pp. 227–31, 244–248, and the relevant notes in each case.

upon divine begetting, of the children of God upon the only-begotten One.

At verse 9 of St John's prologue we pass to a fresh phase of the argument. The reference to the Baptist brought the two images of our diagram together by reminding us that the Word became the Lamb. On the other hand, when we turn from '*a* man sent from God' (verse 6) to 'every man' (verse 9) we are moving in the opposite direction. It will be recalled that (as the diagram shows) in the first figure the source of light surrounds the created object, whereas in the second figure the source of light is within the city, at its centre. There lies the whole difference between the beginning and the end of that divine drama which is spread out successively through the order of creation and through the epochs of history. It is as though, at the beginning, the divine Word approaches the world of his creation from the outside, respecting those creaturely rights of autonomy which he himself has bestowed. The Creator will only penetrate into creaturely existence just so far as its creaturely response opens out to receive him. This respect for creaturehood explains the slow movement of divine revelation in history. God will not force the pace. He is willing to move at *our* pace, as we slowly learn to make our response to him.

Nevertheless, it is equally clear that the slowness of the movement is a direct consequence of the fall of man. As the light of the Word penetrates beneath the outer crust of our humanity, so too the conflict between the light and the darkness develops. In verses 9–14 this development is shown proceeding through stages corresponding to three concentric circles of human life which the Word enters successively. The first of these is the whole world of his creation wherein the Word made 'the order which came to be through him'. Here, however, man has introduced disorder, so that the Word which 'was in the world' remained unrecognized by the world.[1] There is in this situation a paradox which, nevertheless, corresponds to what has been said concerning human response. The light of the Word is ever 'coming into the world', and every human person is illuminated by that light, and lives by it. Yet the source of light may, and does, remain

[1] Throughout this Gospel *cosmos* is 'the order which is disordered', the world of God's creation, alienated by sin and so separated from, yet still loved by, its Creator.

unrecognized. Thus response is withheld; and so the Word is constrained to adopt an alternative method of penetration, more intensive in its character. He chooses a particular people, and imparts to it a special revelation.

At verse 11 it would appear that we have reached a second concentric circle: 'He came unto his own (territory), and his own people did not receive him'. There is a marked change of language here. 'The world did not recognize' . . . 'his own people did not receive him'. The latter phrase implies something more deliberate than non-recognition, something which might be called 'rejection'. As the penetration becomes more intensive so does the conflict become more tragic. As in the first creation darkness is known by contrast with light, so in the stages of redemptive history there is a cumulative unveiling of evil which came to its climacteric at Calvary. Its full exposure, however, presupposes the fuller unveiling of the light from Pentecost onwards. As Jesus said, the Paraclete convicts the world 'of sin, because they believe not on me' (John 16^9). Regarded from this standpoint verse 11 has about it a certain timelessness which covers all history. What happened at Calvary is in principle that which has been happening from the fall of man onwards, namely a turning away from light to darkness, a refusal of response to the Word.

Yet this universal implication becomes manifest only through the historical rejection by the chosen people. The story of redemption has always cosmic dimensions. That brings us to another facet of this mysterious prologue. At what precise point do we reach the Incarnation? It becomes explicit, of course, in verse 14. But verse 11 could be understood as preliminary indication that it occurred; verses 11–13 would then show its sifting effects. A faithful remnant was called into being in contrast to 'Israel after the flesh'. Verses 12, 13 are most naturally understood as connecting the new-born Christians with their new-born Saviour. We cannot, however, exclude the possibility that the timeless quality of verse 11 looks forwards as well as backwards. All through the story of Israel the Word 'came unto his own' and suffered rejection. Moreover, if we see the old covenant as St Irenaeus saw it we should say that throughout Israel's story a new creation was proceeding, and that the remnant of faithful Israel enjoyed re-birth into the true family of God throughout redemptive history. But if so, they believed 'on his name' in a sense explained later in this Gospel, when Jesus says to the Jews: 'Your father Abraham rejoiced to see my day; and he saw it and was glad' (8^{56}).

The 'timeless' aspect of the prologue, however, can also be regarded as an example of Hebrew 'wholeness', and perhaps more securely. For 'timelessness' suggests something non-temporal, whereas 'wholeness', as here understood, gives fresh significance to all events by virtue of their relation to the all-inclusiveness which characterizes the events of the gospel history. From this point of view verses 11–14 can be seen to be so framed that they are a statement concerning the Incarnation which includes within that mystery the whole order of redemptive history under both covenants, old and new. This, again, corresponds to those higher unities of scripture which were examined in the previous volume.[1] It is only with such a proviso that we can speak of an advance from a second to a third concentric circle at the moment when the Word actually became incarnate. When this took place, however, the conflict was transferred to a new battleground, the most restricted of all, namely the flesh of the incarnate Saviour. He was the promised 'seed of the woman' who came to a dominion of darkness usurped by 'the prince of this world'. When, therefore, he entered the arena he did so in a manner appropriate to the essential nature of his act.

If we are to understand rightly the Johannine conceptions concerning the Word incarnate we must pay close attention to the whole form of the statement which covers verses 12–14. Moreover the statement contains two distinct theses, one referring primarily to the new birth and the other more explicitly to the Incarnation. Yet between these two theses there is a deep inward connexion. At present we are concerned with the former. What is said about the new birth in verses 12 and 13 corresponds exactly to the essential nature of the act described in verse 14. Concerning this act, despite differences of language, there is fundamental agreement between St Paul and St John. For both the apostolic writers the act involved a new creation; for both its purpose was to restore man's filial

[1] See especially I. V., pp. 152–155, for 'wholeness'; and for the 'all-inclusiveness' of the gospel events see I. VII. v, pp. 220 ff.

relation to God. Its whole character, then, was determined by its divine source. It was a creative act of deity proceeding, like all God's acts, from the heart of the divine fatherhood.[1] Accordingly the new birth is here so described as to show its close dependence upon two factors, namely (1) the unique relation of the only-begotten Son to the Father and (2) the manner in which the Incarnation took place. Unless this double connexion is perceived the whole force of the passage will be missed.[2]

Up to this point in the prologue the evangelist has been following leading ideas of the creation-cycle, particularly the 'word' and 'light' motifs of Genesis 1. In that poem there is no mention of sonship; and the actual word 'son' probably does not occur in this Gospel until 1^{34}, where Jesus is identified by the Baptist as Messiah through the descent of the dove.[3] Nevertheless the idea of unique sonship is fully present in 1^{14}; and 'only-begotten' there stands in contrast to 'children of God' in 1^{12}. For the Gospel and the Epistles of St John never call men 'sons of God', reserving the title 'son' to 'the only-begotten one'. We must now notice a close interlocking of these three verses by a careful choice of language. The word employed in verse 12 to denote 'children' comes from a root which commonly denotes the physical engendering of child by parent. In the next verse those to whom the title of 'God's children' has been given are said to owe that title to the fact that 'they were begotten of God'. Finally, in verse 14 the Word incarnate is described as possessing 'glory as of an only-begotten from a father'. The omission of the word 'son' here has the effect of throwing emphasis upon the paternal function of begetting; and the title 'only-begotten' suggests that there is only one 'begetting' in the life which is proper to the deity.

[1] The concept of Father is, in the biblical revelation, prior to that of Creator. On this see I, pp. 254–257.

[2] On the text and rendering of John 1^{13} see Bernard in ICC, *ad loc.*, Vol. I, pp. 17 ff. and Hoskyns, Vol. I., pp. 164 ff. (Detached Note 2).

[3] Son of God = Messiah; and the implied reference is Isa. 11^{2}. If *θεός* be read in John 1^{18}, *υἱός* is first used by the eye-witnesses in the primitive Jewish Christian sense (cp. 1^{49}). Moreover, chapter 3 repeats the latter part of the prologue in more developed form: first the new birth, then 'the only begotten' whom Jesus himself now affirms to be 'the Son' (3^{16}); lastly the corroborative comment of the Baptist, who by accepting the truth of the revelation affixes to it the seal of an eye-witness (3^{33}).

The facts recorded in the last paragraph present the characteristically Johannine view of new birth in its relation to the divine begetting. The thesis implied in this careful choice of language is unmistakable. We become children of God by virtue of our entering into a relationship with 'the only-begotten one'. There is only one divine begetting, that of the Son by the Father. But in the new creation mankind can enter into this one begetting so that they are, in some sense, included within it. Precisely the same doctrine is taught in the First Epistle of St John, as we shall see later. At present, however, we have to examine more closely the thesis thus barely indicated. It will be noticed that we have not yet reached 'the manner in which the Incarnation took place'.[1] We are still examining the close dependence of the new birth upon a 'unique relation' within the Godhead. But we can already see that, if the Incarnation was an 'act of deity proceeding from the heart of the divine fatherhood', its motive was a yearning love of God the Father towards his human family.[2] The evangelist is trying to show us how the filial relationship forfeited by sin must, when restored by the creative Word, be founded upon the filial status of that Word, God's only Son.

iv

The analysis of John 1^{12-14} continued. This statement is parallel in form to that of $1^{3,4}$ concerning the first creation. That parallel is crowned by another which connects the Virgin Birth of the Word incarnate with the new birth of Christians. Analogy between mysteries here suggests mutual integration and even inclusion of one mystery in another.

In our analysis of John 1^{12-14} we are now about to pass on from the first of the two factors mentioned to the second, that is from the theme of 'the only-begotten' to 'the manner' of the Incarnation. But in so doing we must notice the close connexion between these two topics. This is brought out by the statement made in verse 12: 'As many as received him to them gave he the

[1] See above the 'two factors' mentioned at the end of the last par. but one.

[2] In Eph. $3^{14,15}$ it is affirmed that the human family (πατρία) derives its 'name' from the heavenly Father (πατήρ). This implies a filial relation of all mankind to God by virtue of creation.

right to become children of God, even to them that believe on his name'. The title to membership in God's family is here limited, as in the other gospels, to those who stand in a certain relationship to Jesus Christ. The fourth evangelist, however, carries the synoptic presentation of this truth a stage further. The right to become God's children was given to those who received God's Word. So far the four gospels agree. But, whereas for the three it is the Word as uttered by Jesus, for St John it is Jesus himself who is the uttered Word. The two affirmations are complementary; but the truth of the former depends upon the truth of the latter which is more fundamental. There was nothing automatic about the new beginning of the world. The co-operation of human faith was, as always, essential to the divine plan. Faith, however, could not bring about the new start. That must come, like the first creation, by an act of the Creator-Word.

In the previous section we emphasized continuity in the stages by which the Word penetrated into our creaturely existence. At the same time it was precisely this factor of continuity which made it difficult to mark the point where the event which we call the Incarnation supervened. From one point of view the most decisive break comes at the beginning of verse 13. For without undue strain of interpretation verse 12 could be understood, at least proleptically, as coming true under the old covenant.[1] There is, however, a quite definite reason why verse 13 should be connected as closely with verse 14 as with verse 12, with the Word-made-flesh as much as with the children of God. The reason is that verse 13 describes the new birth of Christians in language appropriate to the Virgin-Birth of Jesus. The explanation of this peculiar phenomenon must now engage our attention. But before examining the actual language of verse 13 we must take note of the fact that in John 1^{3-14} there is not only continuity but also a certain parallelism between the two ends of the statement, that is between verses 3 and 4 at the beginning and verses 12–14 at the end. This can best be seen in diagrammatic form:

[1] Whereas it belongs to our thesis that verse 13 describes the manner of the Incarnation, that is the Virgin-Birth, in detail. An inclusion of OT characters in verse 13, therefore, could only be envisaged by reading back the new into the old in a yet higher degree (cp. § iii, pars. 4 and 5).

1	2	
1^{3} All things *became* through the Word	1^{14} The Word *became* flesh	1^{13} Who were begotten, not of bloods, nor of the will of the flesh, nor of the will of a man, but of God.
1^{4} All that has *become* was Life in him	1^{12} He gave the right to *become* children of God	

In the first creation all things came into being through the Word, whereas in the second creation the Word himself came into that state of being of which he himself was the Creator. Thus 1^{14} is parallel to 1^{3}. So far there is no difficulty. But at the next stage the elucidation of the diagram becomes more complex because we have to take into account 1^{13} as well as 1^{12}. Moreover 1^{13} binds together the two statements under 2 (1^{14} and 1^{12}). It has therefore been placed alongside both of those two statements to indicate that, although written as an amplification of 1^{12}, it has derived its form from 'the manner of the Incarnation'. The new creation, like the first, could only come by an act of the Creator-Word; that is the initial parallel between 1^{12} and 1^{4}. There is, however, latent here a further parallel which may help us to see why 1^{13} was framed as it was and not otherwise. Readers of Volume I (Chapter VIII, § iii) will remember that Life (*Zoë*) is a Greek name for Eve and that 'Life in the Word' corresponds to 'Eve in Adam'. For the Word is the new Adam; and as Eve received her being from Adam (Genesis 2), so Christians have received their new being from Jesus Christ, the Word incarnate. Here we must also keep in mind the double meaning of *Zoë*. If it be rendered 'life' then 1^{4}, like 1^{3}, is as true of the second creation as of the first. If, again, it is rendered 'Eve', then the identification of Eve with 'the living organism of creation' is as true in the new creation as the evangelist supposed it to be in the old. *Zoë* will then mean 'the new Eve', that is, the bride of Christ who has identity with the living organism of the new creation which is the Body of Christ.

Those who accept my interpretation of 1^{4} will have no difficulty in acknowledging that when the evangelist wrote: 'all that has become was *Zoë* in him' he was thinking in terms of both creations together. But if so, he would have no need to repeat this sentence when he reached the point where he wished to elaborate the analogy with Genesis in the context of the

Incarnation. This may be one reason why, in verse 12, 'the children of God' are introduced instead of 'the new Eve'. In any case 'the children' in verse 12 are the counterparts of 'us' and 'we' in verse 14. In this Gospel as in the others the church exists only in germ as a group of incipient believers. But, further, there is another reason why the children in 1^{12} are the counterparts of *Zoë* in 1^{4}. As we have already seen, there is in verses 12–14 a sustained emphasis upon the divine begetting. The evangelist is writing about the Word and his activity of penetration. As he proceeds he gives, with increasing clarity, an emphatic priority to deity over against his creation, to God over against man, to the Word over against his cosmic bride. In Genesis 2 Eve is created to be a 'helpmeet', and that idea is reflected throughout scripture, wherever the 'mystic bride' motif appears. Accordingly in John 1^{12} this particular image gives place to that of the 'children' who are not so much partners of deity as recipients of divine favour. The only function ascribed to them is that of receptive faith.

We are now in a position to carry forward the parallel between the two creations to its conclusion. In the first creation the Word became the site of all that he made; so also in the second creation the virginal conception of the incarnate Word became, so to speak, the site of our new birth. This is a provisional statement of a mystery which cannot easily be set forth in human speech. For the present let us be content to say that the virgin-flesh in which the Word became flesh is here regarded as the matrix of our new birth. For our new birth depends upon the manner in which he became man; but, more than that, our event somehow lies within his event, as we are included in him. There are other ways of stating the mysterious connexion; but enough has been said to provide a clue to the language employed in verse 13. A contrast is here drawn out between divine begetting and human begetting. So much is certain. But we must add that the elaborate description here given, by means of which a human birth without human agency is described as having its origin in a divine begetting, would be quite pointless unless it were intended to refer to the virginal conception of Jesus as well as to the new birth of Christians.

The divine begetting of believers is affirmed by means of a threefold negative, the purpose of which is to contrast divine begetting with every aspect of human begetting. The first two phrases taken together correspond to 'blood and flesh', an expression which occurs in Ephesians 6[12] as an equivalent of human nature when contrasted with angelic agencies. In Hebrews 2[14] this recurs with the same contrast in the context (2[16]); and in both passages the expression suggests weakness. 'Flesh' by itself would also suggest mortality, whereas in the present context 'blood' would imply the physical facts of generation. The plural form 'bloods' is obscure; and may have a double meaning. In reference to 'new birth' it would correspond to our expression: 'drops of blood,' whereas in reference to the Virgin-Birth it might mean a union of two bloodstreams. 'The will of the flesh' must mean 'natural desire' or 'sexual impulse'; and the third expression should be rendered: 'the will of a man'. For the word used here means 'a member of the male sex', whereas the word employed three times previously in the prologue for 'man' or 'men' (verses 4, 6 and 9) means 'a member of the human race'.[1] The last point is quite decisive. The new birth is defined as the product of a divine act in which natural generation, sensual desire and the will of a human father have had no place; and this was equally true of the Virgin-Birth.[2]

The peculiar technique which we have been examining, by which a phrase is made to convey two different meanings, is thoroughly characteristic of the fourth evangelist. But there are parallels to this form of symbolism in other parts of the New Testament; and always it seems to be employed with the same general purpose in view. Two mysteries are in this way brought together in order that a relationship between them may be suggested, a relationship which illuminates the significance of both the one and the other. In the present instance an analogy is suggested between two events which stand in contrast, the one being historical and the other mystical. But the comparison is made in order to convey a further suggestion. The two events

[1] It is only in verse 6 that the word refers definitely to a male person; and even when context gives this meaning the emphasis is still on 'humanity' rather than on 'maleness'.

[2] But the double meaning of αἱμάτων cannot be adequately conveyed in English. In the text above 'natural generation' must be understood to include 'a commingling of two blood-streams'. Such a connotation may well be without parallel, occurring as it does in a unique statement. A further suggestion on this point will be made later. See below, § v, par. 6.

are not only analogous but also related integrally to one another, and that in a very special sense, since the second is both founded upon the first and also implicitly included within it. From this, still only partial, analysis of John 1[12–14] we must now turn aside for a space to a wider Johannine survey in accordance with the warning given at the conclusion of § i in this chapter. For the topics which we have been handling run through the whole 'Johannine' literature, in different forms, but with an underlying unity which merits serious consideration.

V

The child of the new Eve defeats 'the old serpent'; and 'the rest of her seed' are identified with him in his victory. This is the complement of John 1[12,13]; and other NT scriptures show an underlying unity. But the Johannine writings exhibit a development of the 'new birth' theme from 'the seed of the woman' through the divine begetting to 'the seed' of the heavenly Father sown in the virgin soil of the new Eve's flesh.

In Revelation 12 the seer sees a vision of a 'woman clothed with the sun' who gives birth to the Messiah. The Mother of Jesus is here shewn fulfilling the historic function of Israel. For, as the bride of Jahveh, Israel is the mother of all God's children. But especially Israel was to be mother of the Messiah, God's first-born Son. The messianic motif, however, is here crossed by another drawn from the story of Adam and Eve. This is shewn by the presence of the dragon waiting for the birth of the child. For a few verses later he is identified with 'the old serpent'; and we are at once reminded of the oracle in Genesis 3[15], where, after the fall, God says to the serpent,: I will put enmity between thee and the woman'. The rest of the verse runs thus in the Septuagint: 'and between thy seed and her seed; he shall watch thy head, and thou shalt watch his heel'. Accordingly, in the seer's vision 'the dragon stood before the woman', so that when the child was born his eyes would fasten on the dragon's 'head' immediately in front of him. The other part of the oracle also had its fulfilment. For the child was 'snatched up to God and to his throne'; and the dragon, who had hoped to devour him, merely caught sight of his 'heel' as he ascended swiftly upwards. Jesus, then, is the promised 'seed of the woman'.

In the next verse of Genesis (3^{16}) the woman is told that she shall bear 'children'; and in the Greek version the word used is the same as that which describes the 'children of God' in John 1^{12}. So in the sequel to the seer's vision, after 'the serpent' and his 'seed' have been 'bruised' by the Messiah's angelic host, the ancient enemy seeks to persecute 'the woman', and, failing there, he goes off to make war with 'the rest of her seed' (12^{17}). Thus the story of Eve's downfall is reversed in two ways. For first the messianic child triumphs over the dragon; and then there follows a new chapter of fulfilment. Here the martyr-Christians, persecuted by the dragon, are reckoned amongst the children of the New Eve. Thus they are destined to share the promised victory over the serpent. *Their* victory is already proclaimed as an accomplished fact in the song with which heaven greets the angelic triumph over Satan's hosts (12^{11}): 'They overcame him on account of the blood of the Lamb and on account of the word of their witness, and they loved not their lives unto death'. For they also are 'the seed of the woman'; and as such they have mystical identity with her messianic child in the new creation.

Let us notice how the identification here intimated corresponds to that which we have already examined in the Gospel prologue. There the new birth of 'the children' is identified with the Virgin-Birth of 'the Son'. Here the children are identified with the Son in his victory through death. There the new birth is granted to 'those who believe on his name'. Here the victory of the Lamb is shared by the rest of 'the seed' because they identify themselves with his death; and by this act of 'witness' they give proof that they 'believe on his name'. Thus their death is included in his as their birth was. For the identification is total, and therefore covers the whole pattern of human life from birth to death. So there is one Holy Family of the new humanity, and Jesus is, so to speak, its heart and centre, God's first-born Son 'amongst many brethren' (Romans 8^{29}). This phrase of St Paul's, however, takes us over to the other side of the mystery. The new human family has a heavenly origin. Accordingly the contrast drawn in John 1^{13} is a contrast between earthly generation from the human seed of the man whom 'in the beginning' the Word created and, on the other hand, heavenly regeneration by inclusion in the divine begetting of the Word himself.

In all of this there is a deep underlying unity of witness between the various parts of the New Testament. Quite early in the present volume we found the one family of which Jesus is the centre adumbrated in the synoptic gospels.[1] Similarly it would seem that the Pauline contrast between inclusion in Adam and inclusion in Christ is complementary, if not actually contributory, to the contrast emphasized in John 1^{13}. The doctrine of 'the man from heaven' (1 Cor. 15^{47}) corresponds to the Johannine teaching of a birth 'from above' (John 3^{3-8}).[2] Moreover, the discourse to Nicodemus which thus emphasizes the heavenly origin of the new birth is simply unfolding what is already more tersely said in the prologue. So too, the mysterious character of the new-born Christian, as described in 3^{8}, is later seen to conform to the mysterious coming and going of the Christ.[3] The new birth stamps upon its recipients a 'character' which corresponds to that of the Virgin-born Saviour. The 'children' are moulded in the image of the divine Son; and this act of new creation is a restoration, a return to 'the Beginning'. At this point we must take note of differences as well as likenesses. In the 'Johannine' treatment of these themes there is a definite movement of thought which has a somewhat dialectical character.

The movement which I have in mind starts from the biblical doctrine of the promised Seed. Jesus is the one Seed of promise in whom all Christians are included (Galatians 3^{16}). He fulfils the promise because he is the new Adam, who is 'from heaven', whose seed we are (1 Cor. 15^{36-49}). In Revelation 12 the promise is fulfilled in 'the Seed of the Woman' according to Genesis 3^{15}. In all of these instances it is the human descent of 'the Seed' which is emphasized; but in the gospels there is an alternative line of thought. In Luke 8^{11} the parable of the sower is declared

[1] Ch. I, § ii.

[2] Which, in turn, is connected with the heavenly Son of Man, who came down ($3^{13,31,32}$) and goes up (3^{13}, 6^{62}); so the new birth of the blind man in John 9 is completed in his confession of 'the Son of Man' (9^{35-38} where WH have the best authenticated reading).

[3] On which the Johannine irony plays, e.g. 7^{27}, 7^{33-36}, 8^{21-23}, $9^{29,30}$.

to mean that 'the seed is the word of God' uttered by Jesus. In St John, however, Jesus himself is the uttered Word of the Father; and it must be presumed that the evangelist intended this doctrine to be presupposed in his own version of the sower parable. In 12^{24} Jesus himself is the seed which 'falls into the ground and dies' in order to live again. In short we have now passed right across from 'the seed of the woman' to 'the seed' of the Father; and it is this complete change of emphasis which becomes explicit in the First Epistle of St John. Before turning to that final phase of Johannine thought, let us glance once more at the intermediary stages in which a transition is made from human to divine Seed.

In Romans 1^3 Jesus is declared to have been 'made of the seed of David according to the flesh', that is, by an act of condescension he entered into a lineal descent of human seed. So too in the same epistle the begetting of Isaac (prototype of the promised Seed) is a creative act of God overcoming human infirmity (4^{16-25}). In St John's prologue the 'Seed' doctrine has been altogether superseded by the divine begetting. The 'seed' language is avoided, and apparently this is deliberate. It would have been easy for the evangelist to make his first negation in 1^{13} take shape as 'not of human seed'; or, in accordance with contemporary theory, he could have reversed the description of Solomon's begetting in Wisdom 7^2, where 'from the seed of a man' the child is said to have been 'compacted' in its mother's blood. This, however, would have obscured his chosen contrast which sets aside 'the will of a man' in favour of the divine act of begetting. Accordingly he preferred to give his own meaning to current language about 'blood' descent by an unprecedented use of the plural form: 'bloods'. In 12^{24} the context is wholly different. Jesus is here the Servant who is now 'glorified' by the request of the Greeks and is about to die and rise again like a grain of corn in the Pauline parable (1 Cor. 15^{36ff}). Yet this Johannine application prepared the way for a fusion of seed imagery with the doctrine of the divine begetting.

The teaching of 1 John 3^{8-12} is set in the framework of Genesis 2–4. This appears from the references to the devil who 'sinneth from the beginning' (verse 8) and to Cain who 'slew his brother' (verse 12); possibly also (in verse 1) 'called children of God' refers to John 1^{12} on the background of names 'called' (that is, given) by God through his Word and his Adam in the creation cycle. Thus we might expect some reference to 'the seed of the woman'. What is actually said, however, in verse 9, is something quite different. For the doctrine of the prologue concerning the divine begetting is now combined with a new application of the Johannine phraseology concerning 'abiding':

> Everyone who has been begotten of God does not commit sin, for his seed abideth in him, and he cannot sin because he has been begotten of God.

Here the individual Christian has received the status of God's child through a divine begetting, as in John 1[12,13]. But we now have a fuller explanation of what this means. The divine Seed has been sown in the neophyte and continues to 'abide' in him. This language is unique in the New Testament; but there are approximations to it. In John 15 there is mutual abiding of vine and branches in one another. Again in Galatian 4[19] the apostle addresses his 'little children, of whom I am again in travail until Christ be formed in you'. Here the spiritual father stands *in loco dei* in accordance with a Hebrew idiom of identification.[1]

In this section of 1 John there is a blending of various scriptural strands. But, speaking generally, the Epistle does no more than carry one stage further the tendency observable in John 12[24]. What is, perhaps, most striking, however, is the use made of Genesis. At first sight 'the seed of the woman' has been replaced by the seed of deity. But, on further consideration, it may be suggested that we have here a new interpretation of Genesis in the light of the fulfilment. In Genesis 4[1], at the birth of Cain, Eve exclaims: 'I have gotten a man with Jahveh' (Septuagint: 'through God'). In view of the primitive notion that birth is due to the action of a 'spirit' upon the mother, the saying might be taken to mean that the first human birth was believed to have been a special act of deity. Moreover the saying should surely be connected with 3[15]. Eve is represented as supposing that the child now born is the promised seed which will bruise the serpent's head. In fact, however, her supposition was doubly mistaken. The child was Adam's seed, and in due course became, not a Saviour but a murderer. So far from

[1] Explained in I. IX. v.

being 'begotten of God' he was a child of the devil. This explains the language of 1 John in $3^{8,12}$. What then is the implication?

The answer is not in doubt. The supposition attributed to Eve came true when a new Eve could say with truth: 'I have gotten a man with the Lord'. For in the fulfilment 'the seed of the woman' conquered the serpent precisely because he was the seed of the Father sown in the virgin soil of Mary's flesh.[1] If I have rightly understood the teaching of this epistle the dialectical factor in the Johannine movement of thought stands revealed. For the earlier phases of that movement are taken up into the thought of the epistle. Moreover there is a typical oscillation between the One and the Many which corresponds to that of the Pauline writings, although presented in a different set of images. Instead of the inclusive Seed of promise we have, in the Johannine cycle, a family of the new Eve in which 'the rest of her seed' are somehow an extension of the one Seed. But so also for St Paul the one Christ is reproduced in his members by indwelling. For the Christ so 'formed' in us we have a Johannine counterpart, the divine Seed abiding in us. This language makes explicit the enigma of John 1^{13}. As the form of the Christ is reproduced in his members by 'repetition' of his death and resurrection, so the virginal character of the unique Birth is reproduced by a 'repetition' of the one divine begetting in the many children of God. Moreover a distinction remains between each one 'who has been begotten' and 'him who was begotten' (1 John 5^{18}).[2]

vi

The cumulative character of Johannine thought, as sketched above. Its wholeness in development illustrated. Its twofold prophetic message. If pride is crushed, faith is exalted; and every

[1] For the development of this theme by St Irenaeus see I. V. ii, pp. 137 ff. In his version, however, the 'seed' imagery of Gen. 3^{15} has given place to the 'moulding' of Gen. 2^{7}.

[2] A more speculative deduction from Gen. 4^{1} would connect *kanah* ('to get') in Eve's exclamation with *kanah* in Prov. 8^{22}, where wisdom says: 'The Lord *gat* me as the beginning of his ways'. The seed sown in the new Eve is Logos-Wisdom. He who was always begotten by the Father (*γεννηθείς*) is the beginning of those 'who have been begotten'.

new birth signifies the cosmic new beginning. Transition to fresh aspects of the divine conflict.

The movement of thought analysed in the last section is cumulative in the sense that everything significant in the earlier stages is included in the final presentation. But further, the statements in 1 John throw light upon relevant contributions in the fourth gospel, which can be seen to belong to the same type of thought as we have found in the epistle. For example, it is not as 'seed of the woman' that Jesus destroys the works of the devil, but as 'Son of God' (1 John 3^{8}); and our share in the victory is due to the indwelling of the divine seed. The immunity which we thus enjoy is more fully explained in 5^{18-21}, where, however, the image is turned round. It is now the new-born Christian who is 'in the true God, even in his Son', preserved from the touch of the evil one and illuminated by the teaching of him in whom we dwell. Compare this with the discourse in John 8^{31ff}. Here the human 'seed of Abraham' stands opposed to the divine seed of the Word. The former cannot assimilate the latter from the lips of Jesus (8^{37}); and the explanation is that, while boasting their human descent, these children of Abraham are in reality children of the devil. Significantly, also, they bring forward the traditional slander of Jewry against the manner of our Lord's birth, and that too in a form which exhibits the Johannine irony at its highest intensity.

Here are their words: 'We were not begotten of fornication; we have one Father, even God' (8^{41}). Their claim mounts higher as they depress his in the scale. The seed of Abraham can claim God as its father of right. Complacency could scarcely go further; and such complacency quite naturally substitutes a blasphemous calumny for the mystery of virginal conception by which the only-begotten Son of God appropriately entered this world. The whole discourse harmonizes perfectly with the prologue on the one hand and with the epistle on the other. Notwithstanding its developing movement Johannine thought remains a single whole; and upon this particular theme it has a prophetic message for the modern world. Scepticism concerning the unique mode of our Lord's birth has flourished most naturally in an age which has set man at the centre of things and which, at the same time, has pushed God out to the circumference. For this great mystery passes judgement upon our fallen nature. The new beginning of the world could not come from mortal flesh. For 'that which has been begotten of flesh' is flesh and no more (John 3^6), The new creation, therefore, could not, and did not, proceed from a man's capacity to propagate his species.

This point of view is pressed home repeatedly by the evangelist. For 'he who is from the earth' (as all the race of Adam are) will leave the stamp of his earthly origin upon all that he says and does.[1] So all purely human attempts to re-make the world can do no more than rebuild the tower of Babel, whereas the New Jerusalem comes down 'out of heaven from God', the bride following the downward path previously marked out by the divine bridegroom. Thus the incarnation of the Word, by the manner in which it was effected, dealt a crushing blow at human pride, behind which the serpent ever lies concealed. But secondly, if the struggle between light and darkness is essentially a divine conflict, yet we have identity with the divine Word in the mystery whereby his penetration to the heart of humanity was effected, and in which the conflict was renewed. If 'the Son of God was manifested to destroy the works of the devil', he has also enfolded us within his total response to the Father by which the serpent's head is bruised. The inclusion of 'the children' within the response of the Son is effected by an act of God alone, in which the creaturely will has no part. Yet, none the less, that divine act could not take place without, on our side, that form of human receptivity which scripture calls 'faith'.

This is the precise point at which we can perceive the parallel between the Son's way of entry into our earthly life and the children's way of entry into his heavenly life. Thus it is that if pride is crushed faith is also exalted. As the divine act by which creation is restored required the assent of a new Eve, so the response of the Son to the Father within the restored creation requires our response as its complement. So, finally, the new birth of every believer corresponds to, and signifies, the new beginning of the world in Christ. When man transgressed the primal law of obedience he entered a realm of darkness

[1] 3^{31}; and cp. the irony of $6^{41, 42}$, developed further in reference to 'the seed of David' (7^{42}) until finally it reaches back, as we have seen, to the father of the chosen people.

where 'the light which lighteth every man' was obscured. But 'in the beginning was the Word'; and 'in the beginning' man received life from the Word. To that beginning, therefore, he must return by a new birth which makes him once more a child, but also a child of God. Now if man was to return in lowliness to the beginning, this could happen only through a descent of the Word himself to the lowliness of man's first beginning. So the Word became flesh, that is mortal man, thereby taking to himself all that this word 'flesh' signifies in biblical speech.

We have been surveying a particular aspect of Johannine thought, namely restoration through conflict. The subject will be continued in the next chapter; and there we shall examine the implications of John 1[14] from the same point of view. Until that task has been undertaken our exposition not only of that verse but also of the prologue as a whole remains radically incomplete. There is a reason for this. In the present chapter we have confined our attention to those aspects of the divine conflict which hinge upon the scriptural version of the creation-cycle as seen from the standpoint of the new creation in Christ. We have found the conflict at the heart of both creations, and inevitably so. For in the Johannine creation doctrine, which here reflects very ancient human notions, a new world is created through the conquest of evil. Beyond the creation-cycle, however, in the scriptural record stretch the epochs of redemptive history. As we pass into that sphere we shall find other aspects of the conflict presented to us which may throw further light both upon the Johannine prologue and also upon the New Testament as a whole. This at least is what might be expected; for, although for purposes of exposition we may sometimes find it convenient to treat of them separately, the facts themselves will not allow us to forget that the three strands of creation, history and revelation are woven inextricably into a single pattern.

CHAPTER V

THE DIVINE CONFLICT; (2) IN REDEMPTIVE HISTORY

i

The Word identified himself with 'flesh' in its weakness, mortality and exile. In his 'tent' of flesh he recapitulated Israel's pilgrimage through the wilderness, and took upon him Israel's vocation to restore lost sons through the testing of sonship in a sacrificial ordeal of obedience. Two aspects of 'flesh' in NT.

In becoming 'flesh' the Word made himself one with 'all flesh', that is, with all creaturely life in this world of his creation. He who is in the bosom of the Father, he who himself holds this living cosmos in his embrace, having penetrated to its heart, became its offspring. In St Paul's words: He 'who is the image of the invisible God' became 'the firstborn of all creation'. When the Creator thus entered into his creation and identified himself with it, he became its 'Head' in a new sense. These Pauline titles are not employed by St John. But their meaning is substantially conveyed in the Baptist's witness (1^{15}), where the priority of Jesus to his forerunner is, as in the Hebrew meaning of 'firstborn', a matter of headship or superior status.[1] The primary declarations of 1^{14}, however, emphasize identification, even though the significance of this fact depends upon the status of him who so condescends, that is, one who is 'only-begotten from his Father'. We have, then, to consider next the consequences of this identification, confining our attention at present to those consequences which affected the Word incarnate himself. The two opening phrases of 1^{14} suggest a whole world of associations which will carry us into the heart of the subject.

In becoming 'flesh' the Word took upon himself all the frailties and creaturely limitations of our nature. He became subject to that earthly state which is emphasized in the story of

[1] Not temporal precedence. Cp. Ps. 89^{27}.

Adam, whose bodily frame was formed from the dust of the ground. The 'flesh' which the Word took corresponds to the 'flesh' mentioned in 1^{13}. This flesh, endowed with volition as well as life, nevertheless, could not provide the generative power which might inaugurate a new creation. It was for that very reason that the Word must enter into it. 'For it is the Spirit that quickeneth, the flesh profiteth nothing' (John 6^{63}). In the beginning flesh was inbreathed by Spirit. So quickened, it has its place in the divine plan and can become instrumental to the highest ends. But where its proper dependence upon Spirit has been weakened or dislocated, there it becomes unprofitable for the Creator's purpose. It is precisely this dislocation of our nature which is implied in the phrase 'will of the flesh'. This brings us to another aspect of the consequences flowing from our Lord's identification of himself with us. He identified himself with a fallen race whose dispositions are no longer controlled by the divine Spirit.

Thus he became subject to those conditions which, in the story of the first creation, were imposed upon Adam as a divine judgement upon his sin. The first of these was physical death. 'Dust thou art, and unto dust shalt thou return'. But there was also a second consequence of Adam's transgression, namely, the cursing of the ground for his sake. This indicated a frustration or partial suspension of the dominion over creation originally accorded to Adam. For an effectual sovereignty of man over creation would make all nature to be a garden of Eden where our humanity would enjoy the fruits of the earth and participate in the eternal sabbath-rest of the deity. On the other hand, man dispossessed of effectual dominion has left nature bereft of its proper caretaker. Thus, in place of the garden there appears a wilderness of thorns and thistles, where man during his brief earthly sojourn eats bread in the sweat of his face. There he engages perforce in a task beyond his powers, the endless task of endeavouring to turn chaos into cosmos. The fall, then, laid upon man a burden of the flesh which has two aspects, namely, first mortality, and secondly exile from his true home which is the paradise of God's creative design.

It was precisely this twofold burden which the divine Word assumed when he became flesh; and that fact is now indicated. In becoming flesh the Word made the flesh to be a 'tent' in which he took up his abode. Now a tent can be easily taken down and taken to pieces. Compared with a house it has a makeshift character; it is not a permanent abode. St Paul had this contrast clearly in mind when he wrote: 'We know that if our earthly tent-house is dissolved we have in process of building from God a house not made with hands, eternal in the heavens' (2 Cor. 5^{1}). The contrast here is between the 'flesh' which must die and the body of the resurrection in which we shall live for evermore. The 'tent', then, is a symbol of mortality, but also of something else. A tent, being movable, is a suitable dwelling for anyone on the move, for one who by choice or perforce is without a permanent home. This aspect of the tent is fastened upon in the Epistle to the Hebrews ($11^{8-10,\ 13-16}$), where the author describes the patriarchs as 'strangers and sojourners'.[1] Like St Paul, he draws a contrast between the tent and the permanent dwelling-place. But here the tents of the patriarchs symbolize not mortality but present homelessness by contrast with the city of God for which they look.

Both mortality and homelessness are characteristic of our fallen nature in its present condition with which our Lord has associated himself. But they also signify our present state of pilgrimage as sojourners in a world which is not our true home. From the call of Abraham onwards the people of God has been in this state of pilgrimage. But the classic symbolism of the 'tent' in Israel's story is associated with the forty years of wandering in the wilderness. There the deity identified himself with the fortunes of his people. So the tabernacle or tent erected by Moses in the wilderness was a fitting shrine for the God of Israel, when his people were travelling through desert places to the Holy Land. These facts also made the sacred tent of those desert wanderings a fitting type of the flesh in which the Word took up his abode when he left his heavenly home and became the Son of Man who had not where to lay his head (Luke 9^{58}). That this parallel is clearly intended by the evangelist is evident from the immediate transition which he makes in 1^{14} from 'the tent' to the Shekinah-glory of the only-begotten Son who dwells in the tent. To that point we shall return. For

[1] So St Stephen in his speech says that Abraham had no inheritance in the land of promise, 'not so much as to set his foot on' (Acts 7^{5}).

the present let us keep to that aspect of the symbolism which signifies Israel's pilgrimage.

Israel in the wilderness, journeying to the promised land, symbolized the return of all the scattered children of God[1] to the holy land of paradise regained. They were chosen out to be God's sons[2] that they might lead the return of all lost sons from the far country to the Father's home, that they might embody the resolve of all penitent sinners: 'I will arise and go unto my Father'. Such was the divine intention; but how different is the record of what happened! Here we have a pilgrimage, not of penitents but of rebels who preferred the flesh-pots of Egypt to the milk and honey of their true inheritance. But the rebels, for their disobedience, received the sentence of death which is the lot of fallen Adam. Their carcases were strewn in the wilderness, and they entered not into the rest to which they were called.[3] Thus they foreshadowed Israel's rejection of the Word; and thus, when the Word became flesh and made for himself an earthly tabernacle, he placed himself in the wilderness of a fallen world and surrounded himself with the camp of rebellious Israel. In so doing he took upon himself the consequences of the curse pronounced in Eden. By identifying himself with a race of lost sons, in exile from their true home, he also accepted for himself that burden of the flesh which is our just inheritance.

But further, in the same act he also took upon him that proving of human sonship which Israel had refused. For the filial relation of man to God, broken by disobedience, had been partially restored by the call of Israel, in order that in and through the people of his choice the honour of the divine name might be vindicated. What, then, did that call signify? Israel was selected to bear vicariously the burden of man's lost sonship in a life of sacrificial response to the divine will. Sonship was to be restored through suffering by ever-renewed testing. Such a life would participate in the divine faithfulness and make due response to the divine love. It would thereby make recompense for the broken fellowship of man with God and with his neighbour. But it would also manifest the divine righteousness to

[1] cp. John 11^{52}.
[2] Exod. 4^{22}, Wisd. 12^{21}, 16^{26}, 18^{4}.
[3] 1 Cor. 10^{1-11}, Heb. 3^{7}–4^{2}.

mankind, and in so manifesting would also vindicate it. Finally, such a life would have redemptive power to restore the plan of creation and with it the earthly paradise. For the dutiful oblation of filial love, so rendered to the Father of spirits, is precisely the glory for which creation was planned. The prophetic interpretation of Israel's mission, which we have thus summarized, reaches its culminating point in the second Isaiah and his school. Moreover, the gospels, particularly in their accounts of his temptation, show that our Lord identified himself with Israels' vocation as thus interpreted.[1]

In the Epistle to the Hebrews the identification of the Christ with Israel's mission so interpreted is connected with the restoration of Adam's dominion as set forth in Psalm 8. It finds the connecting link between these two things (the mission and the restored dominion) in the perfecting of sonship through an ordeal of obedience offered as a sacrificial oblation in mortal flesh.[2] In particular, at three definite points the epistle touches the Johannine teaching now under consideration. The first of these points is to be found in the epistle's insistence upon the identity between Christ and his people in their mission and its ordeal, in chastisement and suffering, in scandal and reproach. The second point of affinity lies in the emphasis which the epistle lays upon the flesh which Jesus shares with us, as being the indispensable *locus* of his conflict and of his sacrificial action on our behalf.[3] Thirdly for both writers, despite wide differences of treatment, the new tabernacle is the sphere in which we are identified with Christ's action. In one passage, where two of these points coalesce, the writer appears to identify the flesh of Jesus *either* with the veil of the tabernacle *or* with the way through the veil. Either rendering is possible;[4] but both meanings may be intended, and either would fit the symbolism of the rent veil in Mark 15^{38}. Taken together they illustrate the two aspects of the word 'flesh' as used in St John's Gospel. To this we will now turn.

[1] see especially his use of Deut. 6 and 8 in reply to the tempter.

[2] Heb. 2^{5}–5^{10}; cp. 10^{5-14}.

[3] Heb. 2^{14}, 5^{7}, 10^{20}; cp. 'body' in 10^{10}, and for the connexion of this point with the first see the whole of 10^{32}–12^{13}. See also 1 Pet. $4^{1,2}$.

[4] For the construction in 10^{20}, on the second alternative, there is a close parallel in 12^{11} (peaceable fruit . . . of righteousness).

ii

In St John's Gospel the flesh of Jesus is both the veil which hides the glory and also the way of access to the glory. The flesh of the Word, being both his and ours, is inevitably the place of conflict. Mosaic typology. What the brazen serpent represented the uplifted Saviour became, thus revealing the difference between the Law and his own 'grace and truth'.

When the Word became flesh he veiled the glory of the only-begotten Son under a lowly tent of flesh, just as the glory of the divine presence (*Shekinah*) was hidden from Israel in the wilderness behind a veil in the 'tent of meeting'. Yet Moses entered the tabernacle; and with him 'the Lord spake face to face as a man speaketh with his friend'.[1] So for St John the flesh of Jesus is not only the veil which hides the glory, but also the way of access to the glory. For this evangelist the veiling and the unveiling are concurrent. While Moses passes through the veil the people remain without. The flesh of Jesus has this double effect for all time.[2] The fourth gospel as a whole is dominated by the twofold thesis thus indicated. Its symbolism, however, depends in part upon the implications of the next phrase in the prologue. The Word 'tabernacled' or 'pitched his tent'. Where? The next two words could mean 'amongst us' or 'in us'. It seems that here, as in verse 13, the evangelist is declaring a double truth. The entry of the Word into mortal flesh placed him 'amongst us' and so distinguished him from us, leaving men free to accept or to reject him. He would not force his claim upon anyone. Some, however, discerned the glory under the humiliation, and so entered upon the path which led to the new birth.[3] Like Moses, they were admitted to the secrets of the tabernacle.

But this could happen because 'the flesh' which 'the Word became' is our flesh as well as his. For 'flesh' is human nature. So by entering human nature he 'tabernacled in us'.[4] He had

[1] Exod. 33^{9-11}; cp. Num. $12^{7,8}$, Deut. 34^{10}.

[2] If we allow for differences of symbolism, this corresponds to the teaching of 2 Cor. 3^{7}–4^{6}.

[3] The language of 1^{12} implies a process.

[4] The double meaning arises naturally from a difference between the Hebrew text and LXX in two passages of the Pentateuch. See below, § iii, second note to last par. but one.

entered our race and made himself one with all mankind. He had obtained for himself a bridgehead leading into the entire human territory. He had placed the leaven in the lump, the new order within the old. His presence constituted the magnetic centre of disturbance which leaves nothing as it was. Thus the Word identified himself completely with all mankind without in any way diminishing the contrast between him and us, that is between God and man, between the Saviour and the world which he came to save. Men must be free to co-operate. So the identification of the Saviour with all could come to fruition only through the specific response of some,—those who by faith were admitted to the secrets of the holiest place, where the glory is unveiled. In those who, in this sense, 'beheld his glory' the bridgehead into enemy-occupied territory had already been enlarged, the leaven had already begun to transform the lump of fallen humanity, the Church of the new creation had already been formed, the magnetic centre of disturbance had been extended.

In the second creation, as in the first, the going forth of the Word brought light; but it was veiled under the weakness of the flesh. So the flesh of Jesus is the place where, as of old, the light is divided from the darkness. For the light is manifested only to those whose eyes are opened by Jesus; it remains concealed from the blindness of the proud (John 9^{39-41}). In the story of Israel in the wilderness the glory manifested *to* Moses in the tabernacle was also manifested *from* the tabernacle in judgement upon sinners. So too the flesh of Jesus is both the place of illumination and the place of judgement. It is clear, then, that the flesh of the Word incarnate is the place where the divine conflict of light and darkness has its centre in human history. This thesis is specially prominent in the Johannine writings, but is not peculiar to them. It is developed by means of the Old Testament types, which are always partly like and partly unlike their fulfilment in Christ. But the types also coalesce. Thus the psalmist connected the glory crowning 'the son of Adam' with man's destiny as head of the lower creation. But glory was also reflected for a while on the face of Moses when he brought to Israel the light of the Law. So Moses descending from the mount with the tables of stone is a type of the divine Word descending from heaven to embody the new Torah-Wisdom.

Moreover, as Moses veiled from Israel's sight the glory shining upon his face, so too 'the glory of God in the face of Jesus Christ' was veiled under the weakness of the flesh.[1]

The types are like and unlike; so for St John the disciple of Jesus is likened to Moses in the tabernacle (1^{14}), whereas Moses as mediator is superseded by Christ (1^{17}). Another Mosaic type has been thought to lie just beneath the surface in St Paul, whereas it becomes explicit in St John. This is to be found in the figure of the brazen serpent which, under divine direction, Moses lifted up to be gazed upon by the rebels in the wilderness. He who looked upon this emblem was cured from the poisonous bite of a live serpent (Numbers 21^{4-9}). The Book of Wisdom (16^{6}) calls the brazen serpent 'a token of salvation to bring to remembrance the commandment of thy law'. In this admirable comment the whole Law is summed up as man's duty of obedience to God. The figure on the standard reminded the rebellious murmurers of the judgement which falls upon sin, namely death in the wilderness instead of life in the land of promise. Thus Israel's story renewed the pattern of man's first disobedience with its double consequence of death and exile. We are reminded of that other serpent in the garden and of the curse occasioned by his bite; in both stories the bite brings death and exile from the home appointed for God's children.[2]

But the uplifted serpent was 'a token of salvation'. It confronted the sinner with the very form of the divine judgement, that, convicted of his sin, he might repent and be saved from destruction. Now 'as Moses lifted up the serpent in the wilderness so must the Son of Man be lifted up, that everyone who believeth may in him have eternal life' (John $3^{14,15}$). The analogy is clear. In Jesus uplifted on the cross there is a revelation of sin and its consequences. In those who are saved by that spectacle the uplifted figure effects a repentance which makes forgiveness possible. There is, however, a fundamental difference between the type and the antitype. The writer of Wisdom contrasts the uplifted serpent with God 'the Saviour of all', with whom, in the Gospel, the uplifted Son of Man is identified. In the type no visible object effected the cure, but

[1] Exod. 34^{30-35}, 2 Cor. 3^{7}–4^{6}. For St Paul the 'weakness of the flesh' (Rom. 8^{3}) is characteristic of the Law and its achievements.

[2] see also I. VI. i, pp. 162 f., note 5.

'thy Word, O Lord, which healeth all things' (Wisdom 16[7, 12]). In the antitype the healing power flows from the form uplifted on the cross which is none other than the incarnate Word of God. The difference here disclosed is precisely that to which St John refers, when he draws a contrast between Christ and Moses in the prologue (1[17]).

Let us get this point clear. The Law 'saves' those who obey its commandment. The serpent, therefore, as a representation of sin and its consequences, was a 'token' of that kind of 'salvation' which the Law offered. In fact the incident of Moses uplifting the brazen serpent represented in picture form the truth that 'the law was given through Moses'. Jesus, however, embodied the Law by fulfilling it. Thus he became the true mediator to which the Law with its types and tokens merely pointed. He who is God 'the Saviour of all' condescended to identify himself with his sinful worshippers, whereas when Israel identified the 'piece of brass' with the true object of worship they stood convicted of idolatry (2 Kings 18[4]). When the Word 'tabernacled in us' he identified himself (in us) with sin and its consequences. What the brazen serpent merely represented the uplifted Saviour had actually become, as St Paul clearly states: 'Him who knew no sin' God 'made to be sin for us' (2 Cor. 5[21]). The obedient man identified himself with disobedient man in his state of disobedience. So Jesus was bitten for us with the bite of the old serpent and received in himself the curse of the Law. Identification was complete. 'Grace and truth came through Jesus Christ' who possesses their fulness (1[14,17]); and by this means God gave himself wholly to us.

iii

Symbolism of the uplifted serpent. Light is darkened, and the healer becomes like the hurt. The scandal of sin removed by the double scandal of the cross and new birth. The Johannine plan connects salvation with judgement, the serpent with the Servant, humiliation with divine glory. Affinity with the Word, despite sin, shewn in the magnetism of Christ's sacrifice. The two orders of being, differentiated in Jesus, are like wrestlers interlocked in a new conflict upon Penuel.

By this identification of the Word with sinners in the flesh which is theirs the conflict between the light and the darkness became intensified a thousand-fold. For, in order that his bright rays might reach to us the Light of the world was utterly encompassed by our darkness, just as, when the beams of a torch stream outwards, the torch itself remains a darkened object. So in the conflict of the new creation the light entering the darkness is absorbed into its maw until it seems to be wholly swallowed up. What remains is surely just the monstrous serpent, the old dragon himself! But no; the light still shines; the darkness did not master it. The dragon has overreached himself.[1] As in the story of the Exodus, it is the enemy serpent which is swallowed, while the messianic Rod-turned-serpent is restored to its former estate (Exodus 4^{2-4}, 7^{8-12}). We shall see later that this 'serpent' symbolism has a vital bearing upon the character of that mission to the world with which the Church has been entrusted. For here as elsewhere everything that matters for Christians runs up into Christology. So let us carry our scrutiny a little further into the enigmatic truths which are wrapped up in this typological mystery.

Jesus is the one whole Man, who sought to restore all men into the unity and wholeness of their true being in which he originally created them, that unity and wholeness which exists only in him. He healed the sick victims of the serpent's bite by drawing the poison out of them. In so doing he inevitably drew the poison into himself. He was like one who in ministering to lepers becomes himself a leper, and therefore an outcast. To heal the serpent's victims he must himself become like the serpent; the healer must become like the hurt. Now that very malady of sin which disintegrates our nature causes us to resist the painful process by which alone it can be restored. So by identifying himself with all men the Son of God made himself strange to all. 'The contradiction of sinners against themselves', which he endured, became inevitably a contradiction against him also, as the variant reading in Hebrews 12^{3} testifies. In order to remove the scandal of sin he had to embrace the

[1] The last clause of John 1^{5} is, word for word, a negation of the dragon allegory in Jer. 51^{34}, as read in LXX (28^{34}). To this, apparently deliberate, allusion we shall return later in this chapter in connexion with the 'Jonah' typology.

scandal of the cross. Thus the glory was veiled under the burden of the flesh. It is from this point of view that we can best understand the symbolism of the serpent in St John's Gospel.

The figure of the brazen serpent is introduced by our Lord in reply to the incredulous question of Nicodemus: 'How *can* these things be?' Doubtless the enquirer would not have disputed the thesis that Abraham's seed are in a peculiar sense God's children (8^{33-41}). Why then this talk of a birth 'from above'? Here, as in 1^{12-14}, the doctrine of the new birth cuts at the roots of human pride. 'No man can ascend into heaven' by his own efforts or merits. But heaven has come down to us in the person of the Son of man; and he brings to us the divine Breath by which, as of old, man is re-created. Thus, in the mind of the evangelist, the whole prelude to the 'serpent' statement of 3^{14} registers the scandal caused by a doctrine of new birth, a doctrine of necessary return to our first lowly beginning in the Word. It would seem then that the scandal of the new birth is justified by the further scandal of the uplifted serpent. Clearly the two mysteries belong together. In fact they are one mystery which is all comprised in the scandal of the cross. We shall find presently that the evangelist offers further elucidation when he identifies our Lord with the suffering Servant.

There is, however, something more to be said about the sequel to the new birth doctrine. For the statement about the serpent is followed immediately by an explanation of its significance (3^{15ff}). The 'lifting up' had to take this form, the glory had to be veiled under the flesh, in order that faith might be free to operate. So great was God's love that he gave his Son in a manner which required the response of faith, and which thus made rejection possible. For salvation must always involve the possibility of judgement. The light is abhorred by the darkness, and therefore the coming of the light must divide the 'sons of light' from the sons of darkness.[1] In St John's view the glory of the Son was manifested to the believing disciple on Mount Calvary. Yet the crucifixion was accompanied by a 'darkness over the whole land' (Mark 15^{33}). Even so, the flesh of Christ crucified is for some the flaming beacon which irradiates the whole earthly scene, whereas for others it is like a dark cloud

[1] cp. the contrast in Eph. 5^{6-14} between 'children of light' and 'sons of disobedience'.

which hides the light from their earth-bound eyes. St John concludes the first half of his Gospel with a statement of that double truth (12^{32-47}). This passage has, as we have seen, a verbal connexion with 1^{5}. It has also close affinity of thought with 3^{14ff}; and both sections start from the 'uplifting' of the Son of Man which unites the two images of the serpent and the Servant.[1]

When Jesus speaks of 'the uplifting' which means both death and glory ($12^{32,33}$), his hearers can make nothing of it. But the mystery cannot be unveiled by further explanations; for a veil is on their hearts. So he takes up the prophetic words of Isaiah $50^{10,11}$. Let them cease to walk by their own feeble lights; let them 'obey the voice of the Servant'. If they believe in *that* light they will become 'sons of light' (cp. 1^{12}). His final word, however, was unheeded. So the Light 'was hidden from them' (12^{37}), and the darkness supervened. Then, while the shadows are swiftly falling, the evangelist sums up. As the prologue alludes to the glory seen by Moses in the tabernacle (1^{14}), so this epilogue refers to the glory seen by Isaiah in the temple (12^{41}). The evangelist summarizes the doom which the prophet there heard pronounced upon unfaithful Israel:

> He hath blinded their eyes, and he hardened their heart; lest they should see with their eyes and perceive with their heart, and should turn, and I should heal them.
>
> (12^{40}, paraphrasing Isaiah 6^{10}.)

Then follows this comment: 'These things said Isaiah, because he saw his glory, and he spake concerning him'. So too the first disciples of Jesus saw the glory of the Word made flesh, and they spake of him. For the witnesses of both covenants the judgement issued from the glory manifested; the light exposed the darkness.

The evangelist connects this doom upon unfaithful Israel, heard by Isaiah in the temple, with an utterance of the great Servant prophecy which is to be found in the 53rd chapter of Isaiah's book:

> Lord who believed our report? And to whom was the arm of the Lord revealed? (Isaiah 53^{1}.)

[1] For 1^{5} see above, Ch. IV, § ii, par. 5, first note. For the literary affinities of 3^{14ff} and 12^{32ff} with the Servant songs see my essay in *The Apostolic Ministry*, p. 92.

This second passage refers to the unbelieving attitude of the nations towards the mission of God's Servant, the true Israel. St John sees the two judgements in these two passages as one; he sees in them that single judgement which issues from the glory of God. The two oracles are as one because both find their fulfilment in the Word made flesh. In this way the evangelist identifies the glory of the Lord God seen by Isaiah in the temple with the glory of the Lord's Servant proclaimed in the other prophecy. For in the Greek version of that prophecy he read: 'Behold my servant shall be lifted up and shall be greatly glorified' (Isaiah 52¹³). This text is the key by which St John interprets the passion and death of the Christ. The key shows that Jesus was lifted up and glorified on the cross. But further, the blending of the two prophecies identifies the glory of Jesus manifested upon the cross with the glory of the Lord God manifested to Isaiah in the temple. Moreover, the two halves of the key text give this identification a double application which calls for consideration.

In the first place 'My servant shall be *lifted up*' means that the Son of Man was 'lifted up' on the cross, as the brazen serpent was 'lifted up' in the wilderness. In this aspect of the crucifixion the glory of God the Son was veiled under the weakness of the flesh and hidden from earthly eyes. But, secondly, the other half of the key text is 'My servant shall be greatly *glorified*'; and in the prophecy the Servant was glorified in his humiliation when he was 'led as a lamb to the slaughter'.[1] So, too, in his passion and death Jesus was glorified as the Lamb of God. Thus the Servant prophecy presents a pattern upon which two main threads of this Gospel are interwoven. In this pattern Jesus is identified alike with the brazen serpent lifted up by Moses and with the predestined Lamb to which the Baptist points. The glory of the only Son was, and is, veiled from fleshly eyes in the scandal of the cross. Yet the same glory was, and is, unveiled to the eye of faith in that majestic splendour of sacrifice which is both the source and the crown of creation. To the latter aspect

[1] In the New Testament the servant prophecy is interpreted in more ways than one. But this particular interpretation implies that the announcement in Isa. 52¹³ (LXX), that the servant 'shall be glorified', comes to its fulfilment *throughout* the situations described in Ch. 53, and not only in the triumphant conclusion.

we shall turn in the next chapter after we have completed this survey of the divine conflict through the medium of typical images confronting us in scripture.

Let us conclude this section with some reflexions upon the argument concerning the divine conflict thus far developed, as it bears upon our own situation. The two orders of being have, in the first place, a common origin. The pattern of the first can be restored in the second because each is derived from the Word, and because each exists only in him. 'That which has been made is life' in the Creator-Word; and as such it is brought to its fruition in the incarnate Word. This principle has far-reaching consequences which are yet to be considered. It implies an analogy between the two creations with the possibility that one may represent the other symbolically or sacramentally. To ignore this principle would involve a definite departure from the biblical revelation. Sin has not annulled, and cannot destroy, this ultimate unity of the two creations in their source and ground. Moreover there is the promise of their final integration in the incarnate Word, in whom they are already perfectly united. The light of the Word is in every man, despite the fall. The Incarnation, therefore, was like the introduction of a magnet among objects which are necessarily attracted towards it. As like is drawn to like, so all men, living in him who is the Life and enlightened by him who is the Light, are inevitably drawn by and to him, even though they may be all unconscious of the fact.

On the other hand, the manner in which this drawing becomes effectual is made clear in the saying: 'I, if I be lifted up from the earth, will draw all men unto myself'. The magnetic attraction of the Word became fully operative only through his lifting up on the cross. It is the glory of his sacrifice there manifested which opened the secret of his sonship, thus revealing the preordained form of the elect Servant as the design in which and for which we were created. So the magnet which attracts also and inevitably disturbs. Moreover, the very act by which the Word 'tabernacled in us' was the event which caused the conflict with evil to break forth in its full intensity. For the two orders of creation which are perfectly united in Jesus are also finally differentiated in him. With the sinful flesh of the old Adam is contrasted the sinless flesh of the new Man.

Yet he who came from above entered Adam's fallen stock to make it his own. In so doing he re-created it in himself; but also, by his action, the two orders are now interlocked in conflict. They are like two wrestlers who in their struggle are so closely intertwined that they cannot be separated. The combatants thus engaged are God and the devil, the Light of the world and the prince of darkness, the Lamb and the dragon, the elect Servant and the old serpent, the new Man and the old Adam.

The dispute is about the sick body of the human race,[1] and is both divine and demonic in character. In it the great act of usurpation is countered by the great act of obedience. Moreover, the two combatants are in each case the hub and centre of two opposing armies. Out of the fallen race of Adam enlisted in the usurped kingdom of Satan has been gathered the elect race of the new Israel, enlisted in the restored kingdom of the new Man. But the restored kingdom is also the new organism of the Word incarnate. By his great act of *kenosis* our flesh became his in order that his flesh might become ours. He became flesh that 'all flesh' might become his own flesh, as it should be. We, therefore, are 'one flesh' with Jesus in the new creation that all creation may be reintegrated into his 'sinless flesh'. So being identified with him in his flesh we share with him that conflict which has its centre in his flesh, the testing trial of the wilderness, where the tent of meeting is pitched. Moreover, as he 'tabernacled in us' the Israel of God does not merely surround the sanctuary as formerly; for the new Israel is within the tabernacle, in accordance with the promise which was transformed in its fulfilment: 'I will dwell in them and walk in them'.[2] Nevertheless, the old Adam, although stricken, has not yet lost his power of raising rebellious murmurings within the camp.

In all this it is impossible to make a simple identification between the visible church and the kingdom of God or the *civitas dei*. On that question St Augustine's judgement still

[1] Symbolized in the legend of which we get a glimpse in Jude 9. See also Matt. 24^{28} where the gathering vultures are destined to be disturbed by divine agency. Cp. the scene in Gen. 15^{9-11}.

[2] 2 Cor. 6^{16}, paraphrasing Exod. 29^{45} and Lev. $26^{11,12}$; in both passages the Hebrew text has 'in the midst of'. The LXX phrase: 'I will walk in you' paved the way for St Paul's transformation of the thought.

holds the field. Christ has taken the whole of sinful humanity into his embrace. It is a loving embrace which has the characteristics of conflict only just so far as sinners will have it so. The place of encounter is the flesh of Jesus where the Israel of God is situated. It is therefore Bethel and Penuel.[1] Here the old Adam wrestles with the new, but also the new Man with the old, the conflict extending in ever widening circles to include in its grasp the whole of that fallen race of which 'the One Man Jesus Christ' 'taketh hold'.[2] In this strange wrestling match the story of Jacob repeats itself. The new Israel, like the old, is wounded in the struggle, and yet prevails. The type, however, is fulfilled after a different fashion. For here the divine wrestler also prevails and that completely, since it is only the victory of the new Man over the old Adam which can establish the new Israel. When the old Adam is finally done away, then and only then will the identity of the new Israel with the victorious new Man be complete and final. Until that event the conflict within the soul of the Church is like a vanguard action. For the new Israel serves as the spearhead of the new Man in his penetration of the hostile army. The interior conflict is a microcosm of a vaster conflict of cosmic dimensions. Its issue will not be commensurate with a mere *pax civitatis terrenae*. For it will continue until the sun rises over Penuel,—that is until the dawn of that unending day when God is seen face to face.

iv

A supposed contrast in NT between 'new birth' and 'death and resurrection' disappears with fresh knowledge. Hebrew idioms of identification: (1) In child-birth the matrix of life is the underworld, and safe delivery is a return from death. This implies (2) an identification of motherhood with fruitful earth. So (3) re-birth of nature (reviving plant-life) includes within its cycle a resurrection of man.

Within recent memory a contrast was not uncommonly drawn between the Johannine doctrine of regeneration and the Pauline association of baptism with Christ's death and resurrection, the former being supposed to have a pagan back-

[1] Gen. 28^{11} and 32^{24ff}. [2] Rom. 5^{15}, Heb. 2^{16}.

ground.[1] This theory gravely over-simplified the evidence of the New Testament, and completely ignored the Old Testament background, in which the two modes of expression are, as we shall see, closely interwoven.[2] Here, as elsewhere, anthropology has lengthened our perspectives, penetrated surface impressions, smoothed out supposed antitheses, and gone far towards a vindication of unity in the biblical revelation. Such new light is welcome; for the concept of 'new birth' does not, in itself, suggest to the modern mind any content of thought in the least akin to the death and resurrection of Jesus. In the present volume, however, the ground has been prepared in two respects. In Book I we analyzed the biblical ideas of 'return to the beginning' and found a connexion with 'humiliation'.[3] Then, in Book II the new birth has been found to be associated (*a*) with the cosmic conflict of the divine Word and (*b*) with his historical humiliation as he identified himself with sinful humanity. The latter of these two associations, first manifested in John 1^{12-14}, confronted us again in the discourse with Nicodemus where the double scandal of new birth and uplifted serpent appeared to form one mystery.

Nevertheless, we might still be tempted to suppose that a conjunction of the brazen serpent with teaching about new birth was purely fortuitous, unless we had some evidence of a quite unmistakable character which showed their essential congruity. This is precisely what the Old Testament actually provides; and to this evidence, therefore, we now turn. In so doing we make a leap forward from the story of Israel in the wilderness to the era of the 'writing' prophets. The starting point of our investigation is to be found in the Book of Hosea. Our previous discussion of Hosea's prophecies was concerned with his allegorical treatment of his unhappy marriage, the prophet's faithless wife providing a type of Israel the unfaithful spouse of Jahveh. In chapter 13 he returns to this kind of imagery. But now he is preoccupied, not with the ethics of

[1] W. L. Knox, however, in the judicious note at the end of his Schweich lectures, could find no adequate explanation along these lines (*Some Hellenistic Elements in Primitive Christianity* pp. 90 *ff.*)

[2] For some aspects of the Semitic background see I. IX. §§ iv and v, pp. 274–286. For St Paul see especially *ib.* p. 282 with note.

[3] Ch. II, § i, pars. 6 ff.

marriage, but with the crisis of childbirth which is its natural sequel. Here the possibility of Israel's conversion and regeneration is realistically envisaged in terms of an actual physical birth. The description oscillates in characteristic Hebrew fashion, so that 'Ephraim' (the northern kingdom) is alternatively identified first with the mother and then with the unborn son.

We follow here the American Jewish rendering:

> The throes of a travailing woman shall come upon him; he is an unwise son; for it is time he should not tarry in the place of the breaking forth of children.
>
> Shall I ransom them from the power of the nether-world? Shall I redeem them from death? Ho, thy plagues, O death! Ho, thy destruction, O nether-world! Repentance be hid from mine eyes!
>
> (Hosea $13^{13, 14}$, quoted from the Jewish Soncino commentary.)

In this image successive generations of a people are linked under the figure of child-birth. Each generation gives birth to the next. An unworthy people are unlikely to produce a new generation which is better than its forefathers. The image, however, is not a vehicle of moral generalities. It exhibits a crisis of destiny. The issue is not simply one of 'better or worse'; it is a question whether there is to be any future for Israel at all. For, unless Israel is re-born with a new outlook, judgement will fall, and the holy people will be finally rejected. Under the chosen image disaster might be attributed to the fault either of the mother or of the child. Here the unborn child is defective; the new generation has not learnt its lesson from the past. At the crisis of child-birth 'tarrying' in the womb endangers the lives of both mother and child. So 'the old order will perish and a new one will be powerless to come into existence'. In another time of crisis the allegory is repeated from the mouth of King Hezekiah in a form which attributes disaster to the mother's side.[1] In view of his second chapter Hosea would not have repudiated that form of the image. 'Like mother, like child.' The faithless bride of Jahveh was to blame, if her issue had no future.

In the rendering of verse 14 adopted here it is manifest that the prophet offers no hope of a successful birth taking place.

[1] 'This day is a day of trouble, and of rebuke, and of contumely: For children are come to the birth, and there is not strength to bring them forth.' (2 Kings 19^3).

In other words Israel has 'tarried' too long already, and there will be no regeneration. This gloomy picture agrees with the tone of the passage as a whole (verses 12, 15); it also agrees with a similar outlook in that version of chapter 2 which the weight of modern scholarship allows to be original.[1] For our present purpose, however, what is important is not the original tone of the prophet's words, but the pattern of imagery which he employs. In particular what is the connexion between the birth-image of verse 13 and the awesome picture of the nether-world in verse 14? If the child dies unborn, then the womb, the matrix of life, has become an abode of death. From this point of view a successful birth would be an escape from death and a return to life. Here then we seem to have the starting-point of an idiom which finds in birth a resurrection from the dead.[2] But behind this identification of birth with return from Sheol (the Hebrew underworld) there lies another identity idiom of equal importance.

It will be remembered that in our treatment of Hosea's second chapter it was pointed out that 'in the Semitic world a people was commonly identified with the land in which it dwelt'. So to be born from the people would have the same meaning as to be born from the land. As Israel the bride is Israel the land, so every mother in Israel would and could represent the land by an idiom of identification. There are several examples of this mode of expression. In Psalm 139^{13-15} the psalmist gives thanks to God for his creation in the prenatal period of existence. In the first of these three verses the creative activity is described as taking place in the mother's womb; in the third verse it is declared to have been 'wrought in the lowest parts of the earth'. So also in Job 1^{21} we read: 'Naked came I out of my mother's womb, and naked shall I return thither'. One such instance might be dismissed as metaphor, but not three, all expressed differently, yet all containing the same identification. Moreover we shall find this same idiom

[1] see above, Ch. II § i, par. 5.

[2] Although the belief in a resurrection of the dead does not become *explicit* earlier than Ezekiel's vision (Ch. 37).

There is an instructive parallel to Hos. $13^{13, 14}$ in Jer. 20^{14-18}, where the prophet curses the day of his birth and regrets that he did not die an unborn babe: 'so my mother should have been my grave.'

fully alive in the New Testament. In Hebrew cosmogony Sheol is 'the pit' under the earth to which the departed descend after death. It is, therefore, not incorrect to describe it as 'the lowest part of the earth'. Yet Job finds it natural to say that, at death, he will 'return' to his mother's womb.

There is another idiom which we must notice here, closely akin to that which identifies mother-Israel with mother-earth The children of the former are identified with the fruit of the latter. So Jeremiah's picture of Israel the bride passes immediately into the following image: 'Israel is the Lord's hallowed portion, his first-fruits of the increase' (2^{3}). We may compare the exclamation of St Elisabeth to our Lord's mother in Luke 1^{42}: 'blessed is the fruit of thy womb'. This use of the word 'fruit' is normal in the Old Testament and it reflects a primitive world in which man is still very close to the earth and the rest of the 'all flesh' which earth sustains, a world in which man has not yet become sharply separated from 'nature'.[1] Another facet of this primitive outlook appears in the description of Solomon's birth set forth in Wisdom 7^{1-3}. It begins with a reference to his origin 'from one born of the earth, the first-formed' (Adam), and concludes with Solomon's descriptive phrase: 'I fell upon the kindred earth'. The latter idiom for birth is also employed in Isaiah 26^{19}, where the text quite possibly applies this birth-idiom to the miracle of resurrection promised in the preceding half-verse.

Isaiah 26^{17-19} is a particularly important example of the group of idioms which we have been examining. Although there are obscurities about the last two lines (19^{b}) the passage as a whole is clearly in line with the thought of Hosea $13^{13, 14}$. There is the same idiom of child-birth; and here Israel acknowledges her inability to bring forth offspring. According to the present text of verse 18 this frustration of hope is expressed in the cry: 'We have as it were brought forth wind'.The last line of this verse may be read as an acknowledgement that 'the new age has not dawned in a re-birth *or* as a statement that the hoped-for resurrection has not taken place. This confession of human failure, however, is answered by a divine promise of resurrection in the first two lines of verse 19. There follows a difficult

[1] This is one of the most far-reaching differences between ancient and modern cultures, on which see I. IV., *passim.*

reference to 'thy dew' which the most recent commentator takes to mean 'the vivifying principle which God sends to bring the dead to life as the dew revives vegetation'.[1] The parallel between a revival of plant life and a human resurrection is here fairly certain; and this corresponds to a constant tendency of primitive culture noticed in the preceding paragraph. We are here still in the world of fertility cults, where the annual re-birth of nature includes within its scope a 'death and resurrection' of the gods, and a promise that human life will be renewed.[2]

V

The idioms of identification in NT. In St Paul re-birth imagery takes three forms: (1) the risen life issues from filial status in a new family; (2) the birth of Isaac a type of Christ's resurrection; (3) cosmic restoration identified with the travailing of Mother Eve and her children. In the Johannine cycle the messianic birth includes death and resurrection, and embraces the whole messianic community within its orbit.

In Chapter I (last paragraph) it was pointed out that 'any state of misery can be identified with descent into the under-world of Sheol'; and this use of language is not infrequent in the psalter. A more precise instance of the idiom is furnished in Isaiah $5^{13, 14}$. According to the present text it is suggested that Israel going into exile is all one with Israel descending into Sheol; and the latter is represented as a monster opening its mouth to receive its victims and to swallow them up. To a de-

[1] The Soncino Comm. (1949), p. 121. This rendering would cover either of two alternative readings: 'dew of lights' or 'dew of herbs'. The latter phrase has been defended by J. W. Jack in *The Ras Shamra Tablets, their bearing on the Old Testament* (Edinburgh. 1935). He explains 'the custom of placing flat hollowed stones at the entrance to tombs, in order to gather the rain as dew' as an example of sympathetic magic. 'It was believed that these forces of Nature would ultimately bring about the resurrection of the deceased, just as they revive a plant.' (*op. cit.*, Ch. vi, p. 47.)

[2] If LXX has preserved the correct reading in 19^b, we should render 'thy dew is the dew of their new flesh', which Gray (in ICC) explains thus: 'as God revives the vegetable world by dew, so he will cause new flesh to sprout (Isa. 58^8), and cover the skeletons (cp. Ezek. 37^6) of the Jews now lying in the grave, thus preparing them for a re-birth'. He compares Ps. 139^{12-16}, referred to in the text above (*ib.*, p. 447).

vout Israelite the state of exile in an unclean land is like a living death, and this is expressed mythologically. For us such language would be used only in metaphor. But primitive thought moves in *a world of images where metaphor and reality are all one.* It is from this standpoint that we must understand the idioms of identification, so foreign to our fashions of thought, of which examples were given in the last section. Moreover, in this respect the New Testament belongs essentially to the same cultural world as the Old Testament. The forces which have moulded the modern mind into quite different habits of thought did not gather volume and pace until a much later period of history. These considerations are vital, if we are to recognize the character of the thought-processes which underlie the literary images of primitive Christian writings. The particular illustration from Isaiah mentioned above will prove highly relevant at a later stage of the argument, before the close of the present chapter.

It must now be noticed that the gloomy oracle of Hosea $13^{13, 14}$ is capable of being understood in a more optimistic way. It was so understood by the authors of the Septuagint and in other versions; and St Paul quotes from verse 14 following a version which gives this more optimistic interpretation. His citation of the prophecy occurs at the culminating point of the apostle's argument concerning the resurrection in 1 Corinthians 15. Moreover, the fact that an oracle of re-birth is applied in this way by the principal exponent of a 'death and resurrection' theology in the New Testament is in itself highly significant for the continuity of typical Hebrew idioms. It seems desirable, therefore, to examine the matter more fully. We know from other contexts that St Paul was familiar with the idiom of re-birth. In two passages he uses it, one of them from this same epistle.[1] Now in the more hopeful rendering of Hosea 13^{14} the successful issue of the birth is represented as occurring through an act of God: 'I will ransom thee from the hand of Sheol; I will redeem thee from death'. It is this version which is followed in Isaiah 26, where after the barren efforts of his people, Jahveh carries out a miracle of restoration to life. Thus the new birth through resurrection might be regarded as an act of

[1] 1 Cor. 4^{14-17} and Gal. 4^{19}. For these and other NT examples see I. IX., p. 282 and note.

divine begetting, which is precisely what new birth must be in the Johannine view.

With these facts in mind, let us turn to the argument in 1 Corinthians 15. The quotations in verses 54, 55 show that the apostle connects the promises of the little apocalypse (Isaiah 24–27) with Hosea 13, as we have done. But the argument which here concerns us begins further back. The diversities of creation suggest to him a further diversity between the two creations, the old and the new, between the 'soulish' life proper to the first Adam and his family and the 'spiritual' life which characterizes 'the last Adam' and those whom he quickens. The head of the old Adamic family was earth-born and transmitted an earth-born image to his children. 'The second Man is from heaven' and transmits a heavenly image to his new family. Thus the earth-born family is powerless to 'inherit the kingdom of God'. For it is subject to the divine sentence: earth to earth; 'dust thou art and unto dust shalt thou return'. From such resources there can be no re-birth into immortality. Yet God can bring about this very impossibility, and he will do so. Then there follows (from Isaiah 25^{8}): 'Death is swallowed up in victory', and (from Hosea 13^{14}) 'O death, where is thy victory? O death, where is thy sting?' Thus the promises of resurrection are attached to our entry into the family of the Man who is 'from heaven' (15^{35-57}).

In its main lines this is a continuation of the old Hebrew re-birth pattern. Yet the fulfilment surpasses the type. For, whereas in both resurrection is an act of God supervening upon human failure, in the fulfilment this divine act is the crowning event of a new creation-order. So, whereas the type must show re-birth *in* the event of resurrection, the antitype traces the new birth back to our incorporation into a new family. Later the apostle was obliged to re-think the consequences of this change, with the result that he conceived the new resurrection-event in terms of a process which begins in baptism. Yet the connexion of resurrection with re-birth is maintained in the new setting. This appears from Romans 8^{23} where the process of re-birth into adopted sonship is completed only in the final 'redemption of the body'. Our filial status is not fully achieved until the body is raised from the dead. Thus re-birth and resurrection still belong, in the end, to one pattern. God 'made us sons' by an act of condescending grace. This, however, was no legal formality. It was new life imparted by creative act of fatherhood. It was the beginning of a filial status which is also a birth-process. For even now Christ is being formed in us.

So far we have been tracing a connexion between birth imagery and resurrection in St Paul's thought. Now, however, we must turn our attention to the other idioms of identification which in prophetic oracles were seen to belong to the same pattern. If we find similar phenomena in the apostolic thought-images our case for continuity will be strengthened. Let us take next the identification of motherhood with mother-earth. As in Hosea 2 Israel the foolish bride is threatened with reduction to a condition like that of barren land, so in Galatians 4^{25} Hagar, the inferior wife, is identified quite simply with 'Mt Sinai in Arabia' where the law was given. By contrast Sarah, the proper mother of the faithful, is identified with the heavenly Jerusalem, as representing the higher wisdom of the gospel. After that it occasions no surprise to find a variation upon this theme in Romans 4^{16-25}. Here we have a bold piece of typology which looks like a reversal of Hosea's prediction of unsuccessful birth. The apostle sees the story of Isaac's birth from aged parents as a prefiguring of Christ's resurrection from the tomb. As in prophecy, birth and resurrection have one meaning; and the happy birth of Abraham's son is a sort of dress-rehearsal for the miracle of Easter Day. Moreover, this implies a further identification of Sarah's body with the rock-tomb from which Jesus rose again. The old Greek tag about *sôma sêma* (the body is the prison-house of the soul)[1] had its Semitic counterpart which made the womb to be a tomb. But the ever-open tomb of Jesus is a veritable matrix of new life, a source of new birth to the whole world.

In Romans 5–8 we return from the seed of Abraham to the family of Adam. These chapters should be read on the background of the creation cycle. From the new Adam and his stock we pass in chapter 7 to a vivid temptation scene recalling the serpent's seduction of Eve. In chapter 8, however, defeat is turned into victory, and from 8^{18} onwards the birth-pangs of a new age are set upon the background of Genesis 3. In the old story the curse upon mother-earth ('thorns and thistles')

[1] cp. Wisd. 9^{15}.

corresponds to the travail-pangs of mother-Eve. But in the new version creation is personified and mother earth undergoes the travail of mother-Eve. As in Hosea, so here both sides of the birth-crisis are represented. The new children of God, like Adam and Eve, have their share in the travail of mother-earth. They await the completion of re-birth in that renovation of all things which belongs to the general resurrection. To sum up, as Israel was re-born in the risen Christ (Romans 4) so all creation is re-born in his risen community (Romans 8). The resurrection of Jesus was the re-birth of the world; and the pattern of re-birth is repeated in the family of the new Adam, which is identified on one side with creation as a whole and on the other side with the redeemed community.

When we turn from Romans to Revelation there is development of the pattern, but no clear evidence of discontinuity. The principal development is to be seen in the figure of the new Eve. The vision of Revelation 12 seems to pre-suppose the gospel tradition concerning the Mother of Jesus. In other respects the vision sums up every ancient oracle concerning the promised Seed in a new Genesis-Exodus mystery. Only one point need detain us here. From the Christian point of view there appears a strange gap in the sequence. Why is the messianic child caught up to heaven immediately after birth? Why is there no reference to the Lord's death and resurrection?[1] The answer, surely, lies in the prophetic idiom of re-birth. For this has two aspects: (1) On the one hand this idiom defines resurrection in terms of birth into filial status; (2) on the other hand, and from another point of view, a birth is regarded as a consequence of death and resurrection. We have seen that St Paul finds our filial status fully attained only in 'the redemption of our body', that is the final resurrection. But it appears from Romans 1^4 that (on the authority of certain messianic texts) he held an analogous belief concerning our Lord himself.[2] The messianic sonship was inaugurated officially when Jesus rose from the dead. On Easter Day Jesus was, in his manhood, accepted as God's messianic son in a sense foretold to David by Nathan.[3]

[1] This feature of the vision completely baffled R. H. Charles (see his IC Comm: Vol. I, p. 320, last par.), although he had all the OT facts before him (e.g. *ib.* p. 317).

[2] Details in *The Common Life*, pp. 270 ff.

[3] 2 Sam. $7^{12\,ff}$.

We in turn are 'adopted' into that messianic sonship through our union with the risen Christ, and now await its fulness. On the other hand the whole virtue of that sonship flows from the death and resurrection, as the language of Romans 1^4 seems to indicate. Similarly in the Apocalypse (chapter 5) the Lion of Judah (Son of David) wields his messianic power in history in his character as the Lamb, that is the Servant who died and rose again.

So we may understand the vision in Revelation 12 as a 'new birth' picture which is inevitably complex because it depicts the antitype in terms of the type. The re-birth of Israel as God's son took place in Jesus. But the fulfilment took actual shape in a life-story, every part of which corresponded in some sense to the original prophetic pattern. Thus the Virgin-Birth of Jesus, as described by St Luke, refers us back to the tabernacle and its cultus in such a way that from his conception onwards Jesus is already the sacrificial victim.[1] From this point of view the birth includes the death and the resurrection. How should it not be so? If God the Son becomes mortal man in a fallen world he has already identified himself with 'the son fallen into the pit'.[2] The virginal matrix of life marks the site of a first step downwards in the 'descent into hell', and there is no way out save through the appointed path of death and resurrection. Similarly in St John's Gospel a comparison of 16^{20-22} with Isaiah 66^{5-14} will show the persisting pattern of re-birth oracles to be once more repeated. For the pattern here is identical in detail. It takes this form in Isaiah: warning of persecution, birth-parable, joy after grief. Beginning at 15^{21} this sequence is reproduced in John 15 and 16 with one significant insertion. As in Romans 8 the sequence of Genesis 3 is interrupted by a victory section (8^{1-17}) after the temptation scene of chapter 7, so in John 15^{23}–16^{15} a promise of the Paraclete to partner the persecuted Christians in their witness is inserted into the new creation picture at the end of Isaiah. The antitype always surpasses the type.[3]

[1] For fuller details on topics in this section see my contribution to a symposium entitled *The Mother of God* (Dacre Press) and *The Common Life* (Addit. Note C), p. 320.

[2] cp. the discussion of Luke 14^5 in Ch. II, § ii and Addit. Note C.

[3] Although even here the insertion may be occasioned by the emphasis upon παράκλησις in the Greek version of Isa. 66^{10-13}.

In the prophetic picture last mentioned the whole nation is reborn; and so it is in the fulfilment. 'In the regeneration' (Matthew 19[28]) the disciples share a common joy with the Saviour because they are partakers with him in the new birth (John 16[22]; 1[13]). In the event another detail of the ancient scheme also comes to fulfilment. 'Your heart shall rejoice and your bones shall rise up as a plant' (Isaiah 66[14]); this corresponds to Isaiah 26[19] with Ezekiel 37 in the background. The re-birth of Israel took place in the death and resurrection of the Messiah; for the new *ecclesia* was initiated through identification with him.[1] So it might truly be said that in the Easter joy of the disciples they became sharers in his risen life. The scenes in John 20, 21 are thus the Johannine way of expressing the Pauline doctrine of mystical union with the risen Lord.

vi

The cosmic drama of creation, conflict and re-birth unfolded in Israel's history and recapitulated in Christ. Israel in exile, the story of Jonah and the biblical pattern of re-birth to be connected. With this agree the Lucan setting of the Jonah typology and the re-birth language of Acts 2[24].

At the end of Chapter IV it was suggested that the theme of conflict in the history of redemption might throw further light upon the Johannine prologue, notwithstanding the fact that the evangelist is writing a new version of the creation-cycle set forth in Genesis. If the reader will turn back to the opening paragraphs of Chapter II, section ii, he will find a fuller explanation in terms of what I there called 'the Genesis-Exodus mystery'. Creation is ever renewed in redemptive history, just as that history is itself creatively repeated or resumed when it is first summed up in Christ and then extended from him in epochs of new creation which are also and equally epochs of redemptive history. From this point of view it would be intelligible that the prologue of St John (like other parts of Scripture) could be read at different levels or depths. In this way John 1[4,5] might be interpreted in more than one way. Initially (according to our

[1] The context of this sentence will be found in Chs. VIII and IX of *The Common Life*.

interpretation) it seems to refer to the story of Adam and Eve in language drawn from the poem of creation in Genesis 1. In this way the dividing of light from darkness is understood as the inauguration of a conflict; and further this conflict of cosmic elements is identified with its more picturesque counterpart, the battle between Eve and the serpent.

By such a device the promise that Eve's seed shall bruise the serpent's head is given a cosmic significance, just as the same effect is produced in Revelation 12 by putting this new version of the original conflict into an astronomical setting. Moreover we have already found reason for thinking that these two pictures, the old and the new, belong together in a single design. For we found a parallel between '*Zoë* in *Logos*' (John 1^{4}) and the contrasted vision of the 'Lamb in the Bride' (Revelation 21)[1] But also, in the second place, we found a further parallel between John $1^{3,4}$ and John 1^{12-14}.[2] It looks as if, in the prologue, the evangelist is drawing together into one three distinct pictures: (1) Eve and the serpent, (2) the new Eve and the dragon, (3) the virgin-born Son and the new-born children. The three pictures, moreover, are drawn together by the promise in Genesis 3^{15} and its fulfilment in Christ and the church. For Genesis 3 points forward to a promised victory of Eve's progeny over the serpent; Revelation 12 gives us a picture of the way in which the promise was fulfilled. John 1^{3-14} completes the unification in a statement which includes implicitly all the picture-images, of which there are more besides the three just now mentioned.

In placing the living organism of creation in the Word the evangelist glances at 'Eve in Adam' (another way of setting the Eden story in a cosmic frame).[3] But he also glances forward through the serpent-conflict to the final picture where the victorious Lamb abides in the new mother-Eve, the city of God. Here there is reflected the customary Hebrew oscillation between Israel the mystic bride and Israel the mother of Messiah. Despite this complication, however, the diagram in Chapter IV, § ii (paragraph 2) received fuller justification through our analysis of a Johannine sequence. For near the end of the

[1] Ch. IV, § ii.
[2] Ch. IV, § iv.
[3] cp. I. VIII., p. 242 and I. IX., pp. 263 ff.

sequence we found the Son of God and those who believe on his name included together in the womb of the new Eve (John 1[12,13]); and that in turn corresponds to their joint-inclusion within the new Jerusalem (Revelation 21). This togetherness of Christ and his people in the new Eve may seem less extravagant, if we remember the biblical pattern of re-birth as a whole. From Hosea onwards the birth-parable is a picture of national regeneration. It is Israel as a whole which is re-born, and in the fulfillment this means Jesus and his disciples together. There is one re-birth just as there is one death and resurrection. As 'all died' in Christ (2 Corinthians 5[14]), so all were included in his birth into the world, and again in his re-birth into a new world on Easter Day.[1]

There is more that could be said concerning this method of interpreting the prologue. We will however, concentrate upon one particular application of the method for which the evangelist has himself seemingly provided the clue. The concluding phrase of John 1[5] corresponds verbally to a phrase in the Greek version of Jeremiah 51[34], where, in a dirge over the fall of Babylon Israel says: '*Darkness* devoured me, divided me, *overwhelmed* me; Nebuchadnezzar, king of Babylon, swallowed me, as a dragon he filled his belly from my delicacy'. To the two italicised words corresponds the phrase in the gospel, but with a negative inserted. Here we notice that the king of Babylon is described as a dragon devouring Israel in the captivity in accordance with Isaiah's prediction (5[14]). But also he is identified with darkness. Similarly in Psalm 74[13,14], recounting the exodus story, Pharaoh and his host are identified with sea-monsters. In both instances the story of Israel's conflict with her enemies is aligned with the ancient conflict of the creation myth, where the slaying of a monster is the prelude to creation.

[1] In the light of these considerations an important distinction must be made concerning our use of the term 'new Eve'. To Israel as bride of God corresponds the church as bride of the God-man. Between these two pieces of symbolism, however, lies a time-interval which is filled by the gospel history. In the two gospel narratives concerning the birth of Jesus the rôle of Israel as mother of the Messiah is filled *not by a symbolic figure but by a historical person*. Mary of Nazareth thus became in a quite definite sense the anti-type of old Israel and the type of new Israel. For the maternal vocation of God's people is first concentrated in her alone, and then extended from her to the bride of her Son.

These facts throw a flood of light upon the Johannine sequence. As the dragon is identified with primeval darkness in Jeremiah, so the evangelist, in referring to a conflict of light and darkness, connects darkness with 'the old serpent', Eve's seducer, the dragon of the Apocalypse.

What, then, is the evangelist telling us? First this, that as creation is interwoven with redemptive history, so too the cosmic conflict is conceived to be continuous with that interweaving. In his version the conflict was inaugurated at creation. For 'the devil sinneth from the beginning' (1 John 3[8]). As the darkness seemed to triumph in Eden, so also in Israel's history. Yet the light which seemed to be swallowed re-appeared. As Israel went down into the monster's mouth and returned to life again, so has there taken place a re-birth of Israel in the incarnation of the Word. The birth of the promised Seed in Jesus is the final return of Israel from the underworld of darkness in a new creation victory. Hosea's gloomy prediction, illustrated in the Babylonian captivity, but never accepted after the restoration of the theocracy, was indeed fulfilled in Israel-after-the-flesh, but also finally reversed in the new Israel, Jesus and his church. With this conclusion we are now in a position to take note of one further chapter in the history of the birth-parable and its fulfilment. The Book of the prophet Jonah, although not referred to directly by St Mark or St John is prominent in the records of our Lord's teaching in the two other gospels. It has also a literary connexion with that section of Jeremiah's prophecies in which we found a verbal link with John 1[5]. Moreover, there are grounds for thinking that St Luke may have connected the figure of Jonah with the theme of re-birth. These points must now be explained.

Running through the Old Testament we find various pictorial representations of Sheol, the Hebrew underworld. We have already noticed that some of these pictures do not easily harmonize, for example, a pit below the earth to which mortals descend and, on the other hand, a monster who catches luckless persons in his mouth or with his hand. The disharmonious character of such alternatives is sometimes seriously perplexing to the modern reader who looks for logical unification where primitive peoples do not find it necessary. The identification of the king of Babylon both with the darkness of chaos and with the ancient dragon is a case in point; but it is also a very pertinent instance. For the dragon is a version of Tiamat, the primeval monster of Babylonian mythology; and the Hebrew counterpart is *Tehôm*, 'the deep', that is the primeval waters referred to at the beginning of the creation-poem (Genesis 1²) in the words: 'there was darkness upon the face of the deep'. Thus there is oscillation between a monster, the watery deep and darkness, the latter being connected with chaos and with Sheol. It is this fluctuation of images which is a main key to the story of Jonah. For one of the great perplexities of that story is the fact that it contains not one monster but two!

This fact is not evident to the average reader, partly because he is not acquainted with the original text, and partly because the idiom and its mythological background are not familiar. Everyone knows that Jonah was swallowed by a fish; and this bizarre incident distracts attention from the event which immediately precedes it (two verses earlier). Yet the language used in Jonah 1^{15} strongly suggests that the sea itself is regarded as a raging monster whose wrath is placated only when Jonah is thrown to it as a 'scape-goat' for the rest of the ship's company. Why then are there two monsters? The answer must be twofold: (1) We have already noticed an etymological connection between 'the deep' and the primeval monster. This connection reaches the point of actual identification in certain passages, notably Job 7^{12} and 26^{12}. The sea is regarded as a raging monster. (2) There are therefore two strata in the book. The fish which swallows a man and ejects him is a typical folk-lore story for which there are parallels. The other stratum belongs to the creation-myth. 'Rahab' (Job 9^{13}, 26^{12}) is the Hebrew name for Tiamat, 'the ocean monster which had to be overcome by God before chaos gave place to an ordered universe'.[1] Finally these two elements remain side by side in the story because identification of sea and monster is accompanied by 'oscillation' in which the two entities remain distinct.[2]

In the final form of the book a prayer is put into Jonah's mouth which he prayed 'out of the fish's belly'. Here it is

[1] Soncino Comm. on Job 9^{13}, p. 41.

[2] On this see the footnote to p. 279 of I. IX., and below, note to next par. but one.

noticeable that, although still in the fish, Jonah speaks as though he were also still in the sea into which he was cast (1^{15}), and yet at the same time 'in the belly of Sheol'.[1] Thus we have now a further identification of Sheol with the sea and the sea-monster! Sheol has a hand (Hosea 13^{14}), a mouth (Isaiah 5^{14}) and a belly (Jonah 2^{3}).[2] A later verse tells us that Sheol is located at the bottom of the sea; and now the ocean-monster is regarded as a subterranean pit, a sort of infernal prison with bars (2^{6} EVV).[3]

This analysis shows that in the Book of Jonah as read by our Lord and his disciples the escape of Jonah from his terrible adventure would be regarded as a return from death to life. But the meaning put upon the story would depend greatly upon its place among various possible parallels in the Old Testament, some of which we have already surveyed. The story dates from some time after the Exile, and would therefore be subsequent to its nearest parallel, the swallowing up of Israel by the dragon-king of Babylon in Jeremiah. Moreover there is a further point of affinity between the two pieces. The divine sentence upon the Babylonian dragon runs as follows: 'I will bring forth out of his mouth that which he hath swallowed up' (51^{44}). That which was thus foretold came to fulfilment in the return from exile; and so the later book duly records Jonah's return from Sheol's belly. In short the story has an allegorical character in so far as it reflects Israel's recent experience of captivity and restoration.[4]

In all this there is nothing about re-birth. Nevertheless the experience of Jonah as portrayed corresponds to that of the

[1] (i) 'The weeds were wrapped about my head' (2^{5} EVV) is the result of the event in 1^{15}, and is inconsistent with the fish story. (ii) LXX intensifies the identification of Sheol with the monster by using *κοιλία* throughout for 'belly' where Heb. has two words.

[2] Jonah 2^{3} (Heb.) = 2^{2} in EVV.

[3] In Job 38, however, Sheol has 'gates' to hold the sea-monster in!

[4] And so has nothing to do with the obscure person whose name is attached to the book at the beginning (1^{1}). The allegorism can be disputed only if the fish-story is abstracted from its mythological background, which is identical with that of Jer. 51.

The quotation from Jer. 51^{44} in the text above identifies the 'dragon' with the Babylonian god Bel, another instance of oscillation exactly parallel to the one referred to in I. IX., p. 279, note.

unborn child in Hosea 13, provided that Hosea's oracle be given a hopeful interpretation. Moreover the affinity of Jonah with the dragon-allegory in Jeremiah links it also with John 1^5 and with the whole biblical pattern of re-birth. If Jonah is Israel, his return to life is a re-birth of God's people. Now our examination of the re-birth pattern has shown that it includes death and resurrection; and that aspect of the pattern is the one which corresponds most obviously to Jonah's experience. It is not surprising therefore that in the tradition of St Matthew's Gospel our Lord represents Jonah as a type of himself exclusively from this point of view. To that we shall return later. Our present concern is with the collocation of conflict and re-birth. It is this collocation which may be implicit in the setting of St Luke's only reference to Jonah as a type of Christ. In Luke 11, from verse 14 onwards, Jesus is in conflict with the Pharisees. Into the midst of this conflict is inserted the short Jonah section (11^{29-32}) and immediately before it an incident which seems at first sight to have no connexion with its context. A woman in the crowd addresses to our Lord these words: 'Blessed is the womb that bare thee, and the breasts which thou didst suck'. Jesus replies: 'Yea rather blessed are they that hear the word of God and keep it' ($11^{27, 28}$).

It is never safe to ignore the order in which subject-matter is arranged in the four gospels. So let us consider. The woman's remark refers to 'the place' which housed the unborn Jesus; and the section immediately preceding tells of an unhallowed place which housed a company of demons. Our Lord's reply to the woman beatifies those who obey God's word, and is almost identical with the saying in which he described the members of his new family (8^{21}). Moreover this blessing of the obedient comes appropriately before a reference to the disobedient prophet who went through the ordeal of a re-birth into life, whereby he became a converting 'sign' to the Ninevites. Next, the word for 'womb' (*koilia*) strikes the eye. It occurs three times in the Greek version of Jonah 2^{1-3} and three times in Luke 1^{41-44}. The latter passage contains the benediction of Saint Elisabeth upon 'the fruit of thy womb', addressed to the mother of Jesus on the occasion of their mutual greeting. The phrase recalls what was said earlier about this use of language in scripture and the connexion of such terminology with the pattern of re-birth.[1] Lastly the collocation of the obedient (members of Christ's new family) with a reference to the birth of Jesus corresponds closely with the parallel collocation in John 1^{12-14}. Moreover it must be assumed that the evangelist saw no conflict between the beatitude of 1^{42} and the antithesis implied in 8^{21} and 11^{28}. Indeed the concluding words of Elisabeth (1^{45}) identify Mary with those to whom her Son's benediction refers.[2]

[1] Ch. V. § iv, par. 6.

[2] St Luke's familiarity with the biblical language of re-birth is evident from Acts 2^{24} (St Peter speaking): 'Whom God raised up, having loosed *the pangs of death*, because it was not possible for him to be holden by it'. This is a Christian version of 'the birth-pangs of the Messiah'. In LXX the phrase *ὠδῖνες θανάτου* occurs in Ps. 17^{5} (=2 Reg. 22^{6}) and in Ps. 114^{3}. The Hebrew expression could refer either to the 'cords' or 'the birth-pangs' of Sheol. The literal meaning is that the Hades monster was in parturition with One whom God loosed from bonds of captivity. The 'travail' of hell could not withhold Jonah's antitype from re-birth.

CHAPTER VI

THE DIVINE VICTORY

i

The all-inclusiveness of saving events, formally stated in the Prologue, is symbolized in the Transfiguration. 'Six days' of new creation in rehearsal and in actuality. The implied recapitulation of scripture and Jewish tradition in the fourfold gospel. The way through Calvary to Easter is like access to glory in the wilderness.

In Chapters IV and V we considered the divine conflict with evil mainly through the medium of St John's prologue. In so doing we found ourselves engaged in a study of the 'wholeness' or 'all-inclusiveness' which characterizes the events of the gospel. Actually the prologue has its centre and pivot in one particular event, namely the Incarnation. When, however, we ask ourselves the question: 'Of what is the Incarnation here seen to be the centre or pivot?' the simplest answer would be 'Of everything in heaven and earth', or more exactly 'of creation and history regarded as a single arena of conflict and redemption'. Thus, for example, we found ourselves looking at the new beginning in Christ in terms of the old beginning in creation (1^{12-14} in terms of $1^{3,4}$); and yet, paradoxically, before that we had already looked at the Beginning as reflected in the End, creation foreshadowing the New Jerusalem (notwithstanding their contrasted features as displayed in diagram).[1] Another conclusion which emerged was what might be called a close interlocking of the various themes involved. We had already found creation and redemption interlocked in 'Genesis-Exodus' mysteries. Similarly we now saw this complex taking new forms of which nothing further need be said beyond a brief reminder.

In the Johannine version of the traditional creation story it could be seen that conflict was included within creativity. The creative activity of the Word is, so to speak, the site of the con-

[1] IV, ii, par. 2 preceding IV. iv, par. 2.

flict between light and darkness. Similarly we found the scandal of the cross to be involved in the fact of new birth; for new birth is new creation, a work of 'restoration' which challenges the powers of evil. Finally we found the same essential features present in the biblical pattern of re-birth. For here re-birth (which is re-creation) takes the form of resurrection from the dead. In the new creation Light emerges out of a pit of darkness, the kingdom of messianic sonship rises victorious from the depths of hell. Moreover the new world of that sonship in which God's children share is itself the product of a filial response which found expression through the fiery ordeal of death and resurrection. Death and resurrection are therefore still the solitary path of adopted sonship into which mankind is ever summoned by the trumpet-call of divine creativity.[1]

The inclusiveness which embraces all the parts within the whole will now receive further illustration from another point of view. In our detailed survey of John 1^{11-14} it was remarked that as a statement concerning the Incarnation those few verses manage to include 'within that mystery the whole order of redemptive history under both covenants, old and new'.[2] In that respect there can be few passages of scripture, if any, which present a formal statement having such a high degree of concentration. Formal statement, however, is not by any means the typical mode in which wholeness of revelation manifests itself. Symbolic pictures, or events symbolically described, would be the more normal medium. Even the statement to which we have just referred derives its concentrated character partly from the rich scriptural implications of its phraseology; and these are charged with suggestive power by virtue of the pictorial images which they evoke. In the first three gospels there is no parallel to the Johannine prologue. But there is one narrative within the synoptic frame which might fairly be regarded as exhibiting the same high degree of concentration, allowing for difference of form. I refer to the story of the Transfiguration. For that very reason this incident must occupy a good deal of our attention in the present chapter.

The Transfiguration of our Lord is represented in the gospels as an event in the sequence of events which comprise the gospel

[1] Exod. 19^{9-19}, Num. 10^{1-10}, 1 Cor. $15^{51\,ff}$.
[2] IV. iii., par. 5.

history. Yet, like some other events recorded, it is highly mysterious in its supra-normal characteristics; and further, it is described in a manner which seems intended to emphasize its symbolical character. Accordingly, much of the discussion which it has called forth has been occupied with the question: Of what did the evangelists suppose this event to be symbolical when they described it as they did? On this subject there has, in modern times, been no general agreement, except indeed to this extent; the Transfiguration has been generally believed to have a symbolic reference to a future denouement. It has been believed to foreshadow, for example, either the glorious conclusion of the gospel story or again a glorious consummation of redemptive history. Recently it has been suggested that it covers both alternatives because there is a profound sense in which they are to be identified.[1] The author of this suggestion also holds that the Transfiguration bears an integral relation, in St Mark's Gospel, to the earlier stages of the evangelical narrative. That, as we shall see, is antecedently probable. For this central event, more, perhaps, than any other in the first three gospels, recapitulates revelation in its fulness. Creation and history, as presented in both covenants, are here epitomized in their fulfilment.

There is, however, this further difference between the Prologue and the Transfiguration. The former shows the pivot of the whole in the event of the Incarnation, whereas (when all necessary qualifications have been made) the Transfiguration points forward to the death and resurrection of Jesus. Thus it appears that there are at least two ways of showing all-inclusive events in the story of redemption. All is included in the beginning, and all is summed up in the end. This ought not to surprise us, since Jesus is both the beginning and the end of all things finite, the Alpha and Omega in whom is comprised the entire sequence of temporal events. What we have to do now is to see how the three evangelists *relate* the Transfiguration in its setting to the story of Holy Week and Easter. If we can retrace the theological implications of that symbolic relation we shall have gone some way towards understanding the form in which the Divine Victory is presented to us in scripture.

[1] *A Study in St Mark* by Austin Farrer, pp. 150–153, 170. This gets us out of many difficulties of the 'either . . . or' type.

Each of the three evangelists has his own way of handling this great theme; yet there are also certain fundamental agreements which underlie all divergences. Some of the details have inevitably been touched upon in this volume and in its predecessor. What we are now concerned with, however, is something wider in scope which will involve a simultaneous reference to two different sections of the synoptic cycle, the one near the middle and the other at the culmination of the whole.

In St Mark's Gospel exact notes of time are to be found at two points only.[1] The story of the Transfiguration is introduced with these words: 'After six days Jesus taketh Peter and James and John ...'. This refers back to the confession of St Peter at Caesarea Philippi and the sayings which followed. If we examine this sequence more closely we find it includes the following: Jesus is acknowledged as 'the anointed one', and predicts his passion and rejection, death and resurrection. He summons men to follow him in the way of the cross and predicts his coming in glory. Then he is transfigured. Now turn to the other point of exact chronology. It is spread over chapters 11–16[8]. Here St Mark keeps a careful record of the days in the last week of our Lord's earthly life. The events of each day are detailed in order, so that we can say with some degree of exactness what happened on each day of the week. There is, perhaps, one point in the middle of the week (14[1]), where we cannot affirm with certainty that we are passing from Tuesday to Wednesday.[2] But the general intention of the evangelist is clear. He is counting off the days of a week. Now in scripture as a whole there is one week which stands out as having significance for every Jew. It is the week of creation which was spread over the six days of creative works followed by a sabbath-rest. So in the week of the Passion St Mark sees 'six days' in which the work of the new creation was accomplished, followed by a sabbath in which the body of Jesus rested in the tomb.

The parallel between the 'six days' of Mark 9[2] and the chronology of the passion history has been drawn in terms of a

[1] The 'forty days in the wilderness' (1[13]) is not 'exact' in the sense here intended, as it is not in exact relation to a sequence of events.

[2] If we accept Dr Farrer's chronology for Chs. 14–16 (Wednesday to Sunday) the break is only apparent; for Tuesday morning is scheduled at 11[20]; and all that follows to the end of 13 is *represented* as occurring on that day.

'creation' week, and that aspect of the parallel will require fuller justification. At this initial stage in the argument, however, the reader is reminded of all that has been said previously concerning the interweaving of creation and redemption as two strands in one pattern. For the most obvious link between the earlier six days and the final week lies in a parallel between the redemptive themes adumbrated or enacted respectively in each of these two periods. The parallel, in its simplest terms, is this: each of the two weeks begins with an acknowledgement of Jesus as Messiah, passes through a record of his humiliation and suffering and ends with his glorification. The principal difference between 8^{27}–9^{1} and chapters 11–16^{8} might be expressed by saying that what is rehearsed in speech on the former occasion is enacted in historical reality in the final week. The presumed parallel between the transfiguration and the resurrection stands on a different level. For here the 'rehearsal' of coming events passes from speech into a mysterious symbolism which is itself an event. Moreover it is to be assumed throughout this exposition that in the vision upon the mount death and resurrection are united under a single mystery and in a universal context.

One of the most baffling features of the transfiguration story in its context lies in the many-sided character of the scriptural background which can be invoked to throw light upon its meaning. One important aspect of the 'six days', for example, has been found in a possible alignment with Jewish feasts of 'the seventh month' (*Tishri*) which begins with a New Year festival and passes on to the Day of Atonement (*Tishri* 10) and the feast of 'tabernacles' (*Tishri* 15). St Peter's proposal to make 'three tabernacles' for Jesus, Moses and Elias (Mark 9^{5}) may indicate that the event took place about the time of this, the principal, Jewish feast. The 'six days' would then (according to Jewish reckoning) take us back to the Day of Atonement as the day of St Peter's confession; and this was also the day on which our Lord began to reveal the necessity of his sufferings and death. Thus the sorrowful teaching would correspond to the great fast-day, and the glory on the mount would correspond to the most joyful festival in the Jewish calendar. It is important to remember that the value of this speculation concerning the Jewish associations of the 'six days' does not depend upon an exact coincidence of days. It is sufficient that the proximity of the Jewish festival date put St Peter in mind of its 'booths'. Glory on a mountain belonged to the original revelation on Sinai-Horeb, when Israel dwelt in tents; and the divine glory also descended into a tent to be in the midst of Israel.

The allusion to the tabernacle in the wilderness does not depend upon the festival associations, as in any case the reference to the overshadowing cloud (Mark 9^{7}), repeated by Matthew and Luke, is an unmistakable echo of Exodus $40^{28, 29}$ in the Greek version (EVV: $40^{34, 35}$). It is at this point that the whole story has a clear affinity with John 1^{14}; and some of the implications which we have found in that verse have obvious congruity with the scene on the mount and its immediate sequel. In fact if, as is likely, the fourth evangelist moulded his statement in 1^{14} under the influence of the transfiguration story, he may also have done so with a view to emphasizing precisely the paradox of divine glory tabernacling amongst a 'faithless generation' (Mark 9^{19}).[1] At this point, where the testimony of the four-fold gospel is one, we are looking forward to the resurrection through the shadow of the cross, because, like old Israel, we have some measure of access to divine glory *while still in the wilderness*. The feast of tabernacles was the high-water mark of Jewish joy. It was to them what Easter is to us. It was a foreshadowing of the unfading festival prepared for the righteous in 'eternal tabernacles' (our Lord's own phrase, Luke 16^{9}). Yet, as Easter is approached through the passion and death of Jesus, so did Israel keep fast for sin before entering once more into a grateful remembrance of the discipline endured in the wilderness. The month of Tishri offered a glimpse of glory in the midst of present humiliation.[2]

ii

The 'six days' in St Mark and in Jewish tradition. An 'Adam' Christology crowned by a vision of unfallen Adam provides a creationist background to death and resurrection. But the

[1] In Matt. 17^{17} and Luke 9^{41} this becomes, like Acts 2^{40}, a partial echo of Deut. 32^{5} (quoted in full in Phil. 2^{15}), which in turn seems to refer back to Exod. 34^{5-10}. The latter scene in Exodus is a close parallel to the gospel sequence (a revelation of glory and an unbelieving people).

[2] See further below, Addit. Note D.

symbolism of the Transfiguration embraces the entire gospel cycle in which the Servant's mission restores creation's glories. This gives the clue to the sequence of Mark 9^{8-13} and to the significant incidents of restoration and prediction (9^{14-31}).

When St Peter confessed Jesus to be 'the anointed one', our Lord at once began to teach that 'the Son of Man' must suffer, die and rise again (Mark 8^{29-31}). A few verses later he linked the scandal of the cross with judgement to be executed by the Son of Man when he comes in glory. In the final week this is paralleled by our Lord's confession of his messiahship before the high priest with a 'son of man' quotation from Daniel 7^{13} (Mark 14^{61-64}). Here, as in chapter 8, the use of language clearly implies an identification of Messiah with Son of Man.[1] Daniel in turn has Genesis for its background, and we must here refer the reader back to all that was said in chapter III concerning implications of the Hebrew expression 'Son of Adam'. The fusion of 'Son of Man' with Messiah (Son of David) implies also an identification of the dominion of Christ with a restored dominion of Adam.[2] Moreover we have also seen that our Lord identified himself with the lot of the fallen sons of Adam, and that the great restoration involved, therefore, the inclusion of a third type in the 'fusion' of images from the Old Testament, namely the suffering Servant. We are on the same ground here as in the discussion of Philippians 2^{5-11}; and in the movement of Mark 8 and 9 we appear to be following the same order, that is to say the Son of David is first identified as Son of Adam and then humbled to the Servant's destiny. The types overlap in the radiant figure on Mt Hermon. The details of this sequence must now be explained more fully.

In the scene at Caesarea Philippi Jesus identifies the messianic office with a vocation to accept the 'heavy yoke' which 'is upon the sons of Adam', namely suffering and death. In so doing he reverses the story of Adam's fall. For when Satan tempts the new Adam through friendly lips, as once before in the beginning, the true source of the all-too-human sentiment is instantly

[1] In Mark 14^{62} the Son of Man is 'seated on the right hand of power'. This comes from Ps. 110, and would be accounted Davidic (Mk. 12^{35-37}).

[2] For fuller details see also Farrer, *op. cit.*, Chs. XI and XII, where the connexion of Daniel with Genesis, 1, 2 is fully worked out.

recognized and repudiated (Mark 8^{31-33}). Suffering and death, however, are not ends in themselves. They are indispensible steps to resurrection. The reference to 'three days' may, in the human mind of Jesus, be simply a common form of speech signifying a short time. But it is also possible that it refers us back to Hosea 6^{1-7}, where Ephraim offers a feigned repentance in the hope that 'on the third day he will raise us up'. Israel's formal worship, however, is condemned in these words: 'They like Adam have transgressed the covenant'. To evade the yoke is to repeat Adam's treachery. The yoke of the law must often have involved a criminal's death in the days when Daniel's prophecy was written. Yet only so could Adam's dominion over the lower creation be restored. So when the Son of Adam comes at length to his kingdom there will be shame for those who have evaded the yoke and renewed Adam's treachery. That appears to be the general sense of the words of Jesus as reported in the concluding verses of Mark 8. Thus, when we pass on to the vision upon the mount we are already prepared for a revelation of unfallen Adam and we are not disappointed.

It is worth while to point out here the fact that traditionally the religious observances of the month Tishri were dominated originally by the 'new creation' ideas anciently attached to New Year observance. According to Exodus 23^{16} the feast of 'ingathering' (tabernacles) is assigned to 'the going out', that is 'the beginning' of the year, 'the magical point when, the cycle being completed, the powers of nature begin anew to recreate the world'.[1] Whatever changes may have occurred in Jewish outlook upon 'the feast of booths', this dictum of Exodus remained a governing principle of the Mosaic Law. Moreover, as anciently the king officiated preeminently as Man in the New Year ceremonies, so when the high-priest entered the Holy of holies upon the Day of Atonement 'the whole world' was said to be upon his garment.[2] Thus far the Marcan report of Christ's words during the 'six days' with its emphasis upon an 'Adam' Christology agrees not only with St Paul, but also with the Jewish background now commonly assumed for that crucial week which ushered in the revelation upon the mountain. St

[1] S. H. Hooke, *The Origins of early Semitic ritual* (Schweich lectures, 1935), p. 51.

[2] cp. I. VI, pp. 158, 162 and notes, commenting upon Wisd. 18^{24}.

Matthew (17^1) repeats the reference to 'six days'; but also in Chapter 16 he elaborates the preceding background in a manner which may probably contain a more extended reference to Jewish creationist tradition. To this we shall return presently.

Our analysis of the 'six days' and its teaching, building upon our earlier analyses of the 'Son of Adam' Christology, has placed the prediction of death and resurrection within the framework of a new creation-cycle in which the fall of Adam is reversed. This corresponds to the consistent teaching of St Paul and St John.[1] We shall, therefore, not be surprised to find a similar combination in the details of the transfiguration scene. First, then, the radiant figure of Jesus transfigured recalls once more the vision of Ezekiel in which deity is seen as Adam surrounded by a halo of light. That vision in turn may owe something to the original theophany at Sinai, where 'the appearance of the glory of the Lord was like devouring fire on the top of the mount in the eyes of the children of Israel' (Exodus 24^{16}). Moreover the previous verse refers to 'six days' followed by a seventh in which Moses entered the cloud. In fulfilment of this scene the three disciples, on the seventh day, enter the cloud after seeing the theophany. In Ezekiel the 'devouring fire' surrounds the human form which is also divine. The reserve with which the prophet describes what he sees has enabled Jewish writers to whittle down its full reality.[2] The tension between such a theophany and the divine transcendence as taught by the prophets could be resolved only in the Incarnation for which all such theophanies were preparatory. So, when deity was revealed in the form of unfallen Adam under the new covenant, Law and Prophecy were found to be ancillary to creation restored in its Head.

The references to Exodus and Ezekiel make it evident that for the evangelists the transfigured Jesus has identity not only with unfallen Adam but also with the Creator. Psalm 104[2] completes this aspect of the manifestation. For there the

[1] 1 Cor. 15, Rom. 5–8, John 5^{25-29}. In this last statement Daniel's judgement scene is on the Genesis background. The Son of Adam (who, like the first Adam, has '*Zoë* in himself') exercises the functions of his restored dominion, 'calling' the dead into the new order of risen life, as Adam 'called' the animals into their proper cosmos.

[2] e.g. *The Soncino Comm. ad loc.*, quoting Maimonides in support (p. 8).

psalmist, addressing God, says: 'Thou art clothed with glory and majesty, who coverest thyself with light as with a garment' The context refers to acts of creation as present activities. The deity still wraps himself in the light which his word has brought forth and builds the beams of his chambers. So now the original acts of creation are continued in the Incarnation, when God builds for himself a chamber of flesh and clothes it in light. This continuous creativity, however, has a redemptive purpose; and of that there is evidence in the evangelical narrative which we are considering. Three features of the story appear to indicate the redemptive picture within the cosmic frame. These are (1) the priority of Elias in the Marcan version, (2) the utterance of the divine voice, (3) the white garments. Let us consider these. First. 'Elias with Moses' (Mark 9^{4}) takes us back to Malachi 4^{2-6} upon which we have already commented sufficiently.[1] Like St John in the Prologue, St Mark sees the fulfilment of Malachi's picture in the new creation. Jesus is the Sun of righteousness *rising* at the dawn of a new Day,[2] the Light inaugurating a new creation. The Voice identifies Jesus as 'my beloved Son' (Mark 9^{7}); and this reminds us of Abraham's 'beloved son' made ready for sacrifice (Genesis 22^{16}) and of the baptismal utterance connecting that title with the Servant (Mark 1^{11}).[3]

The other evangelists render the reference to the Servant explicit. In St Mark, however, 'beloved Son' may have a wider significance (as at the Baptism); for the 'Son of Adam' is 'Son of God', the messianic head of the new creation who bruises the serpent's head (1^{11-13}). The white garments, with their unearthly whiteness, correspond to the garments worn, both by the heralds of the resurrection in all four gospels, and by the risen saints of the Apocalypse ($7^{13,14}$). The latter are said to have 'washed their robes and *whitened* them in the blood of the Lamb', repeating St Mark's word (9^{3}). This suggests baptismal purity, in which those who are risen with Christ have been cleansed by

[1] I. pp. 222–224 and 244–248 with notes; and, in the present volume, Ch. I § iv. with the diagram in a note near the end (last par. but three).

[2] As in the New Year ritual the symbolic death of the king was followed by a symbolic 'rising' when the sun appeared above the horizon.

[3] cp. Isa. 42^{1-3}, as rendered in Matt. 12^{18} (=Matt. 17^{5}). Luke 9^{35} also seems to be following a version of Isa. 42^{1}.

blood and water (1 John 5^{5-8}). We seem then, in Mark 9^{3}, to be looking back to the baptism of Jesus as well as forward to his resurrection. In any case the backward glance is evident in the reference to 'my beloved Son'. Here, then, we have an indication that if the transfiguration anticipates death and resurrection it also connects that anticipation with the moment when, on the threshold of his earthly ministry, our Lord accepted the Servant's vocation as the proper destiny of Adam's son. In this way also the whole gospel story in the Marcan cycle is gathered up into the all-inclusive symbolism of the mysterious event upon the mount.

To the central event, however, there are appended a series of episodes, all of which fulfil the same general purpose in that, like the six-day prelude, they illustrate further the symbolism of the central mystery and its inclusive relation to the whole course of revelation in scripture. Strictly speaking the Transfiguration, as a foreshadowing mystery, extends its symbolic effects right on into the Passion. But as we have already handled some of this material we will confine our attention here to the three incidents which follow immediately in St Mark before turning to the further amplifications in the other gospels. Mark 9^{8} is transitional. It completes the symbolism by taking us out of it into the world of mundane events which must lead to the final week. Henceforth Law and Prophecy are to be found in Jesus alone and in his relation to his community. For Jesus in himself is the bearer of the entire scriptural revelation, who restores creation in our nature by fulfilling the predestined plan. In these words we have indicated the light thrown on the central mystery by the ensuing episodes. In verses 9, 10 we are shown the relation of transfiguration to resurrection. The foreshadowing mystery implies its counterpart, the glorious denouement of Easter. Yet that joyous event is here twice described as a 'rising from the dead', as though death and resurrection are in reality one mystery, not two. The disciples fasten upon the phrase as indicating an enigma beyond their present comprehension, and rightly so. For what has been foreshadowed in their presence is a divine 'secret' in the proper biblical sense, a *mysterion* which God alone can and will lay open in his own time and in his own way.

To the organic unity of death and resurrection in a single

mystery correspond other forms of unity now to be considered. In the revelation on the mount the two Old Testament figures are one with Jesus, as the scriptures themselves form one organic whole. St Luke emphasizes this (*a*) by placing the two within the glory which surrounds the One, and (*b*) by recording converse of the three concerning 'the exodus' of the One, as though indeed there were but one glory and one exodus, which latter Jesus only could fulfil. All this implies an identity between the types and the anti-type. We have previously taken note of this relation in respect of the Baptist and the Christ.[1] But in Mark 9^{11-13} we can now see a further application of the same principle. The question of the disciples is evoked by the compresence of Elias with Jesus on the mount. What then of the dictum that 'Elias must first come'? The answer given in verses 12, 13 might be summarized as follows: Elias did precede me in the person of the Baptist; and this implies an identity of the Baptist with the prophet whom Jezebel sought to slay (1 Kings $19^{2,10}$). To John 'they' did what 'they wished to do' at that time. The passion of Elias is thus fulfilled in his representative (*Elias redevivus*). Moreover this identity of the forerunner with his ancient type is due to the fact that both have identity with Jesus, as types with anti-type, as parts with the Whole. For Jesus is the whole action of divine revelation in which each of the actors in turn plays his part.[2]

Accordingly the sufferings of the servants are included in the Passion of the Servant. But the Servant (*pais*) is also the messianic Child (*paidion*). So in coming to an 'unbelieving generation' (9^{19}) he is 'announced as Child'[3] from 9^{21} onwards to 10^{16}. For the healer identified himself with those in need of healing; and thus in the exorcism of the afflicted child Jesus foreshadows his own death and resurrection (9^{25-27}). But further, he also shows here 'death and resurrection' as the law of the new creation in head and members. The healing, therefore, foreshadows every Christian initiation. As Jesus is one with his types, so also he is one with every neophyte grafted into his Body. The incident as told by St Mark is the counterpart of the

[1] See in this Vol. Ch. I § iii, two last notes, Addit. Note A, top of p. 35; and Ch. II. § iii, par. 5 with notes.

[2] I. VII, p. 221.

[3] Isa. 53^2 (LXX). See above, Ch. III, § iii. *et passim*.

baptismal teaching in Romans 6. So finally the prediction which follows ($9^{30,31}$) shows the pattern of the whole 'new creation' organism in terms of the Servant prophecy. This, again, corresponds to the inclusive aspect of the Servant in Romans 8^{31-39}. Jesus on the mount is Son of Adam, and so, implicitly, he is all humanity. But for fallen humanity the Adam vocation is the predestined path of the Servant who is 'delivered up' to death and resurrection. Not until that point is to be made clear is the Servant prophecy explicitly introduced with the key-word *paradidômi* (9^{31}), and repeated in the third prediction (10^{33}). But further, there is an additional reason for this. Looking back from the prediction we see that it comes in its right place at the end of a sequence, as in Isaiah 53^{12}. The sequence which begins with the Transfiguration and ends at 9^{31} corresponds to the whole pattern of the Servant-song. The Servant's exaltation and glory on the mount introduce suffering, death and resurrection leading on to the predestined *paradosis* in which Jesus is 'delivered up' by the traitor.[1]

iii

The 'six days' in Matthew 16. Word-play on names (Bar-jonah and Peter) connects 16^{18} with the typology of 12^{40}. The cosmic stone of the creation myth identified with the temple-rock at Jerusalem. Parallel between the stone closing the chasm over Sheol (Isaiah 28^{16}) and Jonah stopping the mouth of the ocean-monster. Jesus fulfils both types in his 'descent into hell'. Further implications of 'Bar-jonah Peter', and inner meaning of the typology.

We must now take account of some special features in St Matthew's Gospel, which throw further light upon the gospel parallel between the week which was completed by the event of the Transfiguration and the week which was crowned by the Lord's resurrection from the dead. Those special features are to be found at two points, namely (1) in Chapter 16 and (2) in Chapter 21. These take us back, respectively, to the beginnings of the two weeks, the scene of (1) being Caesarea Philippi, and the occasion of (2) being the events of the first 'Palm Sunday' as this evangelist presents them. We will, therefore, take these in

[1] On this point see my essay in *The Apostolic Ministry*, p. 61 with note 1.

order, starting with Matthew 16. It is here that we encounter one of Matthew's references to 'the sign of Jonah' (16^{1-4}).[1] In the corresponding section of the second gospel there is no reference to Jonah (8^{11-13}). But Matthew here fuses 'the sign of Jonah' into one incident with Mark's 'sign from heaven'. Then, a dozen verses later, in reply to 'Simon Peter's' confession, Jesus addresses his leading disciple as 'Simon Bar-jonah'. It appears that this expression is an Aramaic equivalent of 'Simon, son of John' (John 1^{42}). Nevertheless, in our modern Greek Testaments *Iônâ* here is indistinguishable from the name of the prophet whose 'sign' has been introduced a few verses earlier. Moreover, both these features of this particular gospel-section are peculiar to Matthew.

There is, then, at least a possibility that in the first gospel Jesus is represented as playing, in characteristic Jewish fashion, upon the double nuance of Peter's patronymic. For 'the Lord is gracious' (*Johanan*), even though his servant be as 'a silly dove' (*Jonah*) which flies hither and thither, only to be caught in a trap and 'chastised' (Hosea $7^{11,12}$). The Jonah-dove is Israel which will eventually be 'restored' (Hosea 11^{11}. LXX). Our Lord seems to forsee Peter's failure before restoration. But according to Matthew 12^{38-41} Jesus himself is the 'Jonah' who now calls Peter his son (*bar*).[2] Accordingly the 'Petrine text' which follows in 16^{18} is to be connected with the Jonah typology If the Jonah reference is here correctly taken there is a double play upon the apostle's names, Bar-jonah and Peter; and the two word-plays hang together in one frame of thought. What, then, would be the connexion between the Christological interpretation of Jonah's story in 12^{40} and the imagery of the rock or stone and 'the gates of Hades' in 16^{18}? The answer to this question will take us back into the primitive world of creation-myths and to the associations which had traditionally gathered round the temple rock at Jerusalem.

In Ezekiel 38^{12} Israel is said to dwell 'upon the central summit of the earth'. This expression probably meant that, in the eyes of the prophet, Israel was geographically the centre of

[1] $16^{2b,3}$ should be omitted, as a misplaced fragment concerning 'signs which clearly interrupts the dialogue at this point.

[2] In Jewish idiom the disciple is 'son' of his Rabbi, on which see I. IX, pp. 282 ff, and cp. Matt. 12^{27}.

the world. In the versions the word *tabbûr*, which properly means 'height', was rendered 'navel' because the navel is the centre of the body. But more particularly this notion of centrality was associated with the temple at Jerusalem. For it was a common idea of several ancient nations (including Babylon) that their most important shrine stood at the centre of the universe.[1] A Rabbinical saying summarizing this belief continues: 'As the navel . . . so the sanctuary in the centre of Jerusalem, and the holy place in the centre of the sanctuary, and the ark in the centre of the holy place, and the foundation stone before the holy place, because from it the world was founded'. The stone here referred to protruded from the floor of the Holy of holies; and on the Day of Atonement it was believed to have, in a sense, taken the place of the ark in the post-exilic temple. For the ark having disappeared, the stone must receive the sacrificial blood sprinkled by the high-priest. If then the 'six days' referred to by St Matthew (17[1]) were believed to have begun on the Day of Atonement our Lord's reference to a rock or stone upon which he would build his new temple acquires special significance.

The stone, then, was the centre of the universe; but also, 'from it the world was founded'. Here we go back to the creation-myth once more. We recall that 'the ocean-monster had to be overcome by God before chaos gave place to an ordered universe'. To this end it was believed that 'God cast a stone into *tehom*', the watery deep which flows from the mouth of Sheol. This stone became the rock upon which the temple was built. Beneath the rock there still flowed the waters of *tehom*; but now the rock had sealed the mouth of the great deep, so that, the waters being under control, the work of creation could proceed. This gives further significance to the rendering 'navel of the earth' as applied to the stone. As the foetus grows from the navel, so did the earth grow from the cosmic rock. Moreover, we can now begin to see the parallel with Jonah. For as the rock stopped the mouth of Sheol so Jonah stopped the mouth of the 'ocean-monster' when he calmed its raging for

[1] For this and what follows the reader is referred to the essay by Burrows in *The Labyrinth* (ed. S. H. Hooke, 1935). See also G. A. Cooke's Comm. on Ezekiel (ICC), pp. 58 f., and 412 f. from which the following quotation is taken.

his fellow-travellers. There is an illuminating parallel in Isaiah 28, where the idolaters who made a covenant with Death and with Sheol (placating the gods of the underworld) are told to put their trust in their Creator whose tried foundation-stone has securely bottled up the opening of that same underworld. In the Christian fulfilment (1 Peter 2^{6}) Christ is seen to be the Stone, with which believers are mysteriously identified, and in which they put their trust.[1]

The parallel between Jonah and the cosmic rock is in part based upon their common background of ancient cosmogony and topography. In that setting the promise of Matthew 16^{18} is seen to be a remarkably close counterpart of the oracle in Isaiah 28^{15-18}. 'The gates' of Sheol (=Hades) prevail only against those who place themselves outside the genuine Israel. Similarly in Revelation $12^{15,16}$ the *tehom* flood issuing from the jaws of the dragon fails to engulf the new Eve. In the new creation, as in the old, a foundation has been securely laid for the city-sanctuary. In ancient topography a chasm was believed to lead down from the temple-rock to the mouth of Sheol. Yet, though the gates (jaws) of Hades open, the stone has closed the chasm, so that the waters cannot pass through. In Matthew 16^{18}, as in Jonah 2, a 'city of Dis' is presumed to be beneath the waters, located immediately beneath the closed chasm. So, when Jonah sank into the abyss beneath the pillared roots of the mountains he 'went down into the land whose bars are everlasting bolts'.[2] These must be identified with the gates of Hades or 'gates of death', of which Job was asked: 'do they open to thee for fear, and did the porters of Hades, when they saw thee, crouch in fright?'[3] No; but when Jesus became the Jonah scape-goat for mankind and took that perilous journey it was otherwise. Then the picture held up before Job in irony became an awful reality.

[1] cp. Rom. 9^{33}, which combines Isa. 28^{16} with Isa. 8^{14}. In LXX 28^{16} reads: 'I cast a stone' (referring to the creation myth). But NT writers preferred to render the Hebrew by τίθημι with its manifold scriptural associations, e.g. Acts 13^{47}; but see especially John $15^{13,16}$ and my comments in *The Apostolic Ministry*, pp. 102 ff., notes to pp. 103–105 and Addit. Note on pp. 110 f.

[2] Jonah $2^{6,7}$ (LXX).

[3] The whole creation myth is implicit in Job $38^{4-11, 16-20}$. Note especially the taunt in verse 17 (LXX) from which the quotation comes.

In the Christian 'transference of traditions from the Jerusalem temple to Golgotha' the latter (in the Church of the Holy Sepulchre) 'has also its cleft, which is supposed to reach to the centre of the earth'.[1] Here we are clearly on the track of the tradition which constrains Matthew to refer to 'the heart of the earth' in connexion with the dead Christ (12^{40}). For Sheol-Hades, lying below the bottom of the cavernous crevasse into which the stone was let down, was conceived to be immediately beneath the centre of the world. But, secondly, it was also the very pit of the watery underworld, its lowest level. Being beneath the waters it was in 'the heart of the seas' (Jonah 2^{3}). Thus two routes led to 'the heart of the earth'; the one (Jonah's) was marine, the other was terrestrial. The second route led from 'the midst of the earth' (Psalm 74^{12}), where (at Golgotha) the Lord was enthroned as King. Thence it passed through Joseph's rock-tomb in a veritable descent into Hades; that is the thought of Matthew 12^{40}. The same thought could scarcely have been absent from the evangelist's mind when he penned the promise that 'the gates of Hades shall not prevail' (16^{18}). In this respect there is as much anticipation of coming glory in Matthew 16 as in the transfiguration scene which follows.

The Bar-Jonah greeting overshadows our Lord's words to Peter; and Jonah 2 was a synagogue lection for the Day of Atonement. But another scripture for the Tishri season was Psalm 118. Verse 22 stands in contrast to the prophecy against Babylon: 'They shall not take of thee a stone for a corner, nor a stone for foundations' (Jeremiah 51^{26}). The rejected corner-stone is to be connected with Isaiah 28^{16}, and possibly with an ancient new year king-ritual. To a people for whom all natural objects are in some sense alive[2] there would be no difficulty in the parallel between a man and a stone, where the latter is conceived to be the navel from which the world grew. So in the Pauline anti-type the corner-stone is to the temple as head to body. Similarly, in that world of psychological 'wholeness', the identification of Peter with the cosmic rock corresponds to the identification of Jahveh with angelic messengers and of ancient

[1] S. A. Cook, (Schweich lectures, 1925, p. 17) in a note on the temple-rock.

[2] cp. H. W. Robinson's *Inspiration and Revelation in the O.T.*, pp. 12–16.

kings with the gods with whom they form a single totality.[1] But in the gospel the identification is double-edged. For the sacred stone may be treated as a stumbling-block (*petra skandalou*, Romans 9^{33}); and so 'Peter' can become a *skandalon* of unfaith like disobedient Jonah (Matthew 16^{23}). In the fulfilment, however, 'the descent into hell' is unavoidable; and the genuine Jonah takes his 'sons' along with him to Golgotha.

At this point we can see a parallel with Ezekiel's vision in which we found a pre-view of the revelation on the mount. Jahveh took the form of Adam who was his 'likeness', and addressed Ezekiel as his 'son' by creation. Jesus accepted the vocation of Jonah who was his type, and addressed Simon Peter as his 'son' by new creation. In both scenes the 'son' receives a divine commission; and again in both instances the commission is found to involve a 'passion' sequel as the prelude to glory (e.g. Ezekiel 4^{4-6}). In conclusion, the differences between the first and third gospels in their handling of the Jonah theme can be seen to emerge out of a common background: (1) The creation myth and its cosmogony correspond to factors in the inner life of Israel. For Israel is the scene of a conflict in and through which the divine creativity works. In the mission of Israel the victory of creation over chaos is sustained; but also in the tragedy of Israel's unfaithfulness hell is let loose. (2) Creativity overcomes chaos by entering into it, and that continuously. Nature dies to live; and every human birth is like a return from encounter with death. So Israel's hope of resurrection is aligned with the perpetual re-birth of creation's order; and in a manifold order of re-birth the ways of creativity run up from nature into redemptive history. Common to these two themes is the weaving of Israel and creation into a single divinely wrought pattern; and to this both the evangelists are faithful.

iv

'Descent' and 'ascent' (Eph. 4^{8-10}) in Matthew's version of the two weeks (16^{18} and 21^{1-17}). The latter passage shows a recapitulation of David's story foreshadowing universal 'restoration' in

[1] Or the dragon in Jer. $51^{34, 44}$ with the god Bel and with his human representative, the king.

the kingdom of the heavenly Son of Man. The technique of anticipation.

In the Epistle to the Ephesians the author quotes a version of some words from Psalm 68: 'Having ascended up on high he led captivity captive, and gave gifts unto men'. The apostolic writer then comments on the text in a manner which is highly relevant to the present phase of our argument. He says; 'That he ascended, what is it but that he also descended into the lower parts of the earth? He who descended is also he who ascended above all the heavens, that he might fill all things.' The comment corresponds to a current opinion that spiritual mastery of the universe has a realistically geographical character. Jesus had to descend to the kingdom of darkness in order to become its master. But also he had to ascend above the intermediate spheres of the astronomical heavens in order to control the secondary spirits who ruled in those celestial regions.[1] This doctrine of 'descent and ascent' corresponds, of course, to the facts of our redemption. We cannot, as yet, concern ourselves directly with the cosmic aspects of ascent. But the corresponding doctrine of descent clearly agrees with the implications of the Jonah typology as developed by St Matthew. Moreover, whereas in his version the 'six days' begin with an underlying motif of the 'descent into hell', his record of the 'final week' begins with a dramatic presentation of a 'Davidic' ascent to Mount Zion (21^{1-17}).

Both weeks begin with an acknowledgement of our Lord's messianic claim, the one privately at Caesarea Philippi, the other publicly on Palm Sunday; and St Mark especially brings out details of the parallel.[2] But whereas all the gospels emphasize the joyful character of the palm procession and its messianic implications, St Matthew gives to it a special significance which is theologically relevant to the thesis of this chapter. His peculiar contribution is made, partly by assembling on to one day events which, in the Marcan chronology, occupy two days, but partly also by his method of relating these events to the

[1] This corresponds to Rev. 12, where the ascent of the messianic Child to the throne of God secures the expulsion of the dragon from the lower heavens. Cp. also, in Phil. 2^{10}, the 'three-storied' description of the kingdom in which the name of Jesus is acknowledged.

[2] Dr Farrer has worked out the details. *op. cit.*, pp. 105 f., 120–122.

scriptures of the Old Testament. Let us consider these points. St Matthew alone, of the first three evangelists, quotes the prophecy of Zechariah 9, and alone among the four quotes it fully by including the reference to the 'meekness' of the king who rides on the ass. This prepares the way for the paradox of the following incident. The meek Son of David enters the temple-courts in strange contrast to his great ancestor who stormed the stronghold of the Jebusites that he might build there a temple to the Lord. Here the evangelist introduces another special feature not to be found in any of the other gospels. David took away 'the blind and the lame' with whom his enemies alleged that they could hold the stronghold against him (2 Samuel 5^{6-9}). But according to Matthew the Son of David *healed* the blind and the lame when they came to him in the temple-courts. Thus the parallel between type and anti-type is extended, while the contrast between the old and the new is deepened.

In the 'six days' which began on that Sunday the Son of David restored to our nature its integrity and its capacity for worship in the true temple. *In this sense* he took away 'the blind and the lame' when he entered upon his messianic inheritance. The evangelist saw in the Lord's triumphal entry into the temple an anticipation of the Easter victory. But also he saw in that victory something more than a restoration of David's kingdom. This appears from another detail in the story which we are examining, namely the words quoted by our Lord from Psalm 8 in his reply to the remonstrance of the Jewish authorities. When these latter saw our Lord's acts of judgement and mercy in the temple-courts they must have understood, at least in part, the implications. For they had re-instated the Jebusite stronghold by allowing the house of God to become 'a den of robbers'. Zion had become little better than a *grande latrocinium;* and now judgement was come to the sanctuary.[1] So while children greeted their king with 'Hosannas' Jesus met the protest of their elders with these words: 'Did ye never read that "out of the mouth of babes and sucklings thou didst perfect praise"?'[2] In the Greek version of the psalm, from which

[1] Ezek. 9^6. For the relation of Augustine's phrase to Psalm 8 and 'the dominion of Adam' see above, Ch. III, §§ i (last par. but two and preceding quot.) and ii with notes.

[2] Ps. 8^3 (LXX).

the evangelist reports our Lord's words, the poet continues: 'Because of thine enemies that thou mightest destroy the enemy and the avenger'. The Hebrew text, however, means 'cause the enemy to cease', that is (probably) 'reduce him to silence'.

While the enemies of Jesus stood speechless with rage, the children continued to sing 'Hosanna to the Son of David' in the temple which David's heir had just restored to its proper use.[1] 'The enemies' perceived only a threat to their self-interest. Jesus, however, saw an acted parable of the kingdom, in which the lowly acknowledge the lowly, in which the childlike, returning to their true beginning, acknowledge the headship of the Son of Adam,—in short a foreshadowing of that day when 'the meek shall inherit the earth', because that earth has become once more a 'holy land', the paradise of the Creator's design. In the public teaching which followed the three evangelists agree in showing how 'the enemies' were reduced to silence. St Luke says so expressly (20^{26}). But in the reference to the rejected corner-stone, just before, the same evangelist records a note of judgement which corresponds to the Greek rendering of Psalm 8^3 (quoted above):

> Everyone that falleth on that stone shall be broken to pieces; but on whomsoever it shall fall, it will scatter him as dust. (Luke 20^{18}.)

The scene which we have just surveyed is typical, not only of the first evangelist, but also of the New Testament as a whole,—and that both in the presentation of certain great themes and also in their combination into one picture. There is first of all the recapitulation of David's story in David's Son, and secondly the paradox of victorious meekness coming in judgement and in saving power. Thirdly there is the restoration of Adam's dominion'through the meekness and gentleness of the Messiah' (2 Corinthians 10^1). Finally this is seen to involve the renovation of human life and its environment by the reconsecration of both in a new order of worship. But the scene in which all these elements are combined derives its deepest significance from the fact that it introduces the story of Holy Week. The Son of David is the divinely appointed victim who is about to die. The joyful procession of palms and songs is a

[1] And this was fitting. For traditionally David re-ordered the temple cultus and embellished it with choirs of singers.

procession to the altar of the cross; and this, again, means that the death of Jesus is throughout envisaged in the light of the resurrection. Indeed, all four accounts of the passion are told from this point of view. The death of Jesus is neither an end in itself, nor a mere preliminary to a happy ending upon Easter Day. In the plan of redemption death and resurrection form one mystery. Easter is not a happy ending to a tragic story, but the new beginning of that new 'world-without-end' to which we belong.

At the beginning of this section it was pointed out that the ideas of 'descent' and 'ascent' in the text from Ephesians seemed to correspond respectively to the beginnings of the two weeks in St Matthew's version of the parallel which we have been considering. If then the evangelist had in mind some such contrast, can we see further into the mystery at which he may be hinting? In what sense could there be an appropriate correspondence between a Jonah-like 'descent into hell' and a 'Davidic ascent to Mount Zion'? Doubtless it is relevant to recall that David chose the site of the temple which his son built upon the cosmic rock immediately above the very mouth of 'hell'. But if we turn to that text of Psalm 68 which introduces the phrases about 'descent' and 'ascent' in Ephesians we shall, I believe, gain further light. In the first place the title: 'A Psalm of David' supports the possibility that the words of verse 19 carry a 'Davidic' reference. In their original form the text runs thus:

> Thou hast ascended on high, thou hast led captivity captive;
> Thou hast received gifts among men.

Upon this three comments may be made: (1) The text means that the deity ascended to his heavenly throne, after a victory over Israel's enemies, the spoils of victory being tribute laid at the conqueror's feet. (2) The application to deity may have a 'human' counterpart, a victorious ascent of the Davidic king to Mount Zion with captives and spoil. The ancient identification of the deity with the king, his human representative, would render this probable. (3) In its Christian fulfilment the subject is Christ ascending to heaven; and the final clause is transformed into its opposite. The ascended Christ *bestowed* 'gifts' upon his people at Pentecost.

In view of these three points it seems clear that the events of Palm Sunday, as envisaged by the first evangelist, could carry a further implication. Our Lord's recapitulation of David's triumphant ascent to Mount Zion anticipated the inauguration of the messianic kingdom upon Easter Day. But if so, we must surely go a step further. In the messianic psalm (110), quoted twice by our Lord in the final week,[1] the heavenly session is emphasized. Moreover the use made of Psalm 68^{19} in Ephesians 4^{8ff} shows how inevitably a messianic 'ascent' to Mount Zion would suggest to Christian minds the ascension of Christ to heaven. Other texts support this view, particularly in the theological context which the Ephesian passage exemplifies.[2] Thus we can say with some confidence that the exaltation to glory prefigured on the mount of transfiguration is, in this evangelist's view, also prefigured on that other mount which is called Zion. But that is not all. For we found the former prefiguration extended backwards into the promise that 'the gates of Hades shall not prevail' (16^{18}). Thus the technique of anticipation passes on from the beginning to the end of the 'six days' and then bursts forth afresh in a new form at the beginning of the week of fulfilment. From the facts thus assembled we must now pass to a wider survey of their implications.

V

Two aspects of the Son of Adam united in the Servant prophecy, where glory and humiliation, depth and height, form one mystery. All the types come together in the God-man because he fulfils the law of his created world which they partially illustrate. St Luke's handling of typology crystallized in the wording of 9^{51} where the technique of anticipation is stretched to its farthest limit.

The symbolic character of the transfiguration narrative has now been surveyed within the wider context in which the

[1] Mark 12^{36}, 14^{62} and parallels; cp. Matt. 25^{31}.

[2] see above, note to par. 1 of this section. In the Apocalypse the ascended Christ appears on Mount Zion in the midst of new Israel (14^{1ff}). This scene is 'Davidic' and paschal, yet heavenly. It might signify the fulfilment to which Matt 21 points forward.

evangelists seem to place it. There are still details of St Luke's treatment to be considered which are highly important. But they will, I believe, be found to supplement and to support a thesis which we shall next attempt to outline on the basis of the facts already considered. It will be remembered that in St. Mark's Gospel the vision of unfallen Adam upon the mount is introduced by a piece of 'Son of Adam' Christology in which the story of Adam's fall is reversed. He who wears the 'form of God' upon the mount has already accepted 'the form of the slave' which is the appointed lot of Adam's fallen sons. In this way of speaking we can see how perfectly the Marcan presentation fits into the Pauline thesis of Philippians 2^{5ff} which we examined in Chapter III. In that chapter (at the beginning of § vi) a footnote suggested the possibility that the three clauses of verse 7, in St Paul's statement, constituted not so much a causal sequence of events as a complex piece of imagery. The imagery is complex because the three clauses present a picture with three aspects. It is precisely such a picture which is set before us as having been witnessed by the three disciples on the mount.

By acts of condescension God appeared in visible form to Moses (and others),[1] and in the likeness of Adam to Ezekiel. By a deeper act of *kenosis* God the Son 'became in the likeness of men'; and this can now be seen to have two aspects. For on the one hand the 'Adam' form which he took is the image and likeness of God; it is therefore glorious. On the other hand it is in origin earthy of the earth; and its pre-eminence over the other creatures is with a view to service which is in essence lowly, but which self-will has rendered servile. When, therefore, we contemplate the radiant figure upon the mount we see the divine condescension unfolded in its full majesty. *We see both its depth and its height, and each of these in the other.* On the one hand we see God in that human form which, as the theophanies suggest, was from the inception of creation congenial to him in his sovereign lowliness. For God is at home with his creatures; and so he conferred his glory upon one of them. On the other hand that bright form upon which the three disciples gazed was 'the form of the slave'; for it was the flesh and blood of a fallen race destined for death in penalty for sin, notwithstanding its garment of light. It is this twofold situation of the Son of Adam which is

[1] Exod. 24^{9-11}; but contrast 33^{20-23}. See also I. VII, p. 221, note 3.

presented in the Servant prophecy. The vision on the mount exhibits the complete fusion of the two types in their fulfilment. Glory and humiliation here melt together into a single mystery. The Servant is exalted and glorified in the very act of making his soul an offering for sin. It is thus that the evangelists understand the prophecy.

Notwithstanding, they also preserve the order of the prophecy by showing the exaltation and glory on the mount before the *via crucis* begins. Moreover, they take pains to set the revelation in its full context; and this brings us back to St Matthew. He shows us depth and height in his parallel between the two weeks, depth in the Jonah-descent to the underworld, height in the Davidic ascent to Mount Zion. In each case, however, in reality depth and height are once again together in one mystery. For in the former section the vital words are the promise that 'the gates of Hades shall not prevail'; and in the Palm Sunday picture the symbolic 'restoration' through victorious ascent anticipates suffering and death in accordance with the *order* of prophecy. At this point we must try to draw together the various intimations of the manifold typology into something more nearly approximating to a single whole. To this end let us remember once more that the creation-cycle always underlies the images of redemptive history; and with this in mind let us recall one particular parallel between those two spheres, and then draw a conclusion. The parallel in question is that of Jonah with the cosmic rock; the conclusion will follow from the last paragraph of § iii in which that parallel is made.

In the paragraph which has just been mentioned it was said that 'in the mission of Israel the victory of creation over chaos is sustained; but also in the tragedy of Israel's unfaithfulness hell is let loose'. In the former clause the substance of the creation-myth is lodged securely in the heart of redemptive history, whereas the latter clause has obvious reference to the story of Jonah. For the prophet's disobedience is represented as occasioning the storm at sea; and the latter in turn is regarded as an expression of the ocean-monster's rage. But this monster also has identity with Sheol. So the mythological statement of Jonah's adventure is in reality a version of the creation-conflict in terms of Israelite history. Thus we can see that the parallel between Jonah and the cosmic rock is in reality more than a parallel. That is to say, neither type-image becomes fully intelligible until we see them as one reality; and this becomes possible only in Christ who is both Jonah and the sure foundation of the new creation upon which the new city-temple is built. But what follows? Christ as Jonah is like Christ as Son of Adam. In both instances the type represents fallen man suffering the consequences of his sins, whereas Jesus is the obedient Son, the true Israel, sustaining the victory of creation over chaos. In a fallen world, however, he can fulfil his mission only by complete identification with us in our sinfulness, notwithstanding his utter sinlessness.

He must grapple with hell in hell's usurped domain. If chaos invades creativity, creativity in the person of the God-man can overcome chaos only by entering into it. In so acting he is fulfilling the law of his own created order; for nature 'dies to live'. He fulfils that law as the faithful Servant of his Father's purpose, but also, and equally, as the Son 'in whom all things were made'. The law of dying to live is his own law; for he is the mould and archetype of creation's order. Consequently his self-committal to the Servant's mission is glorious; for therein he manifests what deity is, and, further, shows what deity is in terms of that which every child of Adam should be and may yet become. In this way all the types come together upon the mount of transfiguration where majesty is exhibited in the guise of lowliness and servitude is bathed in glory. We must beware, however, of attributing to the vision upon the mount more than it can convey to us. It is reality in symbolic dress pointing us on to the fuller disclosure of reality in that week of events which summed up and fulfilled all redemptive history through a final manifestation of divine creativity. The interrelation between 'the six days' and the final week has, however, still some further significance which demands consideration. It will be convenient to approach this under the guidance of St Luke.

Some of the special features in the Lucan version of the story were touched upon in the previous volume. We shall therefore keep strictly to what bears directly upon our argument. Generally speaking the narrative which begins at Luke 9^{28} appears to be more explicitly typological than is the case in the other gospels. The seventh day after Peter's confession now becomes 'about eight days after', which seems to look forward to the Christian Easter rather than back to the Jewish calendar. But all the other special features in this gospel give prominence to the figures of Moses and Elias in their relation to the Christ. They participate in the glory and converse with Jesus concerning his coming 'exodus'. As they once prayed upon the mount, so now does Jesus. As Moses once entered the cloud (Exodus 24^{18}) so now do the three disciples. This interest in the two saints of the old covenant is, moreover, extended yet further at a slightly later point, when the Marcan epilogues to the main narrative have been briefly summarized.[1] Luke 9^{51}–10^{1}, at least, is deeply typological in its associations; for the whole section seems to be moulded upon incidents in the two ancient biographies.[2] Our main interest, however, must be concentrated upon a single statement which occurs in 9^{51}; it reads as follows:

> When the days of his *being received up* were being fulfilled, he set his face to go to Jerusalem.

The expression here placed in italics renders literally a single Greek word, the meaning of which is fixed by the fairly frequent use of the corresponding verb. The latter is used three times in the Septuagint version of 2 Kings 2^{9-11} in reference to the 'assumption' of Elijah into heaven, and again three times by St Luke in reference to our Lord's ascension into heaven (Acts $1^{2,11,22}$). Clearly the evangelist has in mind a parallel between these two events. But also it is fairly certain that he knew a corresponding legend concerning the 'assumption' of Moses,[3] according to which the lawgiver had a 'spiritual' ascension

[1] Luke 9^{37-50} summarizes Mark 9^{14-40}.

[2] Beginning with the narrative of 2 Kings 1 we pass to the theme of Elisha 'following' Elijah. The homeless Son of Man corresponds to Elijah fed by ravens at the brook. Unlike Elisha the would-be disciple is not allowed to bid farewell to his family. For a sterner precedent had been set to the Levites by Moses (Deut. 33^{9} referring to Exod. 32^{26-29}). From Elisha's plough we pass finally to the seventy elders of Num. 11^{24-30}, the NT MSS showing some doubt as to whether Eldad and Modad are additional to the seventy or not.

[3] And may have had this in mind in the 'bury my father' request ($9^{59,60}$) for reasons which I explained in JTS, Vol. XLVI, No. 181–182, p. 57. For the ἀνάληψις terminology see R. H. Charles, *The Apocalypse of Baruch*, p. 73, note, and his edition of *The Assumption of Moses* (both publ. by A. & C. Black).

after death and burial (the body remaining in the grave). On the other hand Elijah was taken up in the body without death. Jesus, however, comprehended both types; for after death and burial he was taken up in the body. So far we can follow the workings of St Luke's mind with some confidence. But when we compare 9^{51} with Acts 1^{22} we notice a peculiar difference. In the latter St Peter speaks of 'the day on which he was taken up from us', referring to the ascension as a definite event. This corresponds to 'the day when he was taken up' (1^{2}) and the angelic reference to the event of the ascension in 1^{11}. But when we turn back to Luke 9^{51} we are confronted with a plural noun ('days') and a verb which indicates a process rather than a single event. It seems that the period between the transfiguration and the ascension is here regarded as covering a continuous process of 'being received up'.[1]

Here 'the technique of anticipation' is carried further than by either Mark or Matthew. But if 'depth and height' are united in one mystery, then the whole of the humiliation which Jesus underwent might also be regarded as the first stage in the exaltation. If so, then we have here an important clue to New Testament thought as a whole, and that not only in respect of the symbolic relation between the transfiguration and the final events of our redemption. It is this wider implication of St Luke's phrases which we have still to consider; and as a first step let us take note of an expression towards the end of our quotation from 9^{51}: 'He set his face'. The evangelist may possibly have in mind here a slightly later incident in the corresponding Marcan narrative (10^{32}) where on the way up to Jerusalem Jesus was leading the pilgrimage, 'and they were amazed, and they that followed were afraid'. Moreover, St Luke's phrase probably echoes the utterance of the Servant in Isaiah 50^{7}: 'I have set my face like a flint'. If so, we are on familiar ground. The Servant whose glory has already been announced in symbolic vision is now on his way to exaltation by the way of the cross. The days of that exaltation, as predicted, are already being fulfilled as he sets his face towards the place of sacrifice.

[1] There is a corresponding contrast with Acts 2^{1} where 'the day of Pentecost was being fulfilled'.

vi

Aspects of the Transfiguration. The light of the risen Saviour suffuses the gospels and discloses the unity of revelation. In the new 'wholeness' discordant factors are not by-passed but subject to transformation. Two forms of the human element through which God acts; the 'earthen vessel' as a dark torch or as a radiant lamp. Creation redeemed shows 'the two orders of being' united in the adoration of the Lamb.

The transfiguration of our Lord may be said to have two main aspects in relation to the wider topic of redemption. These may be designated, respectively, as *integration* and *transformation*. The second aspect was mentioned in Volume I of this series[1] and has such a wide relevance that it may well be implicit elsewhere. For the two aspects are, in fact, so closely related that it is difficult to separate them. Moreover, as we shall see, this has also a bearing upon those topics which will be handled in the third volume of the series and which lie beyond the scope of our present argument. In this concluding chapter, however, our attention has been given to that aspect of the subject which I have called 'integration'. For the present volume has been devoted very largely to the theme of a restoration of Adam's dominion in Christ, a restoration which takes the form of integration; that is to say a return of our nature to that wholeness of being for which we were designed. Now when we are seeking to envisage what such wholeness means, it is not easy to avoid overlooking some essential factor without which 'the whole' in question is imperfectly conceived. This, moreover, would be likely to occur if we thought of integration in Christ as something less mysterious and less transcendent to our present experience than it actually is.[2]

These considerations shall determine the course of some concluding reflexions with which the present volume is brought to a close. First, then, we will consider briefly that aspect of integration which bears most closely upon the victorious character of the restoration effected in the facts of our redemp-

[1] I. VII, pp. 221 f.

[2] The reader is referred to I. V, pp. 134 ff., for evidence that in this series Revelation is not conceived to be comprehended exclusively within categories of 'integration'.

tion. The aspect in question is indicated in a phrase employed in this chapter which may well be thought to require fuller explanation. A 'technique of anticipation' has been found to be characteristic of that part of the synoptic records which run from the confession at Caesarea Philippi to the resurrection of Christ.[1] In the plan laid down by St Mark the glory of the resurrection casts its light backwards over the whole of the preceding narrative. This does not mean that the tragic grimness of the passion narrative or of earlier incidents in any way lose their essential character. For that grimness with all its agony is being contemplated by the evangelists and their Christian readers as having the redemptive significance which was manifested in the glorious sequel. The technique of anticipation is, it seems, deliberately concentrated at certain points, notably in the Palm Sunday scenes, and earlier still in the transfiguration itself. The light of the resurrection shines backward over the preceding events; but just how far back do its rays penetrate?

It is difficult to resist the conclusion that the final glory suffuses the whole of the four gospels; and it seems probable that in the case of the fourth this factor is dominant. The gospel which does not record the event of the transfiguration might be said to have been written within the orbit of its dazzling radiance. Even there, however, we cannot draw the line. For it is clear from St Luke's version of the vision on the mount that Moses and Elias are partakers in the glory of the central figure; and this is underlined in what follows. As the representatives of the Law and the Prophets were being continuously taken towards a heavenly goal so also was it with the Saviour whom they foreshadowed. At this point two things begin to stand out. One is the continuity and togetherness of all redemptive history when seen in the light of Christ. The other is the fact that this togetherness becomes visible only in the transforming light of the great restoration effected by the death and resurrection of Jesus. This is simply another way of saying that the unity of the scriptural revelation becomes fully manifest only when it attains its goal in Christ. That unity in turn corresponds to the restored wholeness of humanity with which we have been so much

[1] An even wider extension of the same principle has been traced out by Dr Farrer in his *Study in St Mark*.

occupied. Yet both the unity of revelation and the integrating power of redeeming grace include within their compass a whole world of disparate and discordant factors to which full recognition must be given if we are to apprehend rightly the mystery of the Christ.[1]

The possibility that harmony may actually be enhanced by the inclusion of discord within it is doubtless suggestive; but its lack of precision might suggest the wrong things.[2] God is not glorified by the presence of evil in his creation, but rather by the way in which his goodness patiently wears down the power of evil until it is finally destroyed. So too in the gospel story the good news does not lie in the fact of the resurrection taken by itself as a single event, but rather in the transforming character of its relation to all other events, both before and afterwards, including all those factors, not only in the gospel history, but also in *all* history, which might seem most intractable and impervious to the redemptive power of the risen Lord. When therefore we say that 'glory and humiliation melt together into a single mystery' we are not trying to obliterate distinctions. We are simply repeating in another form an earlier statement that in the lowliness of Jesus 'the riches are present in the outward form of poverty'. The 'earthen vessel' of the flesh is aglow with the divine flame of uncreated light. This Pauline expression (2 Corinthians 4[7]) has a relevance which extends far beyond its original application to the Christian life. In its widest connotation the earthen vessel is the human element through which God acts in all his dealings with us, whether it be in scripture, in the Incarnation, or in the people of God.

In itself the earthen vessel might remain a dark object like a torch from which light streams forth.[3] On the other hand, as a lamp, it might so contain the light as to be transfigured by its rays. These two alternatives represent two aspects of our Lord's human nature. It might be said that in the Johannine writings these two aspects correspond respectively to the brazen serpent

[1] cp. above, Ch. V, § iii, *passim.*

[2] Half a century ago idealist philosophers, under Hegelian influence, seemed to be suggesting, not only that evil was an inevitable factor, but also that its inclusion within 'the Absolute' somehow enhanced the splendour of that mysterious entity.

[3] cp. above, Ch. V § iii, par. 1.

and to the Lamb of God. In the book about the last things the Lamb, who is for evermore the sacrificial victim, is shewn triumphant in heavenly scenes, and finally as the radiant source of light in the city of God. But in the book about the earthly life of Jesus the two symbolic figures are simply set over against each other (John 1^{29}, 3^{14}); and it is only by close attention to the thought of the Gospel as a whole that we can see how, and in what sense, they correspond to the two alternatives referred to above. If, however, we are right in assuming that the Gospel presupposes the Apocalypse then the glory of the Servant will be discerned in the forerunner's testimony to one who already 'taketh away the sin of the world'. The two figures, indeed, present facets of truth which are not disparate; for the serpent is 'lifted up', and the Lamb as luminary is for evermore the price of sin. But the latter figure is also a perfect symbol of the entire Christian mystery. For, first, the two covenants here meet and interpret one another, a matter of vital import, since we do not perceive either rightly unless we see it in relation to the other. So 'the lamp is the Lamb'. But, secondly, this truth revealed to the seer of the Apocalypse in the final vision (21^{23}) is the counterpart of another previously disclosed (Chapters 4 and 5). Some reflexions upon the latter will fitly conclude our argument.

The two orders of being which we have been considering are perfectly integrated in Jesus, and yet also perfectly differentiated in him. He is the source and site of both creations; yet he also unveils the chasm which now divides the old from the new. But still a third relationship comes into view. Christ came to restore the first creation in the second, and actually achieved that restoration by his victory over the hostile powers through death and resurrection. Moreover, restoration, once for all effected, set in motion processes and effects which will occupy us in a further volume. For our Lord is not only the Beginning to which we return but also the End to which we are to attain. In the new creation all the treasures of the original design are to be recovered from misuse and distortion and reshaped to their true form in the harmony and unity of the Creator's plan. The relationship thus indicated between the two orders is adumbrated in the vision of heavenly worship to which the seer of the Apocalypse was admitted. Here the praises of the Creator are at first sung antiphonally by the representatives of the two creations. Each order bears its own distinctive testimony to the living God; and further, this differentiation in the modes of their witness enhances its unanimity, since each corroborates the other.

But the scene unfolds; and as we turn from creation to history (symbolized by the sealed book) the key to human destiny is not found in the ranks of created being. The inner meaning of history is laid bare only through the all-prevailing sacrifice of the predestined victim, the victorious Lamb of God. His actual mastery over events and his inherent right to universal dominion are now acknowledged by the consentient and simultaneous witness of both creations together. Moreover this merging of voices, representing a universe redeemed, into a single volume of praise is answered and corroborated by the whole court of heaven. Thus the alternating witness of the two creations to the source of their being is succeeded by the concentrated and concurrent witness of all creaturely orders to the person of the Redeemer before the culminating point is reached. The dramatic sequence here is deeply significant. The two creations which render diverse witness to the Creator confess with one voice the headship of the Redeemer; for he has restored to the servants of God that sovereign dominion which is their true destiny in creation (5^{10}). The stone which became 'the head of the corner' became also the key-stone of the arch in the edifice of the universe. Finally in a world thus reconstituted by its Saviour every creature severally attains its true end, thus contributing its quota to the universal adoration which is rendered 'unto him that sitteth upon the throne and unto the Lamb'.[1]

[1] *πᾶν κτίσμα* (5^{13}) may suggest the original meaning of *κτίζειν* (to 'found' or 'build'). Creation redeemed becomes the City of God.

Additional Note D.

The Transfiguration and the Jewish-Christian Calendar

A copy of Dr. Carrington's *The Primitive Christian Calendar* (Vol. I) reached me after the present work had gone to press. This important treatise by the Archbishop of Quebec has an obvious bearing upon my treatment of the Transfiguration in Chapter VI. Briefly, the Archbishop connects that event *liturgically* with a midsummer festival of corn-harvest corresponding to the old Syrian feast of Tammuz-Adonis. Further, from the same point of view he connects St Mark's story of the Passion with the month Tishri. With this arrangement my own thesis is by no means incompatible. For if the 'six days' of Mark 9^2 are, as I have suggested, a fore-shadowing or 'dress-rehearsal' of Holy Week, then there would be symbolic cross-connexions between the two weeks, so that, for example, the associations of Tishri would be applicable to either.

INDEX

The numbering of biblical chapters and verses follows RV. except where, in (i) (*a*) a different numeration may be indicated by the letters G(LXX) or H(Hebrew text); similarly a number in brackets is that of LXX. The letters '*n*' or '*nn*' indicate the footnotes of this volume.

(i) REFERENCES

(ii) PERSONS

(iii) SUBJECTS